DISEASES OF PLANTATION CROPS

DISEASES OF PLANTATION CROPS

By

Dr. G.P. Gupta

Reader

Department of Botany

Gurukul Kangri University

Haridwar (Uttaranchal)

(India)

DISCOVERY PUBLISHING HOUSE PVT. LTD.

NEW DELHI-110 002

Published by:
Tilak Wasan

DISCOVERY PUBLISHING HOUSE PVT. LTD.
4383/4B, Ansari Road, Darya Ganj
New Delhi-110 002 (India)
Phone : +91-11-23279245, 43596064-65
Fax : +91-11-23253475
E-mail : parul.wasan@gmail.com
discoverypublishinghouse@gmail.com
web : www.discoverypublishinggroup.com

First Edition: **2013**

ISBN: 978-93-5056-251-2

Diseases of Plantation Crops

Printed at:
Aditi Fine Art Press
Delhi

PREFACE

Earlier forms of plantation crops were associated with large disparities of wealth and income, foreign ownership and political influence, and exploitative social systems such as indentured labor and slavery. The history of the environmental, social and economic issues relating to diseases of plantation crops are covered in this book that focus on these subjects.

Prevention is better than cure and it's also applicable when it comes to dealing with most plant diseases. Many diseases cannot be effectively controlled once symptoms develop or become severe. Fall is a good time to launch your preventative management program in the home orchard and garden. This includes a combination of strategies involving sanitation, cultural practices, and seasonal spray applications.

Citrus diseases affecting the entire tree can be classified into two general categories: parasitic and non-parasitic. Parasitic diseases are caused by fungi, bacteria, viruses and nematodes. Some disease-causing agents are restricted to certain parts of the plant, such as the root, trunk or fruit, while others may affect several or all parts of the plant.

Cereals are at risk from numerous diseases due to the level of intensification necessary for profitable production since the 1970s. More recently varietal diversification, good plant breeding and the availability of effective fungicides have played a prominent part in cereal disease control. Use of break crops and good rotations are also good cultural control measures. The demise of UK straw burning in the 1980s also increased the importance of good disease control.

Wheat is subject to more diseases than other grains, and, in some seasons, especially in wet ones, heavier losses are sustained from those diseases than are in other cereal crops. Wheat may suffer from the attack of insects at the root; from blight, which primarily affects the leaf or straw, and ultimately deprives the grain of sufficient nourishment; from mildew on the ear; and from gum of different shades, which lodges on the chaff or cups in which the grain is deposited.

This book is the outcome of long innings of research work in library and Internet. I also consulted foreign authors book on this topic. The editorial staff of this publication along with publisher also helped me in every possible way. I am highly indebted to all these resources for publishing this book on scheduled time in eye-pleasing format.

—Author

CONTENTS

Introduction to Plantation Crops

Plantings of a number of trees or shrubs grown for food or beverage, including tea, coffee, and cacao are generally called 'plantations'.

A plantation is always a mono-culture over a large area and does not include extensive naturally occurring stands of plants that have economic value. It is a large artificially established forest, farm or estate, where crops are grown for sale, often in distant markets.

Crops grown on plantations include fast-growing trees (often conifers), cotton, coffee, tobacco, sugar cane, sisal, some oil seeds (notably oil palms) and rubber trees. Farms that produce alfalfa, Lespedeza, clover, and other forage crops are usually not called plantations. The term "plantation" has usually not included large orchards except for banana plantations, but does include the planting of trees for lumber.

Because of its large size, a plantation takes advantage of economies of scale. Protectionist policies and natural comparative advantage have contributed to determining where plantations have been located.

Among the earliest examples of plantations were the *latifundia* of the Roman Empire, which produced large quantities of wine and olive oil for export. Plantation crops grew rapidly with the increase in international trade and the development of a worldwide economy that followed the expansion of European colonial empires. More than five thousand plant diseases have so far been recorded from India, though all of them do not cause the same degree of damage to crop plants.

The economical loss caused by the disease in India has not been made, it must be considerable and varying from crop to crop. Smut diseases cause an annual loss worth 3.25 lac tons of grain; whete rust alone causes crop loss worth Rs. 6 crores every year. There is no doubt that for sustainable higher productivity fungal diseases have to be controlled in the most effective and effecient manner on a long term basis.

FORMS OF PLANTATION CROPS

Like every economic activity, it has changed over time. Earlier forms of plantation crops were associated with large disparities of wealth and income, foreign ownership and political influence, and exploitative social systems such as indentured labor and slavery. The history of the environmental, social and economic issues relating to plantation agriculture are covered in articles that focus on those subjects.

Crops may be called plantation crops because of their association with a specific type of farming economy. Most of these involve a large landowner, raising crops with economic value rather than for subsistence, with a number of employees carrying out the work. Often it referred to crops newly introduced to a region.

In past times, it has been associated with slavery, indentured labour, and other economic models of high inequity. However, arable and dairy farming are both usually (but not always) excluded from such definitions. A comparable economic structure in antiquity was the *latifundia* that produced commercial quantities of olive oil or wine, for export. One plantation crop is bananas and there are others as well.

Prevention is better than cure and it's also applicable when it comes to dealing with most plant diseases. Many diseases cannot be effectively controlled once symptoms develop or become severe. Fall is a good time to launch your preventative management programme in the home orchard and garden. This includes a combination of strategies involving sanitation, cultural practices, and seasonal spray applications.

Clean Up Programme

Crop sanitation aims to remove the source of future disease infections by means of a thorough clean up programme. Common fungus diseases such as peach leaf curl, brown rot, apple scab, camellia petal blight, and black spot on roses will reappear the next season because the fungus spores survive over winter in dead leaves, rotting or mummified fruit and other plant debris left behind the previous Fall.

Disease pathogens can also survive in older mulching material laid out in previous years. If a serious fungus infection exists, such as Camellia Petal

Blight, remove old mulch and replace with fresh material. Grab a rake and get out into the garden for a clean up day before first rainfall for best results. Dispose of any suspect plant debris.

Removal of diseased plant tissues on the plant itself is your next line of defense. Prune out diseased foliage, twigs or branches, hand pick blighted camellia blossoms as they appear and dispose of these in the trash. Avoid unnecessary pruning; pruning causes wounds, which can be entry sites for decay and disease organisms. Sanitize pruning equipment to avoid transmitting disease to healthy plants.

Avoid overhead irrigation-splashing water spreads fungal spores and wet foliage promotes some foliar and fruit diseases such as leaf spots, rusts, anthracnose, and brown rot.

Finally, follow up with preventative applications of a fungicidal spray. This is an especially critical step in the control of peach leaf curl and other recurring diseases. Synthetic and organically acceptable spray materials are available to control certain plant pathogens, primarily fungi. Products such as Bordeaux mixture, sulfur, fixed copper, and fungicidal soap sprays protect plants from pathogen infection.

These organically acceptable fungicides generally only prevent the infection of healthy, spray-covered tissue and do not act systemically to kill existing pathogens; therefore repeated applications may be necessary during critical growing stages. Synthetic fungicides are often more effective, easier to apply, and are less likely to damage susceptible plants; some have systemic activity. Fungicides require careful timing to be effective. Consult a qualified nursery sales person to determine an appropriate spray product for you. Wear protective gear such as goggles and gloves, and use as directed on the product label.

Tropical and plantation crops include important crops for food security and alternative energy resources. Even so, there are few studies on the impact of climate change on diseases of these crops. Findings from scientific studies concerning some climate-change effects on diseases of coffee, sugarcane, eucalyptus, cassava, citrus, banana, pineapple, cashew, coconut and papaya have been summarized to provide a context.

By reviewing available methods to evaluate the impact of climate change on diseases of tropical and plantation crops, we present trends for some diseases and their management strategies, identify critical gaps in knowledge, and suggest experimental and analytical approaches to advance knowledge. As the projected climate conditions will probably vary greatly in the future from continent to continent and from developed to developing countries, studies must be conducted under tropical regions considering their specific environmental conditions.

Future Considerations

Multifactor studies under realistic field situations, such as free air CO_2 enrichment with increasing CO_2 and O_3 concentrations incorporating spectral reflectance measures *in situ* for realistic assessment of plant growth, are a way forward. Effects of a changing climate on chemical and biological controls are discussed in the context of changing global outlook on environmental demands for the future.

INDUSTRIAL PLANTATIONS

Industrial plantations are established to produce a high volume of wood in a short period of time. Plantations are grown by state forestry authorities and/or the paper and wood industries and other private landowners (such as Weyerhaeuser and International Paper in the United States, Asia Pulp and Paper (APP) in Indonesia). Christmas trees are often grown on plantations as well. In southern and southeastern Asia, rubber, oil palm, and more recently teak plantations have replaced the natural forest.

These are actively managed for the commercial production of forest products. Industrial plantations are usually large-scale. Individual blocks are usually even-aged and often consist of just one or two species. These species can be exotic or indigenous. The plants used for the plantation are often genetically improved for desired traits such as growth and resistance to pests and diseases in general and specific traits, for example in the case of timber species, volumic wood production and stem straightness. Forest genetic resources are the basis for genetic improvement. Selected individuals grown in seed orchards are a good source for seeds to develop adequate planting material.

Wood production on a tree plantation is generally higher than that of natural forests. While forests managed for wood production commonly yield between one and three cubic meters per hectare per year, plantations of fast-growing species commonly yield between 20 and 30 cubic meters or more per hectare annually; a Grand Fir plantation at Craigvinean in Scotland has a growth rate of 34 cubic meters per hectare per year, and Monterey Pine plantations in southern Australia can yield up to 40 cubic meters per hectare per year. In 2000, while plantations accounted for 5 per cent of global forest, it is estimated that they supplied about 35 per cent of the world's roundwood.

Growth Cycle

In the first year, the ground is prepared usually by the combination of burning, herbicide spraying, and/or cultivation and then saplings are planted by human crew or by machine. The saplings are usually obtained in bulk from industrial nurseries, which may specialize in selective breeding in order to produce fast growing disease- and pest-resistant strains.

MAJOR DISEASES OF SOME CROPS

Crops	Common Name of Disease	Dosage/ha in 7750-1000 Litres of Water
Banana	Leaf spot Fruit rot	2.50 kg 2.50 kg
Betel	Leaf rot Foot rot	2.50 kg 2.50 kg
Chillies	Fruit rot Leaf rot	2.50 kg 2.50 kg
Citrus	Canker Foot rot	2.50 kg 2.50 kg
Coffee	Black rot Rust	3.50 kg 3.75 kg
Cotton	Blight Wilt	2.50 kg 2.50 kg
Paddy	Brown leaf Spot Smut	2.50 kg 2.50 kg
Potato	Early blight Late blight	2.50 kg 2.50 kg
Sugercane	Red rot Smut	2.50 kg 2.50 kg
Tea	Blister blight Black rot	1.50 kg 2.00 kg
Tomato	Red rust Blight	1.50 kg 1.50 kg
Wheat	Leaf curling Leaf rust	1.50 kg 2.50 kg

In the first few years until the canopy closes, the saplings are looked after, and may be dusted or sprayed with fertilizers or pesticides until established.

After the canopy closes, with the tree crowns touching each other, the plantation is becoming dense and crowded, and tree growth is slowing due to competition. This stage is termed 'pole stage'. When competition becomes too intense (for pine trees, when the live crown is less than a third of the tree's total height), it is time to thin out the section.

There are several methods for thinning, but where topography permits, the most popular is 'row-thinning', where every third or fourth or fifth row of trees is removed, usually with a harvester. Many trees are removed, leaving regular clear lanes through the section so that the remaining trees have room to expand again.

The removed trees are delimbed, forwarded to the forest road, loaded onto trucks, and sent to a mill. A typical pole stage plantation tree is 7–30 cm in diameter at breast height (dbh). Such trees are sometimes not suitable for timber, but are used as pulp for paper and particleboard, and as chips for oriented strand board.

As the trees grow and become dense and crowded again, the thinning process is repeated. Depending on growth rate and species, trees at this age may be large enough for timber milling; if not, they are again used as pulp and chips.

Around year 10-60 the plantation is now mature and in economic terms is falling off the back side of its growth curve. That is to say, it is passing the point of maximum wood growth per hectare per year, and so is ready for the final harvest. All remaining trees are felled, delimbed, and taken to be processed.

The ground is cleared, and the cycle is repeated.

Some plantation trees, such as pines and *eucalyptus*, can be at high risk of fire damage because their leaf oils and resins are flammable to the point of a tree being explosive under some conditions. Conversely, an afflicted plantation can in some cases be cleared of pest species cheaply through the use of a prescribed burn, which kills all lesser plants but does not significantly harm the mature trees.

Main Drawbacks

In contrast to a naturally regenerated forest, plantations are typically grown as even-aged mono-cultures, primarily for timber production.

Plantations are usually near or total mono-cultures. That is, the same species of tree is planted across a given area, whereas a natural forest would contain a far more diverse range of tree species.

Plantations may include tree species that would not naturally occur in the area. They may include unconventional types such as hybrids, and genetically modified trees may be used sometime in the future. Since the primary interest in plantations is to produce wood or pulp, the types of trees found in plantations are those that are best-suited to industrial applications. For example, pine, spruce and eucalyptus are widely planted far beyond their natural range because of their fast growth rate, tolerance of rich or degraded agricultural land and potential to produce large volumes of raw material for industrial use.

Plantations are always young forests in ecological terms. Typically, trees grown in plantations are harvested after 10 to 60 years, rarely up to 120 years. This means that the forests produced by plantations do not contain the type of growth, soil or wildlife typical of old-growth natural forest ecosystems. Most conspicuous is the absence of decaying dead wood, a crucial component of natural forest ecosystems.

What is Fast-food Plantations ?

In the 1970s, Brazil began to establish high-yield, intensively managed, short rotation plantations. These types of plantations are sometimes called fast-wood plantations or fiber farms and often managed on a short-rotation basis, as little as 5 to 15 years. They are becoming more widespread in South America, Asia and other areas. The environmental and social impacts of this type of plantation has caused them to become controversial. In Indonesia, for example, large multi-national pulp companies have harvested large areas of natural forest without regard for regeneration. From 1980 to 2000, about 50% of the 1.4 million hectares of pulpwood plantations in Indonesia have been established on what was formerly natural forest land.

Replacement of Natural Forest

The replacement of natural forest with tree plantations has also caused social problems. In some countries, again, notably Indonesia, conversions of natural forest are made with little regard for rights of the local people. Plantations established purely for the production of fiber provide a much narrower range of services than the original natural forest for the local people.

India has sought to limit this damage by limiting the amount of land owned by one entity and, as a result, smaller plantations are owned by local farmers who then sell the wood to larger companies. Some large environmental organizations are critical of these high-yield plantations and are running an anti-plantation campaign, notably the rainforest action network and greenpeace.

Farm or home plantations are typically established for the production of timber and fire wood for home use and sometimes for sale. Management may be less intensive than with industrial plantations. In time, this type of plantation can become difficult to distinguish from naturally regenerated forest.

Teak and bamboo plantations in India have given good results and an alternative crop solution to farmers of central India, where conventional farming was popular. But due to rising input costs of farming many farmers have done teak and bamboo plantations which require very little water (only during first two years). Teak and bamboo have legal protection from theft. Bamboo, once planted, gives output for 50 years till flowering occurs. Teak requires 20 years to grow to full maturity and fetch returns. Indirectly it also contributes to the positive impact on the climate change problem.

Tool of Environmental Restoration

These may be established for watershed or soil protection. They are established for erosion control, landslide stabilization and windbreaks. Such plantations are established to foster native species and promote forest regeneration on degraded lands as a tool of environmental restoration.

Probably the single most important factor a plantation has on the local environment is the site where the plantation is established. If natural forest is cleared for a planted forest then a reduction in biodiversity and loss of habitat will likely result. In some cases, their establishment may involve draining wetlands to replace mixed hardwoods that formerly predominated with pine species.

If a plantation is established on abandoned agricultural land, or highly degraded land, it can result in an increase in both habitat and biodiversity. A planted forest can be profitably established on lands that will not support agriculture or suffer from lack of natural regeneration.

The tree species used in a plantation is also an important factor. Where non-native varieties or species are grown, few of the native fauna are adapted to exploit these and further biodiversity loss occurs. However, even non-native tree species may serve as corridors for wildlife and act as a buffer for native forest, reducing edge effect.

Environmental Factor

Once a plantation is established, how it is managed becomes the important environmental factor. The single most important factor of management is the rotation period. Plantations harvested on longer rotation periods (30 years or more) can provide similar benefits to a naturally regenerated forest managed for wood production, on a similar rotation.

This is especially true if native species are used. In the case of exotic species, the habitat can be improved significantly if the impact is mitigated by measures such as leaving blocks of native species in the plantation, or retaining corridors of natural forest. In Brazil, similar measures are required by government regulations.

Plantations and Natural Forest Loss

Many forestry experts claim that the establishment of plantations will reduce or eliminate the need to exploit natural forest for wood production. In principle this is true because due to the high productivity of plantations less land is needed. Many point to the example of New Zealand, where 19 per cent of the forest area provides 99 per cent of the supply of industrial round wood. It has been estimated that the worlds needs for fiber could be met by just 5 per cent of the world forest.

In the well-known Kyoto Protocol, there are proposals encouraging the use of plantations to reduce carbon dioxide levels (though this idea is being challenged by some groups on the grounds that the sequestered CO_2 is eventually released after harvest).

PLANTATIONS AND PLANTER

Plantations were an important aspect of the history of the American South, particularly the antebellum (pre-American Civil War South).

The owner of a plantation was called a planter. While the term "planter" has no universally accepted definition, historians of the antebellum South have generally defined it in the strictest definition as a person owning property and 20 or more slaves, as noted by Peter Kolchin in his 1993 survey of American slavery. The wealthiest planters, such as the Virginia elite with plantations on the James River, had more land and slaves. This was particularly true of what evolved as the Upper South, the original Chesapeake Bay Colonies of Virginia, Maryland and Delaware; and the Carolinas. The later development of cotton and sugar cultivation in the Deep South had different characteristics, in which planters typically owned greater amounts of land and hundreds of slaves.

In the "Black Belt" counties of Alabama and Mississippi, the terms """planter" and "farmer" were often synonymous, a "planter" was generally a farmer who owned many slaves. While most Southerners were not slave-owners, and while the majority of slaveholders held 10 or fewer slaves, planters were those who held a significant number of slaves, mostly as agricultural labor. Planters are often spoken of as belonging to the planter elite or planter aristocracy in the antebellum South.

The historians Robert Fogel and Stanley Engerman define large planters as owning over 50 slaves, and medium planters as owning between 16 and 50 slaves. In his study of Black Belt counties in Alabama, Jonathan Wiener defines planters by ownership of real property, rather than of slaves. A planter, for Wiener, owned at least 10,000 dollars worth of real estate in 1850 and 32,000 dollars worth in 1860, equivalent to about the top eight per cent of landowners.

In his study of southwest Georgia, Lee Formwalt defines planters in size of land holdings rather than slaves. Formwalt's planters are in the top 4.5 per cent of land-owners, translating into real estate worth six thousand dollars or more in 1850, 24,000 dollars or more in 1860, and eleven thousand dollars or more in 1870.

In his study of Harrison County, Texas, Randolph B. Campbell classifies large planters as owners of 20 slaves, and small planters as owners of between ten and 19 slaves. In Chicot and Phillips Counties, Arkansas, Carl H. Moneyhon defines large planters as owners of twenty or more slaves, and six hundred or more acres.

Plantation Crops

Crops cultivated on antebellum plantations included cotton, tobacco, indigo and rice. By the late 18th century, most planters in the Upper South had switched from exclusive tobacco cultivation to mixed-crop production.

In the low country of South Carolina, even before the American Revolution, planters holding large rice and cotton plantations in South Carolina typically owned hundreds of slaves. (In cities such as Charleston, South Carolina and Savannah, Georgia the Southern urban elite held slaves to work as household servants). The 19th century development of the Deep South for cotton cultivation depended on large plantations with much more acreage than was typical of the Chesapeake Bay area, and for labor, planters held hundreds of slaves.

Plantation Architecture

Antebellum architecture is seen in many plantations, especially in the "plantation house", the stately residences of planters and their families. The largest and wealthiest planter families, for instance, those with estates fronting on the James River in Virginia, constructed mansions in brick and Georgian style, e.g. Shirley Plantation. Common or smaller planters in the late 18th and 19th century had more modest wood frame buildings, such as Southall Plantation in Charles City County.

High Value Food Crops

Some spice and high value crops grown from permanent perennial stock, such as black pepper may also be so called. When the holding belongs to a single individual, that person may be called a *planter*.

Sugar Plantations

Sugar plantations were highly valued in the Caribbean by the British and French colonists in the 19th and 20th centuries and the use of sugar in

Europe rose during this period. Sugarcane is still an important crop in Cuba. Sugar plantations also arose in countries such as Barbados and Cuba because of the natural endowments that they had. These natural endowments included soil that was conducive to growing sugar and a high marginal product of labor realized through the increasing number of slaves.

Rubber Plantations

Plantings of para rubber, the tree *Hevea brasiliensis*, are usually called plantations.

Orchards

Fruit orchards are sometimes considered to be plantations.

Arable Crops

These includes tobacco, sugarcane, pineapple, and cotton, especially in historical usage.

Before the rise of cotton in the American South, indigo and rice were also sometimes called plantation crops.

Fishing Plantations in Newfoundland and Labrador

When Newfoundland was colonized by England in 1610, the original colonists were called "Planters" and their fishing rooms were known as "fishing plantations". These terms were used well into the 20th century.

The following three plantations are maintained by the Government of Newfoundland and Labrador as provincial heritage sites:

- Sea-Forest Plantation was a 17th-century fishing plantation established at Cuper's Cove (present-day Cupids) under a royal charter issued by King James I.
- Mockbeggar Plantation is an 18th-century fishing plantation at Bonavista.
- Pool Plantation a 17th-century fishing plantation maintained by Sir David Kirke and his heirs at Ferryland. The plantation was destroyed by French invaders in 1696.

Other fishing plantations:

- Bristol's Hope Plantation, a 17th-century fishing plantation established at Harbour Grace, created by the Bristol Society of Merchant-Adventurers.
- Benger Plantation, an 18th-century fishing plantation maintained by James Benger and his heirs at Ferryland. It was built on the site of Georgia plantation.

- Piggeon's Plantation, an 18th-century fishing plantation maintained by Ellias Piggeon at Ferryland.

LABOUR CAMPS IN COLONIAL PLANTATIONS

African slave labor extracted from forcibly transported Africans was used extensively to work on early plantations (such as cotton and sugar plantations) in the United States, throughout the Caribbean, the Americas and in European-occupied areas of Africa. Several notable historians and economists such as Eric Williams, Walter Rodney and Karl Marx contend that the global capitalist economy was largely founded on the creation and produce of thousands of slave labour camps based in colonial plantations exploiting tens of millions of abducted Africans.

In modern times, the low wages typically paid to plantation workers are the basis of plantation profitability in some areas with minimal employee-protection legislation. Sugarcane plantations in the Caribbean and Brazil, worked by slave labour, were also examples of the plantation system.

In more recent times, overt slavery has been replaced by "para-slavery" or slavery-in-kind, including the sharecropping system. At its most extreme, workers are in "debt bondage": they must work to pay off a debt at such punitive interest rates that it may never be paid off. Others work unreasonably long hours and are paid subsistence wages that (in practice) may only be spent in the company store.

In Brazil, a *sugarcane plantation* was termed an *engenho* ("engine"), and the 17th-century English usage for organized colonial production was "factory". Such colonial social and economic structures are discussed at Plantation economy. Sugar workers on plantations in Cuba and elsewhere in the Caribbean lived in company towns known as Bateys.

In the American South, antebellum plantations were centered on a "plantation house", the residence of the owner, where important business was conducted. Slavery and plantations had different characteristics in different regions of the South. As the Upper South of the Chesapeake Bay Colony developed first, historians of the antebellum South defined planters as those who held 20 or more slaves. Major planters held many more, especially in the Deep South as it developed.

The majority of slaveholders held 10 or fewer slaves, often just a few to labor domestically. By the late 18th century, most planters in the Upper South had switched from exclusive tobacco cultivation to mixed crop production, both because tobacco had exhausted the soil and because of changing markets. The shift away from tobacco meant they had slaves in excess of the number needed for labour, and they began to sell them in the internal slave trade.

Domestic Architecture on Plantations

There was a variety of domestic architecture on plantations. The largest and wealthiest planter families, for instance, those with estates fronting on the James River in Virginia, constructed mansions in brick and Georgian style, e.g. Shirley Plantation. Common or smaller planters in the late 18th and 19th century had more modest wood frame buildings, such as Southall Plantation in Charles City County.

In the Low Country of South Carolina, by contrast, even before the American Revolution, planters holding large rice and cotton plantations in South Carolina typically owned hundreds of slaves. In Charleston and Savannah, the elite also held numerous slaves to work as household servants. During colonial period, the development of the Deep South for cotton cultivation depended on large plantations with much more acreage than was typical of the Chesapeake Bay area, and for labor, planters held hundreds of slaves.

Until December 1865, slavery was legal in parts of the United States. Most slaves were employed in agriculture, and "planter" was a term commonly used to describe a farmer with many slaves.

The term "planter" has no universally accepted definition but academic historians have defined it to identify the elite class, "a landowning farmer of substantial means." In the "Black Belt" counties of Alabama and Mississippi, the terms ""planter" and "farmer" were often synonymous. Robert Fogel and Stanley Engerman define large planters as owning over 50 slaves, and medium planters as owning between 16 and 50 slaves.

In his study of Black Belt counties in Alabama, Jonathan Wiener defines planters by ownership of real property, rather than of slaves. A planter, for Wiener, owned at least 10,000 dollars worth of real estate in 1850 and 32,000 dollars' worth in 1860, equivalent to about the top 8 per cent of landowners.

In his study of southwest Georgia, Lee Formwalt also defines planters in size of land holdings rather than slaves. Formwalt's planters are in the top 4.5 per cent of landowners, translating into real estate worth six thousand dollars or more in 1850, 24,000 dollars or more in 1860, and eleven thousand dollars or more in 1870.

In his study of Harrison County, Texas, Randolph B. Campbell classifies large planters as owners of twenty slaves, and small planters as owners of between ten and nineteen slaves. In Chicot and Phillips Counties, Arkansas, Carl H. Moneyhon defines large planters as owners of twenty or more slaves, and six hundred or more acres.

Tea *(Camellia* spp.*)* is an important beverage and the world drinks more of it than any other beverage. It is made from the tender or young leaves and unopened buds of the evergreen tea-plant, popular as a 'healthful herb'. The tea plant is in the polymorphic species *Camellia sinensis* Kuntz, but recent findings show that this plant of commerce is derived from more than one species.

Two distinct varieties of tea-plant are generally recognised, the small-leaved China *(sinensis)* and the large-leaved Assam *(assamica)* which have been raised to a specific rank by a well-known tea botanist. Careful field observations, however, reveal that more than one or two species are involved in the evolution of the present-day tea-plant of commerce. Considerable interspecific hybridization has taken place in nature. Thus, the taxonomy of the tea-complex is confounded.

The tea-plant, in the natural state,grows into a small or medium-sized tree, but in commmercial plantations it is pruned and trained to form a many-branched low bush and is encouraged to produce vigorous vegetative growth by adopting an appropriate schedule of fertilizer applications.

The important tree growing countries are India, Sri Lanka and East Africa; Japan and Indonesia also produce sizeable quanties of tea. It is also grown in Bangladesh, China, Georgia, Argentina and some other countries. In India, the crop is grown in Assam, West Bengal, Kerala, Karnataka and Tamil Nadu, and to some extent in Tripura and Himachal Pradesh.

The total area under tea in our country is about 3,58,000 hectares and over 468 million kilograms of product is obtained anually. Over one million workers are employed by the tea industries.

Yeilds have steadily increased during two decades. Tremendous progress has been made on the selection of clones and those with high yeilds and improved quality have been released to the industry. The tea planters are encouraged to uproot poor section of their plantation and replant them with improved planting material.

Tea is grown on plantation scale in many areas of the world in warm and moist climate. These range from Georgia (USSR) to Corrientes (Argentina). It is grown from sea level to about 2460 m. A well distributed rainfall is essential for its cultivation. The rainfall varies from 125 cm to 750 cm in the tea-growing regions in this country.

Tea is planted on soils of widely different geological origin and of almost all physical types. a well drained, deep and friable loam or forest land rich in organic matter is ideal. Tea soils are acidic (pH 4 to 6), low in calcium and generally rich in iron and manganese.

Vegetative Propagation

Tea is propogated from seed, but high yielding clonal material has also become popular. The plants are initially raised in nurseries to produce healthy plants. 1 to 1½ year old nursery seedlings are used for planting in the field. The vegetative propogation of selected tea-plant cuttings, each with a leaf and an internode has been standardized and progressive planters now raise colonial nurseries on a large scale.

The area intended for planting is first cleared of forest growth and adequate steps are taken to prevent soilerosion.Planting lines are traced (as at present on contour on hill slopes) and pits of a convenient size (generally 30-45 cm deep and 24 cm wide) are dug. The normal accepted spacing is 120 × 75 cm, accomodating about 10,000 plants in a hectare. The soil is heavily mulched during the initial one or two years.

In most of the tea areas in our country, a system of shading the tea plants is practised. In southern India , the silver oak (*Grevilla robusta*) is a shade tree of choice (planted 600 by 600 cm, later thinned to 600 cm by 1200 cm or 1260 cm by 1200 cm as required). Other trees used for shading are *Erythrina lithosperma (dadap), Acacia and Albizia.* Albizia species are used in tea gardens in northern India.

Weeds compete with the tea plant for nutrients, and weed control is important in tea plantations. In recent years , the control of weeds with chemicals has gained popularity. Grasses and broad-leaf dicot weeds are kept under check. Pests and diseases are effectively controlled with chemicals.

A manuring scheme is followed from the nursery stage upto maturity. A special 1:1:1 NPK soluble fertilizer mixture is used in the nursery; a 4:3:3 NPK mixture in the first three years in the clearing and thereafter the dosage of the fertilizer applied is varied, depending on the type of tea, its performance, soil fertility and the yield potential of the crop. On an average 10 kg of nitrogen is applied for every 100 kg of the crop.

Tea readily responds to the application of nitrogen and potassium. Potassium is applied at the rate of 40 to 50 per cent of the amount of nitrogen applied, depending on the soil type and weather conditions. In southern India, tea responds to nitrogen upto 300 kg per hectare applied to some high-yielding varieties of tea, whereas in northern India, the application of nitrogen is limited to about 120 kg whereas 30 to 40 kg of phosphate per hectare is adequate.

Zinc deficiency is a limiting factor in crop production in most areas and a schedule of foliar application of zinc sulphate usually 11 kg per hectare in alternate years is recommended.

The tea-plant is initially trained into a small bush by centring low within a few months of planting, by removing the central leader stem in order to encourage development of lateral branches. The lateral branches are cut to a convenient height of 40 to 50 cm and the growth above this is periodically cut.

Thus, a small, compact bush is formed. New shoots are allowed to grow unhampered and these shoots are tipped, leaving a growth of 20 to 30 cm above the pruning cut, depending on that kind of plant. The crop is then harvested at regular intervals.

In southern India, the pruning cycle extends over a period of 4, 5 or 6 years depending on the elevation and growth. In some cases, a 'skiff' is given at a cinvenient height and the pruning cycle extended for two or three years. Pruning and skiffing are done periodically to keep the height of the bush at a cinvenient level for the pluckers to operate and to encourage vegetative growth. Annual pruning is a practice in northern India (Assam), but even there the present trend is toward an extended pruning cycle. After a series of pruning cycle, the bushes are rejuvenated by hard pruning, removing all cankered and diseased portions of the stem.

In northern India, the economic life of the tea bush is generally 40 to 50 years and therefore 2 to 2.5 per cent of the area is uprooted and replanted every year. In southern, such regular uprooting and replanting is not practiced, because economic yields are obtained from sections which are 80 years or more old. Usually plucking is restricted to the terminal bud and two expanded leaves, or to the bud and three succulent leaves, known as fine or medium plucking. Coarse plucking includes extra leaves.

In northern India the tea bush is plucked at weekly intervals from April to December and there is a dormant season during winter. In southern India the crop is harvested during the cold and dry months (December to March).

The shoots may be prepared in several ways to make black or green tea. To make the former, the leaf is usually withered and rolled or distorted by rolling in the conventional tea rollers, or is passed through tea machines, the 'rotorvane' and CTC rollers which exert drastic action on the withered leaves.

The juice of the leaf cells is exposed in the air to oxidize (fermentation) when important changes take place. When the optimum fermentation is reached, the action of enzyme is arrested by drying the fermented leaf in a current of hot air in suitable tea-dryers. In the production of green tea, the shoots are steamed as soon as possible after plucking and the leaf oxidized is soon destroyed so that fermentation does not take place on rolling.

The processed tea is passed through a series of meshes, sorting out leaf grades and dust. The tea leaves are sorted into different grades , for example, pekoe, Orange pekoe, Flowery pekoe, Broken Orange pekoe and Fannings.

Tea intended for export is packed in plywood chests and shipped directly to various centres or sold through auctions at centres like Calcutta and Cochin.

Instant tea, soluble in water, tea bag and ready mix tea are new developments.

Tea is a widely used product in India where tea research is carried out in at two centres: Tocklai Experimental Station of the tea research association , Jorhat (Assam) and the Tea Research Station of the United Planters Association of Southern India (UPASI) Cinchona P.O., Coimbatore district, Tamil Nadu.

Certain short-based schemes on tea research are carried out at centres such as the Central Food Technological Research Institute at Mysore and the Department of Applied Chemistry, Calcutta university.

The Tocklai Experimental Station publishes its findings in its annual reports, bulletin the *Tea Encyclopedia* and in the journal *Two and a Bud*. The UPASI tea Research Station publishes the results of research in its annual reports, bulletins Handbook of tea Culture and in the Planter's Chronicle.

FUNGICIDES

Fungicides are chemical compounds or biological organisms used to kill or inhibit fungi or fungal spores. Fungi can cause serious damage in agriculture, resulting in critical losses of yield, quality and profit. Fungicides are used both in agriculture and to fight fungal infections in animals. Chemicals used to control oomycetes, which are not fungi, are also referred to as fungicides as oomycetes use the same mechanisms as fungi to infect plants.

Fungicides can either be contact, translaminar or systemic. Contact fungicides are not taken up into the plant tissue, and only protect the plant where the spray is deposited; translaminar fungicides redistribute the fungicide from the upper, sprayed leaf surface to the lower, unsprayed surface; systemic fungicides are taken up and redistributed through the xylem vessels to the upper parts of the plant. New leaf growth is protected for a short period.

Most fungicides that can be bought retail are sold in a liquid form. A very common active ingredient is sulfur, present at 0.08 per cent in weaker concentrates, and as high as 0.5 per cent for more potent fungicides. Fungicides in powdered form are usually around 90 per cent sulfur and are very toxic. Other active ingredients in fungicides include neem oil, rosemary oil, jojoba oil and the bacterium Bacillus subtilis.

Fungicide residues have been found on food for human consumption, mostly from post-harvest treatments. Some fungicides are dangerous to human health, such as vinclozolin, which has now been removed from use.

Plants and other organisms have chemical defenses that give them an advantage against microorganisms such as fungi. Some of these compounds can be used as fungicides:

- Tea tree oil
- Cinnamaldehyde
- Cinnamon essential oil
- Jojoba oil
- Neem oil
- Rosemary oil
- Monocerin
- Milk
- Ampelomyces quisqualis AQ10, CNCM I-807

Whole live or dead organisms that are efficient at killing or inhibiting fungi can sometimes be used as fungicides:

- The bacterium Bacillus subtilis
- Kelp (powdered dried kelp is fed to cattle to protect them from fungi in grass)

Resistance

Pathogens respond to the use of fungicides by evolving resistance. In the field several mechanisms of resistance have been identified. The evolution of fungicide resistance can be gradual or sudden. In qualitative or discrete resistance, a mutation (normally to a single gene) produces a race of a fungus with a high degree of resistance.

Such resistant varieties also tend to show stability, persisting after the fungicide has been removed from the market. For example sugar beet leaf blotch remains resistant to azoles years after they were no longer used for control of the disease. This is because such mutations often have a high selection pressure when the fungicide is used, but there is low selection pressure to remove them in the absence of the fungicide.

In instances where resistance occurs more gradually a shift in sensitivity in the pathogen to the fungicide can be seen. Such resistance is polygenic—an accumulation of many mutation in different genes each having a small additive effect. This type of resistance is known as quantitative or continuous resistance. In this kind of resistance the pathogen population will revert back to a sensitive state if the fungicide is no longer applied.

Little is known about how variations in fungicide treatment affect the selection pressure to evolve resistance to that fungicide. Evidence shows that the doses that provide the most control of the disease also provide the largest selection pressure to acquire resistance, and that lower doses decreased the selection pressure.

In some cases, when a pathogen evolves resistance to one fungicide it automatically obtains resistance to others—a phenomenon known as cross resistance. These additional fungicides are normally of the same chemical family or have the same mode of action, or can be detoxified by the same mechanism.

Sometimes negative cross resistance occurs, where resistance to one chemical class of fungicides leads to an increase in sensitivity to a different chemical class of fungicides. This has been seen with carbendazim and diethofencarb.

There are also recorded incidences of pathogens evolving multiple drug resistance—resistance to two chemically different fungicides by separate mutation events. For example *Botrytis cinerea* is resistant to both azoles and dicarboximide fungicides.

There are several routes by which pathogens can evolve fungicide resistance. The most common mechanism appears to be alteration of the target site, particular as a defence against single site of action fungicides. For example Black Sigatoka, an economically important pathogen of banana, is resistant to the QoI fungicides, due to a single nucleotide change resulting one amino acid (glycine) being replaced by another (alanine) in the target protein of the QoI fungicides, cytochrome b. This presumably disrupts the binding of the fungicide to the protein, rendering the fungicide ineffective.

Upregulation of target genes can also render the fungicide ineffective. This is seen in DMI resistant strains of *Venturia inaequalis*.

Resistance to fungicides can also be developed by efficient efflux of the fungicide out of the cell. *Septoria tritici* has developed multiple drug resistance using this mechanism. The pathogen had five ABC type transporters with overlapping substrate specificities that together work to effectively pump toxic chemicals out of the cell.

In addition to the mechanisms outlined above, fungi may also develop metabolic pathways that circumvent the target protein, or acquire enzymes that enable metabolism of the fungicide to a harmless substance.

Fungicide Resistance Management

It has several recommended practices to try to avoid the development of fungicide resistance, especially in at-risk fungicides including Strobilurins such as azoxystrobin.

Products should not be used in isolation but rather as mixture, or alternate sprays, with another fungicide with a different mechanism of action. The likelihood of the pathogen developing resistance is greatly decreased by the fact that any resistant isolates to one fungicide will hopefully be killed by the other—in other words two mutations would be required rather than just one.

The effectiveness of this technique can be demonstrated by Metalaxyl, a phenylamide fungicide. When used as the sole product in Ireland to control potato blight (*Phytophthora infestans*) resistance developed within one growing season. However in countries like the UK where it was only ever marketed as a mixture resistance problems developed more slowly.

Fungicides should only be applied when absolutely necessary, especially if they are in an at-risk group. Lowering the amount of fungicide in the environment lowers the selection pressure for resistance to develop.

Manufacturers' doses should always be followed. These doses are normally designed to give the right balance between controlling the disease and limiting the risk of resistance development. Higher doses increase the selection pressure for single site mutations that confer resistance, as all strains but those that carry the mutation will be eliminated, and thus the resistant strain will propagate. Lower doses greatly increase the risk of polygenic resistance, as strains that are slightly less sensitive to the fungicide may survive.

It is also recommended that where possible fungicides are only used in a protective manner, rather than to try to cure already infected crops. Far fewer fungicides have curative/eradicative ability than protectant. Thus fungicide preparations advertised as having curative action may only have one active chemical; a single fungicide acting in isolation increases the risk of fungicide resistance.

It is better to use an integrative pest management approach to disease control, rather than relying on fungicides alone. This involves the use of resistant varieties and hygienic practises, such as the removal of potato discard piles and stubble on which the pathogen can overwinter, greatly reducing the titer of the pathogen and thus the risk of fungicide resistance development.

What is Plant Pathology?

It is the scientific study of plant diseases caused by pathogens (infectious diseases) and environmental conditions (physiological factors). Organisms that cause infectious disease include fungi, oomycetes, bacteria, viruses, viroids, virus-like organisms, phytoplasmas, protozoa, nematodes and parasitic plants. Not included are ectoparasites like insects, mites, vertebrate or other pests that affect plant health by consumption of plant tissues.

Plant pathology also involves the study of pathogen identification, disease etiology, disease cycles, economic impact, plant disease epidemiology, plant disease resistance, how plant diseases affect humans and animals, pathosystem genetics, and management of plant diseases.

PLANT PATHOGENS

Plantations are replacing natural forest, for example in Indonesia. According to the Food Agricultural Organization (FAO), about 7 per cent of the natural closed forest being lost in the tropics is land being converted to plantations. The remaining 93 per cent of the loss is land being converted to agriculture and other uses. Worldwide, an estimated 15 per cent of plantations in tropical countries are established on closed canopy natural forest.

Fungi

The majority of phytopathogenic fungi belong to the Ascomycetes and the Basidiomycetes.

The fungi reproduce both sexually and asexually via the production of spores and other structures. Spores may be spread long distances by air or water, or they may be soil borne. Many soil inhabiting fungi are capable of living saprotrophically, carrying out the part of their lifecycle in the soil. These are known as facultative saprotrophs.

Fungal diseases may be controlled through the use of fungicides and other agriculture practices, however new races of fungi often evolve that are resistant to various fungicides.

Biotrophic fungal pathogens colonize living plant tissue and obtain nutrients from living host cells. Necrotrophic fungal pathogens infect and kill host tissue and extract nutrients from the dead host cells.

Significant fungal plant pathogens includes:

Ascomycetes

- *Fusarium* spp. (causal agents of Fusarium wilt disease)
- *Thielaviopsis* spp. (causal agents of canker rot, black root rot, Thielaviopsis root rot)
- *Verticillium* spp.
- Magnaporthe grisea (causal agent of blast of rice and gray leaf spot in turfgrasses)

Basidiomycetes

- *Rhizoctonia* spp.
- *Phakospora pachyrhizi* (causal agent of soybean rust)
- *Puccinia* spp. (causal agents of severe rusts of virtually all cereal grains and cultivated grasses)

Oomycetes

The oomycetes are not true fungi but are fungus-like organisms. They include some of the most destructive plant pathogens including the genus Phytophthora which includes the causal agents of potato late blight and sudden oak death.

Despite not being closely related to the fungi, the oomycetes have developed very similar infection strategies and so many plant pathologists group them with fungal pathogens.

Significant oomycete plant pathogens are:

- *Pythium* spp.
- *Phytophthora* spp. [including the causal agent of the Great Irish Famine (1845-1849)]

Bacteria

Most bacteria that are associated with plants are actually saprotrophic, and do no harm to the plant itself. However, a small number, around 100 species, are able to cause disease. Bacterial diseases are much more prevalent in sub-tropical and tropical regions of the world.

Most plant pathogenic bacteria are rod shaped (bacilli). In order to be able to colonize the plant they have specific pathogenicity factors. Five main types of bacterial pathogenicity factors are known:

1. *Cell wall degrading enzymes* - used to break down the plant cell wall in order to release the nutrients inside. Used by pathogens such as Erwinia to cause soft rot.
2. *Toxins* - These can be non-host specific, and damage all plants, or host specific and only cause damage on a host plant.
3. *Effector proteins* - These can be secreted into the extracellular environment or directly into the host cell, often via the Type three secretion system. Some effectors are known to suppress host defense processes.
4. *Phytohormones* - for example Agrobacterium changes the level of auxins to cause tumours.

5. *Exopolysaccharides* - these are produced by bacteria and block xylem vessels, often leading to the death of the plant.

Bacteria control the production of pathogenicity factors via quorum sensing.

Significant bacterial plant pathogens are:

- *Burkholderia*
- *Proteobacteria*
- *Xanthomonas* spp.
- *Pseudomonas* spp.

Phytoplasmas ('Mycoplasma-like organisms') and spiroplasmas

Phytoplasma and Spiroplasma are a genre of bacteria that lack cell walls, and are related to the mycoplasmas which are human pathogens. Together they are referred to as the mollicutes. They also tend to have smaller genomes than true bacteria. They are normally transmitted by sap-sucking insects, being transferred into the plants phloem where it reproduces.

Viruses, Viroids and Virus-like Organisms

There are many types of plant virus, and some are even asymptomatic. Normally plant viruses only cause a loss of crop yield. Therefore it is not economically viable to try to control them, the exception being when they infect perennial species, such as fruit trees.

Most plant viruses have small, single stranded RNA genomes. These genomes may only encode three or four proteins: a replicase, a coat protein, a movement protein to allow cell to cell movement though plasmodesmata and sometimes a protein that allows transmission by a vector.

Plant viruses must be transmitted from plant to plant by a vector. This is often by an insect (for example, aphids), but some fungi, nematodes and protozoa have been shown to be viral vectors.

Nematodes

Nematodes are small, multicellular wormlike creatures. Many live freely in the soil, but there are some species which parasitize plant roots. They are a problem in tropical and subtropical regions of the world, where they may infect crops. Potato cyst nematodes (*Globodera pallida* and *G. rostochiensis*) are widely distributed in Europe and North and South America and cause $300 million worth of damage in Europe every year.

Root knot nematodes have quite a large host range, whereas cyst nematodes tend to only be able to infect a few species. Nematodes are able to cause radical changes in root cells in order to facilitate their lifestyle.

Protozoa

There are a few examples of plant diseases caused by protozoa. They are transmitted as zoospores which are very durable, and may be able to survive in a resting state in the soil for many years. They have also been shown to transmit plant viruses.

When the motile zoospores come into contact with a root hair they produce a plasmodium and invade the roots.

Parasitic Plants

Parasitic plants such as mistletoe and dodder are included in the study of phytopathology. Dodder, for example, is used as a conduit for the transmission of viruses or virus-like agents from a host plant to either a plant that is not typically a host or for an agent that is not graft-transmissible.

PHYSIOLOGICAL PLANT DISORDERS

Significant abiotic disorders can be caused by:

- Natural
- Drought
- Frost damage, and breakage by snow and hail
- Flooding and poor drainage
- Nutrient deficiency
- Salt deposition and other soluble mineral excesses (e.g. gypsum)
- Wind (windburn, and breakage by hurricanes and tornadoes)
- Lightning and wildfire (also often man-made)

Man-made (arguably not abiotic, but usually regarded as such)

- Soil compaction
- Pollution of air, soil, or both
- Salt from winter road salt application or irrigation
- Herbicide over-application
- Poor education and training of people working with plants (e.g. lawnmower damage to trees)
- Vandalism

Quarantine

Wherein a diseased patch of vegetation or individual plants are isolated from other, healthy growth. Specimens may be destroyed or relocated into a greenhouse for treatment/study.

Another option is to avoid introduction of harmful non-native organisms by controlling all human traffic and activity (for e.g., AQIS) although legislation and enforcement are key in order to ensure lasting effectiveness.

Cultural

Farming in some societies is kept on a small scale, tended by peoples whose culture includes farming traditions going back to ancient times. An example of such traditions would be lifelong training in techniques of plot terracing, weather anticipation and response, fertilization, grafting, seed care, and dedicated gardening. Plants that are intently monitored often benefit not only from active external protection, but a greater overall vigor as well. While primitive in the sense of being the most labour-intensive solution by far, where practical or necessary it is more than adequate.

Plant Resistance

Sophisticated agricultural developments now allow growers to choose from among systematically cross-bred species to ensure the greatest hardiness in their crops, as suited for a particular region's pathological profile.

Breeding practices have been perfected over centuries, but with the advent of genetic manipulation even finer control of a crop's immunity traits is possible. The engineering of foodplants may be less rewarding however, as higher output is frequently offset by popular suspicion and negative opinion about this "tampering" with nature.

Chemical

Many natural and synthetic compounds exist that could be employed to combat the above threats. This method works by directly eliminating disease-causing organisms or curbing their spread; however it has been shown to have too broad an effect, typically, to be good for the local ecosystem.

From an economic standpoint all but the simplest natural additives may disqualify a product from "organic" status, potentially reducing the value of the yield.

Biological

Crop rotation may be an effective means to prevent a parasitic population from becoming well established, as an organism affecting leaves would be starved when the leafy crop is replaced by a tuberous type, etc. Other means to undermine parasites without attacking them directly may exist.

Integrated

The use of two or more of these methods in combination offers a higher chance of effectiveness.

Rusts and Smuts Fungi

Rusts and smuts are fungi belonging to the orders *Urediniales* (rusts) and *Ustilaginales* (smuts) which are basidiomycete fungi. The rusts have complicated life cycles which involve the infection of two different plant species. The most well-known members of these groups are wheat rust (*Puccinia graminis tritici*) and corn smut (*Ustilago myadis*). Rust fungi attack plants such as ferns, gymnosperms, and flowering plants. When a wheat plant is infested by *Puccinia graminis tritici*, the infestation may become obvious during the summer growing season when rust colored growth appears on the stems of infected plants.

Fungal hyphae are composed of groups of spore generating structures (sporangia) called *uredinia* that rupture the stem and become visible. It is the spores released from the uredinia (called *urediniospores*) that infect new wheat plants and spread the disease. In the fall, *Puccinia* produces black sporangia (called *telia*) and the infected wheat plants have distinct black patches on their stems. Spores from the telia (called *teliospores*) do not attack other wheat plants but instead infect barberry plants.

Teliospores which land on barberry leaves germinate and form small cup-shaped structures called spermagonia. Each spermagonium produces long filaments called receptive hyphae which extend above the spermagonium and spermatia, which are sexual gametes. The spermagonium also produces a nectar-like substance which is attractive to flies. Spermatia are mixed with this nectar and flies transfer the spermatia from adjacent spermagonia as they feed.

New fungal mycelia, resulting from the union of the spermatia with the receptive hyphae of spermagonia of different genetic strains, grow on the underside of the barberry leaf. There, the mycelium produces a larger bell-shaped sporangium called an aecium, which generates aeciospores which in turn infect new wheat plants.

CORN SMUT

It is a disease of maize caused by the pathogenic plant fungus *Ustilago maydis*. *U. maydis* causes smut disease on maize (*Zea mays*) and teosinte (*Euchlena mexicana*). Known in Mexico as *huitlacoche,* it is eaten, usually as a filling in quesadillas and other tortilla-based foods.

In Mexico, corn smut is known as *huitlacoche*, sometimes spelled *cuitlacoche*. This word entered Spanish in Mexico from classical Nahuatl, though there is debate as to which Nahuatl words huitlacoche derived from. In modern Nahuatl, the word for *huitlacoche* is *cuitlacochin*, and some sources deem "cuitlacochi" to be the classical form.

Some sources give the etymology as coming from the Nahuatl words *cuitla* ("excrement" or "rear-end") and *cochtli* ("sleeping", from *cochi*="to sleep"), thus giving a combined meaning of "sleeping/hibernating excrement."

A second group of sources deem the word to mean "raven's excrement". These sources appear to be combining the word *cuitlacoche* for "thrasher" with *cuitla*, meaning "excrement". However, the avian meaning of *cuitlacoche* derives from the Nahuatl word *cuicatl* ("song"), itself from the verb *cuica* ("to sing"). This root then clashes with this re-construction's second claim that the segment *cuitla-* comes from *cuitla* ("excrement").

One source derives the meaning as "corn excrement", using "cuitla" again and *tlaole* ("maize"). This requires the linguistically unlikely evolution of *tlaole* into *tlacoche.*

How It Enters?

Although, it can infect any part of the plant it usually enters the ovaries and replaces the normal kernels of the cobs with large distorted tumors analogous to mushrooms. These tumors, or "galls", are made up of much-enlarged cells of the infected plant, fungal threads, and blue-black spores. The spores give the cob a burned, scorched appearance. The name *Ustilago* comes from the Latin word *ustilare* (to burn).

Effects on Crops Yield

Smut feeds off the corn plant and decreases the yield. Usually smut-infected crops are destroyed. Some farmers may also choose to prepare corn silage out of the smutted corn. It is most popular in Mexico, where it is known as "huitlacoche" and can be regularly found as an option in meals. The consumption of corn smut originates from ancient Aztec cuisine and is still considered a delicacy in Mexico, even being preserved and sold for a significantly higher price than corn.

For culinary use, the galls are harvested while still immature — fully mature galls are dry and almost entirely spore-filled. The immature galls, gathered two to three weeks after an ear of corn is infected, still retain moisture and, when cooked, have a flavor described as mushroom-like, sweet, savory, woody, and earthy. Flavor compounds include sotolon and vanillin, as well as the sugar glucose.

The fungus has had difficulty entering into the American and European diets as most farmers see it as blight, despite attempts by government and high profile chefs. In the mid-1990s, due to demand created by high-end restaurants, Pennsylvania and Florida farms were allowed by the United States Department of Agriculture (USDA) to intentionally infect corn with *huitlacoche*.

Most observers consider the programme to have had little impact, although the initiative is still in progress. Regardless, the cursory show of interest is significant because the USDA has spent a considerable amount of time and money trying to eradicate *huitlacoche* in the United States. Moreover, in 1989 the James Beard Foundation held a high-profile *huitlacoche* dinner. This dinner famously tried to get Americans to eat more of it by renaming it the Mexican truffle.

Huitlacoche grows best during times of drought in a 78°F to 93°F (25°C–34°C) temperature range. Aztecs purposely inoculated corn with the spores by scratching their corn plants at the soil level with a knife-thereby allowing the water-borne spores easy entrance into the plant.

When grown in the lab on very simple media, it behaves like baker's yeast, forming single cells going by the name sporidia. These cells multiply by budding off daughter cells. When two compatible sporidia meet on the surface of the plant, they switch to a different mode of growth. First, they send out conjugation tubes to find each other, after which they fuse and make a hypha to enter the maize plant.

Hyphae growing in the plant are dikaryotic; they possess two haploid nuclei per hyphal compartment. In contrast to sporidia, the dikaryotic phase of *U. maydis* requires infection of the plant in order to grow and differentiate and cannot be maintained in the laboratory.

Diseases Symptoms

Proliferation of the fungus inside the plant leads to disease symptoms as chlorosis, anthocyanin formation, reduced growth and the appearance of tumors harboring the developing teliospores.

Mature spores are released from the tumors and spread by rain and wind. Under appropriate conditions a probasidium is formed in which meiosis occurs. Resulting haploid nuclei migrate into elongated single cells. These cells detach from the probasidium; these are the sporidia, completing the life cycle.

Native Americans of the American Southwest, including the Zuni tribe, have used corn smut to induce labor. It has similar medicinal effects to ergot, but weaker, due to the presence of the chemical *ustilagine*.

GENETIC MODIFICATION VIA FUNGUS

The yeast-like growth of *Ustilago maydis* makes it an appealing model organism for research, although its relevance in nature is unknown. The fungus is exceptionally well-suited for genetic modification. This allows researchers to study the interaction between the fungus and its host with relative ease. The availability of the entire genome is another advantage of this fungus as model organism.

U. maydis is not only used to study plant disease. In 1996, a study on *U. maydis* genetics lead to the discovery of synthesis-dependent strand annealing, a method of homologous recombination used in DNA repair. Other studies in the fungus have also investigated the role of the cytoskeleton in polarized growth. It is largely due to work with *U. maydis* that the function of the breast-cancer gene BRCA2 is now known.

In Mexico, huitlacoche is mostly consumed fresh and can be purchased at restaurants, street or farmer's markets throughout the country and, to a much lesser degree, can also be purchased as a canned good in some markets and via the internet. Some farmers markets and organic growers are endeavoring to bring fresh huitlacoche to their customers and local food service trade.

COMMON RUST AND SOUTHERN RUST OF SWEET CORN

Common rust and southern rust occur wherever sweet corn and field corn are grown, but cause no real economic damage on dent corn in the Midwest. In commercial sweet corn, yield losses range from 0 to nearly 50 per cent depending on the environment and the type of resistance in the individual hybrid or variety.

Quality factors and quantity are also affected, such as ear length, ear diameter, percentage of moisture, and per cent soluble solids in the kernel. One important difference between the two rusts is that southern rust may possibly kill the corn plant while common rust seldom does. Southern rust occurs primarily in relatively warm regions.

COMMON RUST SYMPTOMS

Common rust is caused by the fungus *Puccinia sorghi*. Symptoms are circular to elongate (usually 0.2 to 2 mm long), golden or reddish brown to cinnamon brown pustules that appear on the upper and lower leaf surfaces, and less frequently on other above-ground plant parts. Most of the infection is found on the upper leaf surface and may occur in bands. The pustules break through the epidermis early in their development and become powdery as spores (urediniospores) are produced.

Later in the season they become brownish black as a second spore stage (teliospores) develops which also breaks through the epidermis. If severe, chlorosis and premature drying of the leaves may occur, reducing sweet corn yields.

Symptoms may vary slightly depending on the hybrid being grown. Common rust is especially severe on many sweet corn hybrids containing the shrunken-2 (sh2) endosperm mutation for high levels of kernel sugars and on some of the sugary-1 (su) hybrids grown for processing.

Disease Cycle

In warmer climates, urediniospores overwinter and serve as primary inoculum. Urediniospores are windblown into the Midwest following a pathway of infected corn plants starting from southwestern United States and Mexico. Infected corn plants appear in Illinois usually about mid-season, and powdery pustules are formed that produce large numbers of microscopic spores (urediniospores) in what is called the repeating stage.

The urediniospores reinfect the same or additional corn plants, producing more urediniospores. Several repeating cycles may occur during a single growing season. Later in the season, the same pustules produce brownish black teliospores.

The teliospores may overwinter and germinate in the spring to form basidiospores, which will only infect species of wood sorrel (*Oxalis* spp). Two more spore stages are produced in Mexico on *Oxalis*: spermatia (pycniospores) are formed and mate with receptive hyphae. From this mating, aeciospores are formed which are wind-disseminated to infect corn.

However, the alternate host (*Oxalis* spp.) is not considered important in the life cycle of this rust disease in the United States. The only other host of the common rust fungus is teosinte (*Zea mays* subsp. *mexicana*; synonym *Euchlaena mexicana*), a close relative of corn.

Common corn rust becomes a problem under ideal environmental conditions which include cool temperatures of 65° to 75°F (18.3° to 23.8°C), abundant moisture in the form of light rains or heavy dews, and high humidity (98 to 100%).

Optimum temperature for urediniospore germination is approximately 50° to 85°F (10° to 28.5°C). An average time from infection to the production of a new generation of mature urediniospores is 7 to 8 days.

SOUTHERN CORN RUST

Symptoms

The fungus causing southern corn rust is *Puccinia polysora*. This disease is much less common in Illinois than common corn rust and is usually considered of minor importance, but can be widespread in some years. The disease becomes progressively more severe as the plant develops, with the greatest damage occurring in late-season plantings.

In years, where it is severe in the southwestern United States, southern corn rust may cause premature desiccation and death of the corn plant. Symptoms are similar to that of common corn rust, with the pustules being lighter in color, smaller (0.2 to 2 mm long), and circular to oval.

The orange-red to light cinnamon brown pustules are often much more numerous on the upper surfaces of leaves with development being slower and less abundant on the lower leaf surface. The pustules are initially less powdery than common corn rust. The leaf epidermis remains intact covering the pustule for a long time, frequently opening by a longitudinal slit.

Chocolate brown to black teliospores are often produced in a circle around the uredial pustule later in the season than teliospores of common corn rust. It is often difficult to separate these two diseases unless the causal fungi are examined microscopically.

Disease Cycle

Urediniospores of this fungus are windblown from previously infected corn leaves, and are blown progressively northward during the growing season. Although teliospores are produced, they do not rupture the epidermis and have not been shown to germinate, and thus are unimportant in the disease cycle.

Disease progress is most rapid when favourable temperatures of 77° to 80°F (25° to 28°C) and high humidity occur in fields of susceptible varieties. As with the common rust pathogen, free water as dew is needed on plant surfaces for urediniospore germination and initial penetration of the corn leaf. Symptoms appear about three to six days after infection and by seven to ten days, the pustules may rupture to expose mature urediniospores. Southern rust is associated with high temperatures, high relative humidity, and heavy rainfall.

Resistance to Rusts

Plant moderately resistant varieties. Commercial varieties of sweet corn vary in their resistance to both common and southern rusts and are much more susceptible than dent corn. Early season varieties often escape infection due to low levels of inoculums or environmental conditions which are not conducive to disease development.

In susceptible varieties, or when conditions are extremely favorable for development of an epidemic, foliar fungicide applications may be feasible starting when pustules first appear on the leaves, particularly in seed production fields

SMUT FUNGI

Smut fungi differ from rust fungi in several ways. While rust fungi require two different hosts to complete their life cycle, smut fungi may complete their life cycle on only one host, which is always a flowering plant.

Another difference between rust and smut fungi is seen in the way that they infect their host plants. Infections from rust fungi are localized to that part of the plant close to where a germinated urediniospore, aeciospore, or teliospore becomes established.

Smut fungi spread to infest the entire plant from a single initial infection site, often targeting specific organs. This is exemplified by the smut fungus *Ustilago violacea* which attacks plants of the genus *Silene*. *Ustilago violacea* infests the entire plant but its presence within the plant is only apparent where mycelia grow within the anthers of the plant. There, hyphae divide to become teliospores and these take the place of pollen grains. Pollinating insects then carry the teliospores from infected *Silene* plants to uninfected ones.

Teliospores mature along with the *Silene* flower and fall to the ground along with seeds of the host *Silene* plant. When the seeds germinate, the smut fungus teliospores germinate along with them and immediately infect the *Silene* seedlings. *Ustilago myadis,* is a well-known smut fungus that infects corn, where its immature teliospores are enclosed in sacs which replace the kernels of corn. When these sacs burst, *U. myadis* spores are released and cling to normal corn kernels. When these kernels are planted, teliospores are planted along with them, infecting new corn plants when they germinate.

Rust and smut fungi are both of great economic importance due to their destruction of cash crops. An effort to eliminate *Puccinia graminis tritici* by the eradication of barberry was not successful. This rust fungus is now controlled by selection for genetically resistant wheat plants, but rust fungi frequently mutate and override Smut on corn. Wheat resistance, so an ongoing genetic selection programme for wheat is necessary.

Another economically important rust fungus is *Gymnosporangium juniperus-virginiae,* which has as its two plant hosts the common juniper (*Juniperus virginianus*) and the domestic apple, and other species of the rose family. This fungus produces large orange colored spore-generating structures on juniper trees, which then infect apple trees, causing the tree to produce deformed and unmarketable apples.

The best way to avoid ruined apples is to keep apple trees away from juniper trees and to remove all infected juniper trees in the area.

One way that humans have reduced infection of corn by smut has been to wash away any clinging fungal spores from the kernels of corn. In the southwestern United States and in Mexico immature corn smut sacs are fried and eaten as a delicacy.

MEDICINAL MUSHROOMS

Medicinal mushrooms are mushrooms, or mushroom extracts, that are used or studied as possible treatments for diseases. Shiitake, Maitake, and Reishi, have a history of medicinal use spanning millennia in parts of Asia. Medicinal mushroom research has indicated possible cardiovascular, anticancer, antiviral, anti-bacterial, anti-parasitic, anti-inflammatory, hepatoprotective, and antidiabetic activities.

Currently, several mushroom extracts like PSK, PSP and lentinan have widespread use in Japan, Korea and China, as chemotherapy adjuvants. Research with most other extracts, are on cell lines, animals, or limited clinical trials. Fungi that do not produce mushrooms, were the original source of penicillin, griseofulvin, lovastatin and other medicines.

Red Rot of Sugarcane

Sugarcane production greatly influenced many tropical Pacific Islands, including Okinawa and, most particularly, Hawai and Fiji. In these islands, sugarcane came to dominate the economic and political landscape after the arrival of powerful European and American agricultural businesses, which promoted immigration of workers from various Asian countries to tend and harvest the crop. Sugar was the dominant factor in diversifying the islands' ethnic make-up, profoundly affecting their politics and society.

Brazil is the biggest grower of sugarcane, which goes for sugar and ethanol for gasoline-ethanol blends (gasohol) for transportation fuel. In India, sugarcane is sold as jaggery, and also refined into sugar, primarily for consumption in tea and sweets, and for the production of alcoholic beverages.

Today, sugarcane is grown in over 110 countries. In 2009, an estimated 1,683 million metric tons were produced worldwide which amounts to 22.4 per cent of the total world agricultural production by weight. About 50 per cent of production occurs in Brazil and India.

RED ROT OF SUGARCANE

This was first reported from Java (now Indonesia) by Went in 1893. During 1895-1900, the disase assumed epidemic proportion in the Godavari Delata of Andhra Pradesh, India. Butler (1906) published a detailed account of this disease from Pusa, Bihar State and gave it the name 'Red rot'. The disease is caused by the fungus *Colletotrichum falcatum* Went (imperfect state);

perfect/ascigerous state = *Glomerella tucumanensis* (Speg.) von Arx and Muller). The disease is the number one problem of sugarcane in India and entire cane breeding in India is geared around this disease. Today, no sugarcane variety is released for cultivation without resistance to red rot.

The pathogen is mainly sett-borne (goes in the field along with the planting material) and thus affects the cane plant from the germination. The damage starts with germination failure, settling mortality to the dying of the full-grown cane. In full-grown cane the disease appears as the yellowing of the crown leaves.

On splitting open the cane of such affected plants, interrupted red and white patches (white spot) along with sour alcoholic odour are observed. In later statge numerous acervuli develops on the rind. The pathogen mainly spreads during the rainy season and if environement favours it can wipe out entire sugarcane plantation.

Disease Management

The disease is currently managed through host resistance as fungicides do not get adequate entry (conc. is less to effect eradication) into the stalk. Application of biocontrol agents like *Trichoderma* has shown promise in the containment of the disease through antibiosis and induced systemic resistance.

Sugarcane cultivation requires a tropical or temperate climate, with a minimum of 60 centimetres (24 in) of annual moisture. It is one of the most efficient photosynthesizers in the plant kingdom. It is a C_4 plant, able to convert up to one per cent of incident solar energy into biomass. In prime growing regions, such as India, Pakistan, Peru, Brazil, Bolivia, Colombia, Australia, Ecuador, Cuba, the Philippines, El Salvador and Hawaii, sugarcane can produce 20 lb (9 kg) for each square meter exposed to the sun.

Although sugarcanes produce seeds, modern stem cutting has become the most common reproduction method. Each cutting must contain at least one bud, and the cuttings are sometimes hand-planted. In more technologically advanced countries like the United States and Australia, billet planting is common.

Billets harvested from a mechanical harvester are planted by a machine which opens and recloses the ground. Once planted, a stand can be harvested several times; after each harvest, the cane sends up new stalks, called ratoons. Successive harvests give decreasing yields, eventually justifying replanting. Two to 10 harvests may be possible between plantings.

Sugarcane is harvested by hand and mechanically. Hand harvesting accounts for more than half of production, and is dominant in the developing world. In hand harvesting, the field is first set on fire. The fire burns dry leaves, and kills any lurking venomous snakes, without harming the stalks and roots. Harvesters then cut the cane just above ground-level using cane knives or machetes. A skilled harvester can cut 500 kilograms (1,100 lb) of sugarcane per hour.

Mechanical harvesting uses a combine, or chopper harvester. The Austoft 7000 series, the original modern harvester design, has now been copied by other companies, including Cameco/John Deere. The machine cuts the cane at the base of the stalk, strips the leaves, chops the cane into consistent lengths and deposits it into a transporter following alongside. The harvester then blows the trash back onto the field. Such machines can harvest 100 long tons (100 t) each hour; however,'harvested cane must be rapidly processed.

Once cut, sugarcane begins to lose its sugar content, and damage to the cane during mechanical harvesting accelerates this decline. This decline is offset because a modern chopper harvester can complete the harvest faster and more efficiently than hand cutting and loading.

Austoft also developed a series of hydraulic high-lift infield transporters to work alongside their harvesters to allow even more rapid transfer of cane to, for example, the nearest railway siding.

LIST OF SUGARCANE DISEASES

Gumming disease	Bacterial diseases *Xanthomonas campestris* pv. vasculorum
Leaf scald	*Xanthomonas albilineans*
Mottled stripe	*Herbaspirillum rubrisubalbicans*
Ratoon stunting disease	*Leifsonia xyli* subsp. xyli
Red stripe (top rot)	*Acidovorax avenae*
	Fungal diseases
Banded sclerotial (leaf) disease	*Thanatephorus cucumeris* = *Pellicularia sasakii* *Rhizoctonia solani* [anamorph]
Black rot	*Ceratocystis adiposa* *Chalara* sp. [anamorph]
Black stripe	*Cercospora atrofiliformis*
Brown spot	*Cercospora longipes*
Brown stripe	*Cochliobolus stenospilus* *Bipolaris stenospila* [anamorph]

Downy mildew	*Peronosclerospora sacchari* = *Sclerospora sacchari*
Downy mildew, leaf splitting form	*Peronosclerospora miscanthi* = *Sclerospora mischanthi* *Mycosphaerella striatiformans*
Eye spot	*Bipolaris sacchari* = *Helminthosporium sacchari*
Fusarium sett and stem rot	*Gibberella fujikuroi* *Fusarium moniliforme* [anamorph] *Gibberella subglutinans*
Iliau	*Clypeoporthe iliau* = *Gnomonia iliau* *Phaeocytostroma iliau* [anamorph]
Leaf blast	*Didymosphaeria taiwanensis*
Leaf blight	*Leptosphaeria taiwanensis* *Stagonospora tainanensis* [anamorph]
Leaf scorch	*Stagonospora sacchari*
Marasmius sheath and shoot blight	*Marasmiellus stenophyllus* = *Marasmius stenophyllus*
Myriogenospora leaf binding (tangle top)	*Myriogenospora aciculispora*
Phyllosticta leaf spot	*Phyllosticta hawaiiensis*
Phytophthora rot of cuttings	*Phytophthora* spp. *Phytophthora megasperma*
Pineapple disease	Ceratocystis paradoxa *Chalara paradoxa* = *Thielaviopsis paradoxa* [anamorph]
Pokkah boeng (that may have knife cut symptoms)	*Gibberella fujikuroi* *Fusarium moniliforme* [anamorph] *Gibberella subglutinans*
Red leaf spot (purple spot)	*Dimeriella sacchari*
Red rot	*Glomerella tucumanensis* = *Physalospora tucumanensis* *Colletotrichum falcatum* [anamorph]

Red rot of leaf sheath and sprout rot	*Athelia rolfsii* = *Pellicularia rolfsii* *Sclerotium rolfsii* [anamorph]
Red spot of leaf sheath	*Mycovellosiella vaginae* = *Cercospora vaginae*
Rhizoctonia sheath and shoot rot	*Rhizoctonia solani*
Rind disease (sour rot)	*Phaeocytostroma sacchari* = *Pleocyta sacchari* = *Melanconium sacchari*
Ring spot	*Leptosphaeria sacchari* *Phyllosticta* sp. [anamorph]
Root rots	*Marasmius sacchari* *Pythium arrhenomanes* *Pythium graminicola* *Rhizoctonia* sp. *Unidentified Oomycete*
Rust, common	*Puccinia melanocephala* = *Puccinia erianthi*
Rust, orange	*Puccinia kuehnii*
Schizophyllum rot	*Schizophyllum commune*
Sclerophthora disease	*Sclerophthora macrospora*
Seedling blight	*Alternaria alternata* *Bipolaris sacchari* *Cochliobolus hawaiiensis* *Bipolaris hawaiiensis* [anamorph] *Cochliobolus lunatus* *Curvularia lunata* [anamorph] *Curvularia senegalensis* *Setosphaeria rostrata* *Exserohilum rostratum* [anamorph] = *Drechslera halodes*
Sheath rot	*Cytospora sacchari*
Smut, culmicolous	*Ustilago scitaminea*
Target blotch	*Helminthosporium sp.*
Veneer blotch	*Deightoniella papuana*

White rash	*Elsinoë sacchari* *Sphaceloma sacchari* [anamorph]
Wilt	*Fusarium sacchari* = *Cephalosporium sacchari*
Yellow spot	*Mycovellosiella koepkei* = *Cercospora koepkei*
Zonate leaf spot	*Gloeocercospora sorghi*
Miscellaneous diseases and disorders	
Bud proliferation	Undetermined
Bunch top	Undetermined
Cluster stool	Undetermined
Internal stalk necrosis	Undetermined
Leaf freckle	Undetermined
Leaf stipple	
Multiple buds	Undetermined
Stem galls	Undetermined
Nematodes, parasitic	
Lesion	Pratylenchus spp.
Root-knot	Meloidogyne spp.
Spiral	Helicotylenchus spp.
	Rotylenchus spp.
	Scutellonema spp.
VIRAL DISEASES	
Chlorotic streak	Virus (assumed)
Dwarf	Sugarcane dwarf virus
Fiji disease	Sugarcane Fiji disease virus
Mosaic	Sugarcane mosaic virus
Sereh	Virus (assumed)
Streak disease	Maize streak virus, sugarcane strain
Yellow Leaf	Sugarcane Yellow Leaf Virus

PHYTOPLASMA DISEASES	
Phytoplasmas were previously known as 'mycoplasma-like organisms' (MLOs).	
Phytoplasma Diseases	
Grassy Shoot (SCGS), Leaf Chlorosis, Sugarcane Grassy	Early Bud Sprouting, Shoot Phytoplasma

Pests

The cane beetle also known as cane grub can substantially reduce crop yield by eating roots; it can be controlled with imidacloprid (Confidor) or chlorpyrifos (Lorsban). Other important pests are the larvae of some butterfly/ moth species, including the turnip moth, the sugarcane borer (Diatraea saccharalis), the Mexican rice borer (*Eoreuma loftini*); leaf-cutting ants, termites, spittlebugs especially *Mahanarva fimbriolata* and *Deois flavopicta*, and the beetle *Migdolus fryanus*. The planthopper insect Eumetopina flavipes acts as a virus vector, which causes the sugarcane disease ramu stunt.

How Pathogens Infect Sugacane?

Numerous pathogens infect sugarcane, such as sugarcane grassy shoot disease caused by Phytoplasma, whiptail disease or sugarcane smut, pokkah boeng caused by *Fusarium moniliforme*, and red rot disease caused by *Colletotrichum falcatum*. Viral diseases affecting sugarcane include sugarcane mosaic virus, maize streak virus, and sugarcane yellow leaf virus.

Fixing Nitrogen Fixation

Some sugarcane varieties are known to be capable of fixing atmospheric nitrogen in association with the bacterium *Glucoacetobacter diazotrophicus*. Unlike legumes and other nitrogen fixing plants which form root nodules in the soil in association with bacteria, *G. diazotrophicus* lives within the intercellular spaces of the sugarcane's stem.

Red rot is a serious disease of sugarcane in the southern United States. It causes a rot of seed cuttings that commonly results in faulty stands of plant cane or sometimes complete failures, reductions in stands of stubble or ratoon crops because of the rotting of the underground parts of the stem from which the crops arise, and annual losses of sucrose in mill cane from infection of the stalks that usually follows injury by the sugarcane moth borer, *Diatraea saccharalis*.

Besides the loss in tonnage from reduced stands of cane, red rot lowers the amount of recoverable sugar at the factory because of the inversion of sucrose in the stalk, which is accompanied by lowered purity of the juice and other untoward chemical changes.

Because it is most destructive as a rot of seed cuttings, red rot causes little injury to seed cane if conditions favor the early germination of the buds after planting, as in the Tropics. In the subtropics, however, such as India, South Africa, and Queensland, where considerable time may elapse between the time of planting and the establishment of new plants, it frequently reduces stands badly. As a rot of mill cane, on the other hand, it may be more important in the tropical areas, where the longer growing season gives the fungus more time in which to spread through the stalks between the time of infection and milling of the cane.

Red rot was first described in Java in 1893. Shortly thereafter it was identified in the West Indies, where it was considered at first to be a cause of the then prevalent root disease. Within the next 20 years its occurrence was recorded in Queensland, India, Hawaii, and Louisiana. It now is one of the most widely distributed of the diseases of sugarcane.

Decline in Sugarcane Varieties

Red rot has been a major cause of the decline of several varieties of sugarcane in the Southern States. First identified in Louisiana in 1909, it doubtless was a factor in the general downward trend in the average yield that began early in this century in Louisiana. It was one of the causes of the failure of the Louisiana Purple and D-74 varieties in Louisiana in the 1920's and of those and other noble-type varieties in the other Gulf States. It forced the discontinuance as a commercial cane of the variety P. O. J. 2714 in southern Florida.

The noble varieties were replaced in Louisiana with hybrids from Java, one of which, P. O. J. 213, became the leading commercial variety in the State by 1931. Classed as resistant to red rot when it was released, it suddenly failed from red rot in the early 1930's. In the sirup-producing districts of the Gulf States, Cayana 10 and P. O. J. 213 became the most popular replacements of the older canes, but both eventually succumbed to red rot. Some of the other varieties that have succeeded them as important commercial canes have also declined from red rot, but they were tested more rigidly before they were released to growers, and their potential weakness in this respect was recognized at the time of their release.

The Fungus that causes red rot may infect any part of the sugarcane plant. Its principal importance is as a rot of the stalk of standing cane, of seed cuttings, or of the stubble pieces remaining in the ground after the cane is harvested. It produces long lesions on the leaf midribs. The lesions usually cause no serious injury to the plant but are important in the life history of the disease because they are sources of the spores that cause infection of the stalk.

Red rot often cannot be told on external examination of the stalk unless it has rotted the interior so completely as to cause the rind to lose its natural bright colour and to look dull. Plants so affected may be detected by the yellowing, shriveling, and dying of the upper leaves. More certain identification may be made by splitting the stalk or seed cutting. Then one recognizes the disease by the reddening of the normally white or creamy-white internal tissues and cross-barring of the reddened area with occasional white or light patches.

Unless the cross bars are present, identification of red rot may be uncertain without microscopic examination or culturing of the fungus. Almost any sort of wounding causes a reddening of the stalk tissues next to the wound, but when red rot is present the characteristic discoloration usually extends considerably beyond the point of origin. In advanced stages of rotting, the interior of the stalk darkens and the tissues shrink, leaving a cavity, which may be filled with the mycelium of the fungus.

The lesions on the leaf midribs are dark or blood red, and may occur as short, discontinuous blotches or as long ones that extend nearly the length of the leaf. The centers become straw-colored with age and are later covered with the black, powdery masses of the spores of the fungus.

The fungus causing red rot is commonly known by its imperfect stage, *Colletotrichum falcatum*, although *Physalospora tucumanensis* is the perfect stage of the fungus. If a fairly large number of isolates of the fungus obtained from different cane varieties or geographic areas are studied on artificial culture media, considerable variation in the type of growth and color of the fungus colony usually is seen. Some isolates or races are light gray and form a loose cottony colony. Others are dark gray and form a restricted velvety colony. Others are intermediate in those respects. If they are inoculated into stalks of sugarcane, the fact that they differ also in pathogenicity their ability to infect and rot the stalks will be seen.

It is this variability of the fungus that makes it appear that some sugarcane varieties are unstable in their resistance to the disease. Often a new variety, when it is released to growers, may be resistant to the races of the fungus then prevalent. If a race that is virulent toward that variety is present or appears later, however, it may build up on it and eventually cause serious injury.

We have evidence that that occurred with the variety P. O. J. 213 in Louisiana in the early 1930s. Some growers believe this change in predominance of races of disease organisms indicates an inherent change in the sugarcane variety with respect to its disease resistance. The real explanation, though, is to be sought in changes in the prevailing populations of the disease organism.

The infections of the leaf midrib provide the means of dissemination of the disease during the growing season and the source of inoculum for stalk infections. The infections appear in Louisiana in the late spring and continue to develop on new leaves as they are produced during the summer.

On the midrib lesions the fungus produces an abundance of spores, which are carried by wind or splashed by rain to other leaves and plants. Heavy dews and rains wash the spores down the leaf blade to the attachment of sheath to the stalk, where the spore-laden moisture may be held for some time in contact with the nodal region of the stem. The spores may also be washed down the stalk, where they cause infections through the tunnels made by the moth borer.

Bacteria and Fungi on Seedlings

Many people equate bacteria with disease and fungi with rot. But in fact, the vast majority of bacteria and fungi are beneficial to life on earth. These two classes of microbes are irreplaceable parts of the organic web of life. Without them your plantation crop would not grow. Without them, organic plantation would not be possible.

The effects of micro-organisms on a plant can be profound. These organisms, such as bacillus, mycorrhizae and trichoderma all form symbiotic relationships with the plant and are found in soil. Bacillus is used world wide for the control of loopers, fungus gnats, insect pests and opportunistic fungi pathogens. Tricoderma is a fungi that feeds off pathogenic root rot and damping off fungi; it also stimulates the plants root and immune systems, which helps the plant to fight off fungi attacks.

Mycorrhizae is a beneficial fungi which colonizes the root surface; this helps keep the pathogenic fungi from getting a foot hold on the plant's root system. Mycorrhizae also helps the plant take up nutrients that are out of reach of the plant's roots. All of these beneficial organisms feed off plant exudes from the root system and some nutrients in the growing medium.

Bacteria and fungi perform many almost miraculous tasks in the agricultural land. In instance, they lock up plant nutrients until they're needed. This greatly reduces the reducing leeching of those vital nutrients from the soil. They also help retain water in the soil, near your plants' roots where it's needed.

But probably their greatest contribution to your garden—and to the organic web of life—is as the earth's main decomposers. They take dead plant and animal material and break it down into components that other plants and animals are able to "eat".

It's normal to think that eating involves biting, chewing and swallowing (after all, that's how we and other large animals do it). But in fact, all living things need to eat—that is, they need to ingest energy and nutrients in order to grow and reproduce.

To get the maximum benefit from beneficial micro-organisms, the gardener should always provide food for these beneficals. Providing these organisms with food (e.g.: Liquid Karma, Earth Juice Catalyst and Sweet) ensures that they will grow and multiply in your garden, however, the harmful micro-organisms will also use this food to multiply.

This is one of the reasons why your water and growing medium should be well oxygenated. Harmful pathogens tend to thrive in anaerobic conditions whereas beneficial organisms thrive in aerobic conditions.

1. **For clones and seedlings:** Use both Hydroguard (15ml per gallon) and Rhizotonic (15ml per gallon). These two products can be used in clone machines, rockwool cubes and Rapid Rooters. The Hydroguard contains two bacillus strains which secrete anti-biotics which will fight off root rot and damping-off pathogens. The Rhizotonic will help your young plants develop vigorous, healthy, strong roots; it will also provide the bacillus with some food. If your seedlings or clones develop a stem rot Hydroguard can be painted on the affected area (1 part Hydroguard 3 parts water).

2. **For plants in soil:** Most gardeners who grow in soil will use organic nutrients to feed there plants. Mycorrhizae suits plants that are being fed organic nutrients; chemical nutrients, especially when the concentration builds up in the growing medium, will destroy the Mycorrhizae. It is best to apply Mycorrhizae into the soil before planting (1 teaspoon of Rooters Mycorrhizae per gallon of soil). Bacillus and tricoderma can also be used on plants grown in soil. One pouch of Subculture should be mixed into 8 cubic feet of soil. A maintenance application should be reapplied every four to six weeks at one teaspoon per ten gallons of water. A weekly application of Liquid Karma or Earth Juice Catalyst will help keep your plants healthy and also provide the beneficial organisms with essential foods to keep them multiplying. This programme can also be used for plants being grown in coco fiber that are fed organic nutrients.

3. **For hydroponic systems:** Mycorrhizae does not do well in hydroponic systems as it is sensitive to the nutrients that are used for hydroponics. For hydroponic systems it is best to use Subculture or Hydroguard. Both these products contain bacillus strains which are well suited to hydroponics even in systems that have high salt contents. Subculture should be applied at a rate of 1 teaspoon per 10 gallons of water/nutrient solution (1 pouch per 50 gallons). The first application of Hydroguard should be 15ml per gallon and maintenance applications at 5-10ml per gallon of nutrient solution. For coco fibre, rockwool and ready-Gro mediums, both hydroguard and subculture should be reapplied three weeks after first application and thereafter every three weeks. For hydroponic systems that use Hydroton rocks, perlite, NFT or aeroponics, the Subculture and Hydroguard should be reapplied every one week.
4. **Foliar Sprays:** Both Hydroguard and Subculture can be used as a foliar spray to help control mildew that attack the leaves, stems, flowers and fruits of plants. Serenade is another product which contains only Bacillus subtilus. These bacteria will effectively control most leaf fungi pathogens.
5. **Fungus Gnats:** Bacillus thuringienses sub-species israelensis (the active ingredient in Gnatrol) is used for the control of fungus gnats. This bacteria produces a parasporal crystal which is toxic to the larvae of fungus gnats.

Here's how bacteria and fungi carry energy from the sun to plants, animals and you.

The sun provides the ultimate source of energy on earth. Through the process of photosynthesis, green plants convert the sun's light energy, carbon dioxide (CO_2), and water (H_2O) into simple sugars.

These simple sugars contain only carbon (C), oxygen (O), and hydrogen (H). This energy-harvesting process occurs in plants as tiny as one-celled alga and as massive as giant redwoods.

All green plants turn these simple sugars into more complex chemical structures such as starches and proteins. Larger green plants then convert these components into more complex structures like leaves, stems, bark, and roots.

While complex in its details, this process of harvesting the sun's energy for most life on earth might seem straightforward. But there's one huge problem with the way I've described it.

Animals and plants need more to survive and reproduce than sugars and starches. They need proteins, DNA, RNA, fats, vitamins, and other substances that contain elements other than carbon, oxygen, and hydrogen. They need nitrogen, sulfur, phosphorus, potassium, and numerous other minerals.

And the process of photosynthesis does *not* provide these last crucial elements. Where do they come from? Plants are able to absorb most of the sulfur and many soluble minerals directly from the water or soil they live in. But they're not able to absorb all the nitrogen they need that way.

How does nitrogen get into plants? This is where bacteria and fungi come into the picture.

MOLECULAR NITROGEN

Nitrogen is the most common component of air—but in the form of a two-atom molecule N_2 (called molecular nitrogen). Plants can't use molecular nitrogen. They're unable to break the bonds holding the two nitrogen atoms together to release nitrogen in a form plants can use to make proteins.

However, a special class of bacteria called nitrogen-fixing bacteria are able to break this bond. By a special, symbiotic relationship with plants, these bacteria provide them with usable nitrogen.

Problem solved, so it seems. But it isn't. Once nitrogen and sulfur are used by plants to make proteins and other biochemicals, these elements are "locked up." They're locked up inside the animals and other plants that eat them.

Some of these important life-sustaining elements (nitrogen, carbon, sulfur and others) are excreted as waste material. Some remain in organisms the original nutrient providers ate until that organism dies.

These crucial elements would stay in the waste material and the dead organisms if it weren't for bacteria and fungi.

These tiny organisms—in a process we turn our noses up to and call "decay"—release these locked up elements. They recycle them.

You may have heard in elementary school that if it weren't for bacteria and fungi, we'd be walking knee deep in excrement and dead animals and plants. But bacteria and fungi's role is far more important than that.

If it weren't for these tiny recyclers, we wouldn't even be walking around. Without these microbes, animals and most complex plants would not have the nutrients they need to grow and reproduce.

So, the bottom line for you as a conscientious organic gardener: If you want to harness the organic web of life in your agricultural land you must "pamper" the bacteria and fungi that make your agricultural land grow.

That pampering starts with knowledge. So here's your "short course" on the details of the roles bacteria and fungi play in the organic web of life.

UNDERSTANDING BACTERIA AND FUNGI

What they "eat"	• Bacteria decompose both dead plant & animal material and take in nutrients released by the decomposition. • Bacteria do best with "green" material (fresh plants, no woody parts). • Root exudates are favorite foods for some bacteria, so there can be huge populations of these bacteria near roots (called the rhizosphere).
Who they feed	• Other members of the web get food and energy by eating bacteria. If there are not enough bacteria or they're killed by chemicals or over tillage, the entire organic web of life in your garden suffers.
Element recycling	• Bacteria play a crucial role in recycling carbon, nitrogen, and sulfur.
Nutrient retention and release	• Bacteria lock up nutrients in their cells that otherwise would disappear through leeching. Since bacteria attach themselves to soil particles, these nutrients stay in the soil, close to plant roots. • When bacteria die, fungi and other microbes scavenge their bodies, releasing locked-up nutrients back into the soil. • Bacteria don't travel far therefore the nutrients stay close to the roots. • Thus, bacteria can be viewed as living fertilizer containers.
Special considerations	• Bacteria generally prefer alkaline soil conditions pH above 7. Most vegetables, annuals, and grasses prefer bacterially dominated soils.
Special problems and solutions	• Many anaerobic bacteria bacteria that grow in the absence of air are toxic to plant life, other bacteria, and humans. They are usually bad

	smelling, suggesting rotting and putrifaction. Conditions promoting anaerobic bacteria include poor soil texture, lack of soil pore space, standing water, and soil compaction.These conditions can result from excess tillage of the soil. • Artificial insecticides, chemical fertilizers, and non-organic approaches to plant culture can kill bacteria, fungi, and other beneficial microbes. • Solution to these problems: Bacteria compete with each other. When conditions for bacterial growth are well maintained, the "good" bacteria win out against the anaerobic and other dangerous bacteria.
What they "eat"	• Like bacteria, fungi break down both dead plant & animal material. But they also eat dead bacteria, releasing nutrients stored in bacterial cells. • Fungi are the primary decomposers of the organic web of life. • While some fungi prefer easier-to-digest sugars, most prefer hard-to-digest "brown" material like dried leaves and woody parts of plants. • Fungi are able to penetrate hard surfaces including plants, insect shells, and bones. This ability to penetrate surfaces results in release of important inorganic minerals for plant (and ultimately animal) use.
Who they feed	• Some fungi exude nutrients while alive. But most release their stored nutrients when other organisms eat them. They also release their nutrients and feed the soil when they die and decay. • Some fungi called mycorrhizal fungi form a special symbiotic relatio-nship with plant roots. They produce microscopic threads that penetrate root hairs, transporting nutrients from the soil directly into the plant.

	• Without mycorrhizal fungi, plants could not obtain the variety or amounts of nutrients they need to grow optimally. For this reason, your gardening practices should protect these special fungi.
Element recycling	• As with bacteria, fungi play a crucial role in recycling carbon, nitrogen, and sulfur.
Nutrient retention and release	• Fungi lock up nutrients in their cells that otherwise would disappear through leeching. • Like bacteria, fungi immobilize nutrients they take in. These nutrients are released later when the fungi die or other organisms eat them. • So, like bacteria, fungi are living fertilizer containers.
Special considerations	• Fungi generally prefer acidic soil conditions (pH below 7). Most shrubs, trees, and woody plants prefer fungi-dominated soils. • Mycorrhizal fungi unlock and transport copper, calcium, magnesium, zinc, and iron for plant use.
Special problems and solutions	• Artificial insecticides, chemical fertilizers, and non-organic approaches to plant culture can kill fungi. • Tillage of garden soil destroys the microscopic threads of beneficial mycorrhizal fungi, reducing nutrient uptake by plants and trees. • Solution to these problems: Reducing or eliminating tillage, use of organic fertilizers, and avoidance of chemical insecticides and other materials protects the fungi-plant symbiosis while allowing fungi to grow and thrive naturally.

Soil scientists are just starting to gather a significant body of data showing biochar's beneficial effect on soil microbes. But there is an ancient "laboratory" that gives strong evidence that biochar encourages growth of these beneficial organisms.

Terra preta—the dark earths of the Amazon which are rich in biochar—are also significantly richer in microbial activity, composition, and mass than the surrounding areas that lack biochar amendment.

This historical insight provides evidence of the beneficial relationship that exists between biochar and microbes including bacteria and fungi.

But there are some very exciting results from modern experiments as well. Dr. Paul Blackwell has been working since 1988 to improve the soils in Western Australia. At a 2007 International Biochar Initiative meeting in Terrigal, Australia, Dr. Blackwell presented findings reached on his work with biochar.

His results were very positive. He established the biochar probably helped the seed-applied microbes survive better in a dry soil environment at planting.

Another experiment demonstrates visually the direct effect of biochar as seen which show the growth of plants that had been grown in just biochar and in biochar with added mycorrhizal fungi after two and half months.

The plants grown with biochar and added fungi showed significantly darker and more dense plant growth at the 75-day mark than the control plants or those grown just with biochar .

This result is a good indication of the mutually beneficial interaction between biochar and mycorrhizal fungi. The theory behind this positive effect is that biochar improves soil porosity, giving beneficial bacteria and fungi favorable living conditions. It's also suspected that biochar's own pores provide good growing places for beneficial microbes.

More research needs to be done to determine the exact causes for biochar's ability to improve the interaction of beneficial bacteria and fungi in your garden.

Many people enjoy starting their own seeds. Not only is it enjoyable, but it is economical as well. Because starting seeds indoor is so popular, many people can become frustrated if they run into problems. One common problem is the development of a white, fluffy fungus (some people may mistake it for a mold) on the top of the seed starting soil that can eventually kill a seedling. Let's take a look at how you can stop this fungus from ruining your indoor seed starting.

The number one reason that this white, fluffy fungus grows on your seed starting soil is due to high humidity. Most seed growing tips will suggest that you keep the humidity high over the soil until the seeds have fully germinated. Your seedling planter probably has a lid or cover that help with this or you cave covered your indoor seed starting container with plastic. Sometimes, this raises the humidity to a level that is too high and which encourages the growth of this white, fluffy fungus.

Either prop open the lid of the seedling planter about an inch or poke some holes in the plastic over the container you are starting seeds indoor in. This will allow more air circulation and decrease the humidity some around the seed starting soil.

If you have taken steps to increase the air circulation around your seedling planter and have decreased the humidity around the seed starting soil and the fungus is still growing, you will need to take additional steps. Setup a small fan that can blow gently over your indoor seed starting setup. This will help to get the air moving, making it much harder for the fungus to grow.

Be careful though that you keep the fan at very low levels and only run the fan for a few hours each day. If the fan is running too high, this will damage your seedlings.

Starting seeds indoor does not need to be tricky. Now that you can keep the fungus off your soil, you can grow healthy seedlings for your agricultural land.

WAY TO PREVENT DAMPING OFF FUNGUS

Seedlings that wilt and die are usually afflicted by damping off — a disease caused by a fungus. Unfortunately, young seedlings are especially susceptible to fungus. Worse yet, fungi spreads quickly, wiping out entire trays of seedlings.

The best way to prevent damping off is to use sterile potting mix. You'll find mixes specially made for seed starting that are soilless. These soilless mixes are sterile — and your best bet for avoiding any fungus problems.

Never re-use potting mixes. It's just not worth it. And, don't even think about digging up dirt from your garden to start seeds indoors. Garden soil is a triple threat: it becomes too compact in a container, it's also filled with live bacteria, and possibly insects. You don't want to start off your seedlings with these problems.

Use clean containers. If you re-use trays or other containers for starting seeds, wash them thoroughly with soap and water, then allow to dry completely before planting in them. Containers for seed starting need to be clean to prevent contaminating the potting medium.

Avoid overwatering. Fungus thrives in a moist environment. Overwatering seedlings promotes damping off fungus. It's a good idea to water seedlings from below so that the surface of the potting medium doesn't become soggy.

Most seed starting trays have drainage holes to allow the potting medium to soak up water from below. Peat pots, which are made up of compressed peat moss, will also soak up water.

Damping off is a fungal disease that can strike seedlings and quickly kill them. If not detected right away, it will spread and can wipe out every seedling in a tray within hours. Too much moisture and a lack of ventilation help to promote this dreaded disease.

What to Do if Your Seedlings Show Signs of Damping Off

If you find even one of your seedlings lying on the soil, pull it out. Just as a precaution, remove the surrounding seedlings at once.

Is the soil too moist? Do what you can to increase air circulation around the seedlings. Move the tray away from other plants to avoid contaminating them and to help air flow. Use a fan on the seedlings to help dry the soil. If the soil surface is soggy, try gently blotting it with paper towels to wick up the excess moisture.

Once the soil has dried out a bit, you can return the tray back to its former location. Water only when the soil is dry, aiming to keep it only lightly moist. Always water seedlings from the bottom—and don't leave containers to sit in water any longer than it takes to moisten the soil surface.

SOIL LIFE

Soil life is a collective term for all the organisms living within the soil. In a balanced soil, plants grow in an active and vibrant environment. The mineral content of the soil and its physical structure are important for their well-being, but it is the life in the earth that powers its cycles and provides its fertility. Without the activities of soil organisms, organic materials would accumulate and litter the soil surface, and there would be no food for plants. The soil life includes:

1. **Macrofauna:** size range 2–20 mm, e.g. woodlice, earthworms, beetles, centipedes, slugs, snails, ants, and harvestmen.
2. **Megafauna:** size range 20 mm upwards, e.g. moles, rabbits, and rodents.
3. **Microfauna** and **Microflora:** size range 1-100 micrometres, e.g. yeasts, bacteria (commonly actinobacteria), fungi, protozoa, roundworms, and rotifers.
4. **Mesofauna:** size range 100 micrometre-2 mm, e.g. tardigrades, mites and springtails.

Of these, bacteria and fungi play key roles in maintaining a healthy soil. They act as decomposers that break down organic materials to produce detritus and other breakdown products. Soil detritivores, like earthworms, ingest detritus and decompose it. Saprotrophs, well represented by fungi and bacteria, extract soluble nutrients from delitro.

BACTERIA

Bacteria are single-celled organisms, and are the most numerous denizens of agriculture, with populations ranging from 100 million to 3 billion in a gram. They are capable of very rapid reproduction by binary fission (dividing into two) in favourable conditions. One bacterium is capable of producing 16 million more in just 24 hours. Most soil bacteria live close to plant roots and are often referred to as rhizobacteria. Bacteria live in soil water, including the film of moisture surrounding soil particles, and some are able to swim by means of flagella.

The majority of the beneficial soil-dwelling bacteria need oxygen and are thus termed aerobic bacteria, whilst those that do not require air are referred to as anaerobic, and tend to cause putrefaction of dead organic matter. Aerobic bacteria are most active in a soil that is moist but not saturated, as this will deprive aerobic bacteria of the air that they require, and neutral soil pH, and where there is plenty of food (carbohydrates and micro-nutrients from organic matter) available.

Hostile conditions will not completely kill bacteria; rather, the bacteria will stop growing and get into a dormant stage, and those individuals with pro-adaptive mutations may compete better in the new conditions. Some Gram positive bacteria produce spores in order to wait for more favourable circumstances, and Gram negative bacteria gets into a "nonculturable" stage. Bacteria are colonized by persistent viral agents (bacteriophages) which determine gene word order in bacterial host.

Nitrification

It is a vital part of the nitrogen cycle wherein certain bacteria (which manufacture their own carbohydrate supply without using the process of photosynthesis) are able to transform nitrogen in the form of ammonium, which is produced by the decomposition of proteins, into nitrates, which are available to growing plants, and once again converted to proteins.

Nitrogen Fixation

The process of nitrogen fixation constantly puts additional nitrogen into biological circulation. This is carried out by free-living nitrogen-fixing bacteria in the soil or water such as *Azotobacter*, or by those that live in close symbiosis with leguminous plants, such as rhizobia. These bacteria form colonies in nodules they create on the roots of peas, beans, and related species.

These are able to convert nitrogen from the atmosphere into nitrogen-containing organic substances.

Denitrification

While nitrogen fixation converts nitrogen from the atmosphere into organic compounds, a series of processes called denitrification returns an approximately equal amount of nitrogen to the atmosphere. Denitrifying bacteria tend to be anaerobes, or facultatively anaerobes (can alter between the oxygen dependent and oxygen independent types of metabolisms), including *Achromobacter* and *Pseudomonas*.

The putrefaction process caused by oxygen-free conditions converts nitrates and nitrites in soil into nitrogen gas or into gaseous compounds such as nitrous oxide or nitric oxide. In excess, denitrification can lead to overall losses of available soil nitrogen and subsequent loss of soil fertility.

However, fixed nitrogen may circulate many times between organisms and the soil before denitrification returns it to the atmosphere. The diagram above illustrates the nitrogen cycle.

Actinobacteria

Actinobacteria are critical in the decomposition of organic matter and in humus formation, and their presence is responsible for the sweet "earthy" aroma associated with a good healthy soil. They require plenty of air and a pH between 6.0 and 7.5, but are more tolerant of dry conditions than most other bacteria and fungi.

FUNGI

A gram of garden soil can contain around one million fungi, such as yeasts and moulds. Fungi have no chlorophyll, and are not able to photosynthesise; besides, they can't use atmospheric carbon dioxide as a source of carbon, therefore they are chemo-heterotrophic, meaning that, like animals, they require a chemical source of energy rather than being able to use light as an energy source, as well as organic substrates to get carbon for growth and development.

Many fungi are parasitic, often causing disease to their living host plant, although some have beneficial relationships with living plants as we shall see below. In terms of soil and humus creation, the most important fungi tend to be saprotrophic, that is, they live on dead or decaying organic matter, thus breaking it down and converting it to forms that are available to the higher plants. A succession of fungi species will colonise the dead matter, beginning with those that use sugars and starches, which are succeeded by those that are able to break down cellulose and lignins.

Fungi spread underground by sending long thin threads known as mycelium throughout the soil; these threads can be observed throughout many soils and compost heaps. From the mycelia the fungi is able to throw up its fruiting bodies, the visible part above the soil (e.g., mushrooms, toadstools and puffballs), which may contain millions of spores.

When the fruiting body bursts, these spores are dispersed through the air to settle in fresh environments, and are able to lie dormant for upto years until the right conditions for their activation arise or the right food is made available.

Mycorrhizae

Those fungi that are able to live symbiotically with living plants, creating a relationship that is beneficial to both, are known as Mycorrhizae (from *myco* meaning fungal and *rhiza* meaning root). Plant root hairs are invaded by the mycelia of the mycorrhiza, which lives partly in the soil and partly in the root, and may either cover the length of the root hair as a sheath or be concentrated around its tip. The mycorrhiza obtains the carbohydrates that it requires from the root, in return providing the plant with nutrients including nitrogen and moisture. Later, the plant roots will also absorb the mycelium into its own tissues.

Beneficial mycorrhizal associations are to be found in many of our edible and flowering crops. Shewell Cooper suggests that these include at least 80% of the *brassica* and *solanum* families (including tomatoes and potatoes), as well as the majority of tree species, especially in forest and woodlands. Here the mycorrhizae create a fine underground mesh that extends greatly beyond the limits of the tree's roots, greatly increasing their feeding range and actually causing neighbouring trees to become physically interconnected.

The benefits of mycorrhizal relations to their plant partners are not limited to nutrients, but can be essential for plant reproduction: in situations where little light is able to reach the forest floor, such as the North American pine forests, a young seedling cannot obtain sufficient light to photosynthesise for itself and will not grow properly in a sterile soil. But if the ground is underlain by a mycorrhizal mat then the developing seedling will throw down roots that can link with the fungal threads and through them obtain the nutrients it needs, often indirectly obtained from its parents or neighbouring trees.

In the book, Private Life of Plants, David Attenborough points out the plant, fungi, animal relationship that creates a "Three way harmonious trio" to be found in forest ecosystems wherein the plant/fungi symbiosis is enhanced by animals such as the wild boar, deer, mice or flying squirrel, which feed upon the fungi's fruiting bodies, including truffles, and cause their further spread. A greater understanding of the complex relationships that pervade natural systems is one of the major justifications of the organic gardener, in refraining from the use of artificial chemicals and the damage these might cause.

Non-Parasitic and Parasitic Diseases in Plants

Citrus diseases affecting the entire tree can be classified into two general categories: parasitic and non-parasitic. Parasitic diseases are caused by fungi, bacteria, viruses and nematodes. Some disease-causing agents are restricted to certain parts of the plant, such as the root, trunk or fruit, while others may affect several or all parts of the plant.

Non-parasitic diseases are physiological disorders caused by excesses or deficiencies of certain nutrients or by unfavorable environmental conditions. Among the most common non-parasitic diseases of citrus occurring in Texas are iron chlorosis, mottle leaf, salt and chronic water table injury.

In addition to the economic losses that can result if not avoided or corrected, these physiological disorders often predispose the tree to attack by disease-causing organisms, such as the relationship that exists between salt and chronic water table injury and the increased occurrence of several types of gummosis, twig blight, tip-burned yellow leaves and nematode infestations.

Texas root rot is a pathogen fairly common in Mexico and the southwestern United States that causes sudden wilt and death of affected plants, usually during the warmer months. It is a soil-borne fungus of the species *Phymatotrichopsis omnivora* that attacks the roots of susceptible plants. Because the damaged roots are unable to take up enough water to maintain the plant in warm weather, the leaves wilt and the plant dies. The dead leaves usually remain attached to the plant.

A multitude of dicotyledonous tree, shrub and herbaceous plants are susceptible to Texas root rot, including figs, pomegranates, elms, grapes, cotton, alfalfa, oleander, and roses. The largest compilation of hosts, more than 1,700, was made by J. Taubenhaus and W. Ezekiel. It is one of the most destructive fungal plant diseases. Some monocot plants are tolerant and others are immune.

Eradication or control of Texas root rot is difficult, at best. The fungus is known to thrive in moist and alkaline soils. It can survive for long periods in the soil, sometimes lying dormant for decades, and can penetrate to depths of up to twelve feet.

Increasing the organic content of the soil with compost and green manure may help to reduce growth of the fungus. A monograph of this disease, which includes a historical review, was written by Streets and Bloss in 1973.

Fungus Diseases

Cotton Root Rot

This disease, caused by the fungus *Phymatotrichum omnivorum*, affects many plant species. The fungus attacks the underground parts of the citrus tree and occasionally kills young trees. Once trees reach maturity, they are less susceptible to attack. Cotton root rot commonly causes sudden death of susceptible trees, with most of the dried leaves temporarily retained on the tree. The best protection against cotton root rot is to use resistant rootstocks such as sour orange.

Rio Grande Gummosis

This is one of several well-known gumming diseases of citrus. Gum formation on the trunk or branches is a characteristic symptom. Gum exudes from blisters containing gum pockets, usually located on the trunk. The wood beneath the blister shows a pink-orange color.

Several factors such as freeze damage, high water table and salt accumulation contribute to the disease. Gummosis is believed to be a condition of weak and injured trees and is reported to be infectious. Symptoms of the disease were reproduced when healthy trees were inoculated with the fungus *Diplodia natalenris*.

No reliable cure exists for gummosis. Keeping trees vigorously growing is the best way to avoid the problem.

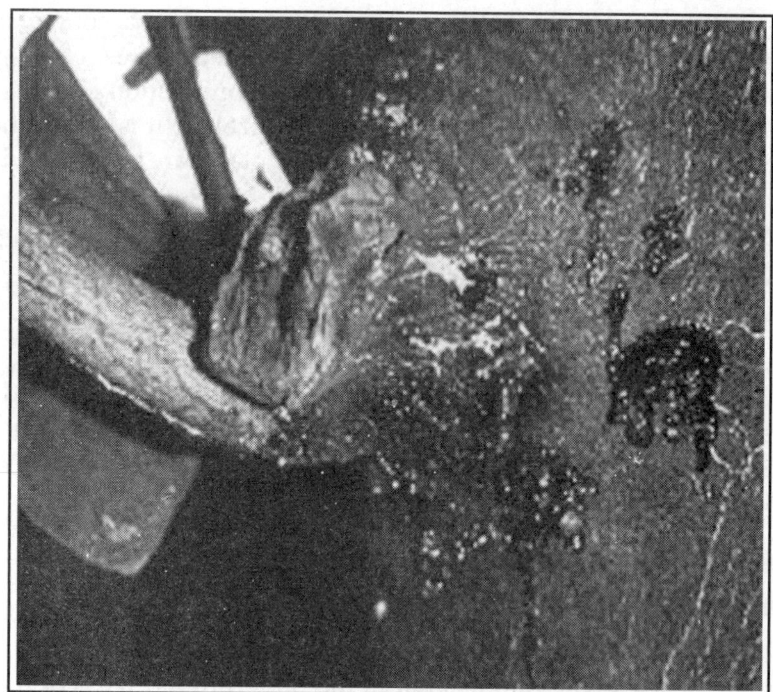

Fig 5.1: **Rio Grande Hummosis Causesamber Exudate to be Secreted Frompockets Beneath the Bark**

Phytophthora Foot Rot

Foot rot, also known as brown rot gummosis, is caused by one or more species of the fungus *Phytophthora*. This disease can affect the root system, the trunk below and above ground, branches, leaves, blossoms and fruit. It is especially troublesome during prolonged rainy periods.

Trees with the bud union beneath or close to the soil and trees in poorly-drained locations are highly susceptible. Foot rot is commonly found in Lower Rio Grande Valley orchards, but becomes a more serious problem under unusual conditions such as those that occur following hurricanes.

Healing is slower if infection occurs below ground level. The fungus may attack young feeder roots, causing them to decay. Infection of lateral and fibrous roots can become widespread in wet soils. This infection results in poor health of the tree, a thin canopy, failure to make new growth and poor fruit production.

Phytophthora sp. also may attack nursery stock and young orchard trees during rainy weather. Examination of the crowns of infected trees shows symptoms similar to those described for older tree.

Fig 5.2: *Foot rot damage from* Phytophthora *sp.*

Phytophthora foot rot can best be controlled by preventative practices, including use of resistant rootstock and planting in well-drained land. Sour orange is the most resistant rootstock for the Lower Rio Grande Valley. Other resistant rootstocks include Swingle citrumelo and Troyer and Carrizo citrange.

Budding seedlings high, avoiding wounds, and keeping soil off the lower trunk are among recommended control practices. Soil fumigation of seedbeds should be practiced in field nurseries.

NEMATODES

Nematodes are the most numerous multicellular animals on earth. A handful of soil will contain thousands of the microscopic worms, many of them parasites of insects, plants or animals. Free-living species are abundant, including nematodes that feed on bacteria, fungi, and other nematodes, yet the vast majority of species encountered are poorly understood biologically. There are nearly 20,000 described species classified in the phylum Nemata.

Plant parasitic nematodes are very small worms that cannot be seen with the naked eye. Several plant parasitic nematodes are known to attack the root system of citrus plants, especially the citrus nematode, *Tylenchulus semipenetrans*. The burrowing nematode, *Radopholus similis*, causes a disease known as spreading decline and is a serious pest of citrus in other production areas. This nematode has been found in the Valley on ornamentals, but not in citrus orchards. Serious losses to the Texas industry could result should it ever become established in citrus groves.

The citrus nematode occurs commonly in Valley citrus orchard soils. Sour orange is rated as highly susceptible to nematode infection. Of the common rootstocks with potential use in the Valley, only *Swingle citrumelo* is rated as highly tolerant to the citrus nematode.

Populations of the citrus nematode usually are higher in older orchards (six years and older). Young trees also may be injured if planted in orchard sites where nematodes previously prevailed. Other plant parasitic nematodes, mainly the lesion nematode (*Pratylenchus spp.*) often have been found associated with citrus roots.

Nematodes are structurally simple organisms. Adult nematodes are comprised of approximately 1,000 somatic cells, and potentially hundreds of cells associated with the reproductive system . Nematodes have been characterized as a *tube within a tube* ; referring to the alimentary canal which extends from the mouth on the anterior end, to the anus located near the tail. Nematodes possess digestive, nervous, excretory, and reproductive systems, but lack a discrete circulatory or respiratory system. In size they range from 0.3 mm to over 8 metres.

Because the presence of the citrus nematode cannot be detected visually, positive diagnosis is based on external symptoms and laboratory examination of root and soil samples. Above-ground symptoms associated with nematode-infected trees are wilting, lack of vigour, poor fruit production and poor response to watering and fertilization. Texas Cooperative Extension operates a Plant Nematode Detection Laboratory at College Station where samples can be sent for analysis and recommendations. County Extension agricultural agents can assist growers in collecting and sending samples.

Losses caused by the citrus nematode in heavily infected orchards can be reduced effectively by applying nematicides to the soil. Before treating an orchard, however, consider the overall condition of the orchard. Application of nematicides to freeze-damaged orchards grown under poor cultural conditions may not be profitable. Soil should be sampled before establishing a new orchard to determine if nematodes are present in damaging numbers. If the analysis reveals large numbers of parasitic nematodes, treating the soil before establishing trees may be profitable. Ideally, nematodefree plants should be used when establishing new orchards.

At present, products cleared for use on established citrus trees are also known to have an effect on mites and other insects. Careful attention must be paid to instructions on the label, not only for directions on how to apply the material, but also for current rates and regulations that may affect the legal use of these products.

Plant diseases in which no foreign organism or parasite is associated are known as non-parasitic diseases. They differ from virus diseases in being non-infectious. Such diseases are induced by certain disorders in the physiology of the plants due to unfavorable environments including the soil conditions.

Black Heart of Potato

Symptoms

1. The disease usually occurs in poorly ventilated rooms in closely packed conditions.
2. It also occurs in the field when temperature of the soil goes above 320C during growth & maturation of tubers.
3. The disease occurs in the transit when the temperature inside the carrying vans rises for sometime above 320 C.
4. Dark gray to purplish or inky black discoloration occurs in the central tissues of the tuber.
5. In advanced stages, the affected tissues may dry out & separate thus forming cavities.

Remedy

(a) The tubers should not be stored at temperatures above 33° C.

(b) Storage of tubers must be made in well ventilated rooms and the bags of tubers should not be piled very high upon each other.

(c) In the field if the temperature seems to go very high the field should be irrigated.

Black Tip or Mango Necrosis

Symptoms

1. The disease is characterized by necrosis of tissues at the distal end of the fruit.
2. The first symptoms is the development of a small etiolated area at the distal end which gradually spreads, turns nearly black, and covers the tip completely.
3. The tip is flattened with the outer skin turning hard and sunken.

4. The inner portion is soft & yields a dark brown liquid due to rotting induced by saprophytic bacteria.

Remedy

Spray of borax 3-4 kg /500 liters of water at an early stage of fruiting substantially reduces the disease incidence.

Tip Burn of Rice

Symptoms

1. The first symptom of the disease is the drying of leaves.
2. Leaves show lack of luster & a tendency of bronzing & later become scorched at the tip.
3. The drying progresses down along the margins & finally the whole leaf completely dries.

Remedy

1. The field should be first drained off in early stage of plant growth & then 30-50 kg/ha of ammonium sulphate is applied.
2. Green manuring could reduce the incidence of disease & increase the yield.

Disease due to Lack of Minerals

1. **Copper (Cu)** – most of the diseases caused by copper deficiency develop symptoms of chlorosis. The leaves may fail to unroll & tend to appear wilted. Leaf margins turn yellow and leaf tips of cereals wither. Citrus trees shows die back symptoms during summer.
2. **Zinc (Zn)** – Due to deficiency of zinc diseases like rosette of apple, mottle leaf of citrus, and little leaf of grapevine are caused. Leaves of zinc deficient plants develop prominent veins, become pale yellow and sometimes bear dead patches. In rice zinc deficiency causes khaira disease. Leaves of diseased plants show chlorosis at the base. Large number of small brown or bronze spots appears on the lamina surface. The disease can be effectively controlled by 2 sprays of a mixture of 2 kg of zinc sulphate & 1 kg of slaked lime in 400 liters of water per acre.
3. **Iron (Fe)** – Although plant needs a very small quantity of iron they develop acute chlorosis when this element is deficient in soil or it is not being absorbed by the plant. The chlorosis of leaves

without any mottling is the most prominent effect. Soil or foliar application of ferrous sulphate often corrects this deficiency.

4. **Manganese (Mn)** – Chlorosis of spinach & bean, spots on potatoes & gray speak of oats are common diseases resulting from manganese deficiency. Manganese sulphate may be used as foliar spray to correct this deficiency.

5. **Boron (B)** – Necrosis of tissues is the most important symptom of boron deficiency. In heart rot of beet the disease is characterized by curling of central leaves, which turns blackish brown & die. In apple fruits, brown necrotic areas in the flesh are caused by boron deficiency. Such deficiencies can be corrected by application of 20kg/ha borax before sowing.

DISEASES OF URBAN PLANTS

Arizona is a large, square-shaped, climatically diverse state of approximately 114,000 square miles within the north latitude lines from 32 to 37 degrees. Geographically the state can be divided roughly into four areas; southwest, central, southeast, and northern. These areas, in general, correspond with four climatic zones. The zones include low desert areas (elevations below 1000 feet) that are found primarily in Yuma, Maricopa and Pinal counties where annual precipitation is low (less than 4 inches), frosts are rare, and high summer temperatures are typical (average daily high temperature during June, July, August, and September are above 100°F). Intermediate elevation areas (elevations from 1200 to 3300 feet) occur primarily in La Paz, Maricopa, Pima, Gila, and Pinal counties.

These areas receive more rainfall (10 to 13 inches annually), occasional frosts and lower temperatures (there is approximately a 3°F drop in temperature for every 1000 foot increase in elevation). The high desert areas with elevations from approximately 3300 to 4500 feet, typically occurring in the counties of Yavapai, Santa Cruz, Cochise, Gila, Graham, and Greenlee, have higher rainfall (12 to 18 inches), 74 to 100 frosts per year, and colder temperatures. The northern counties of Arizona including Coconino, Navajo, Apache, and certain areas in Mohave, Yavapai, Gila, and Greenlee are, in general, higher in elevation with colder winter climates. The growing season in some of these locations averages only about 150 days a year.

A large and diverse number of plants are grown for landscaping purposes in Arizona. They include perennial and annual ornamentals, evergreen and deciduous vines, deciduous and evergreen shrubs and trees, conifers, palms, bamboos, turf and other ground covers, citrus, fruit trees, and native plants.

Interestingly, in our desert environment many of the parasitic diseases in landscape plants are caused by a limited number of plant pathogens. Most of the important fungal plant pathogens survive in the soil and cause root, crown and wilt diseases of a large number of unrelated plants. These include *Phymatotrichopsis omnivora* (Cotton or Texas root rot), *Phytophthora* sp. (root and crown diseases), *Pythium* sp. (seedling and root diseases), *Rhizoctonia solani* (seedling, root and stem diseases), and *Verticillium dahliae* (wilt diseases). Other soil fungi including *Fusarium* sp., *Thielaviopsis basicola*, and *Macrophomina phaseolina* are occasionally involved as root and crown pathogens of a number of landscape plants. However, they are insignificant when compared with the previously listed pathogens. They will not be discussed in this publication.

Fungi that cause foliage diseases in our dry environment are rare. Two groups, however, are important. They include the powdery mildew fungi (species of *Uncinula, Spaerotheca, Erysiphe, Microsphaera, Phyllactinia, Podosphaera, Oidiopsis* and *Oidium*) and the rust fungi, including species in several genera including *Phragmidium* and *Puccinia*. Other important plant pathogenic fungi, involved as causal agents of wood decay and canker diseases in woody perennials, include *Cytospora* sp. (Cytospora canker), *Hendersonula toruloidea* (sooty canker), and genera of wood rotting basidiomycetes such as *Ganoderma*.

Only a few bacterial plant diseases are of significant importance to discuss in detail. They include crown gall (*Agrobacterium tumefaciens*), oleander gall (*Pseudomonas syringae* pv. *savastanoi*), fire blight (*Erwinia amylovora)*, bacterial necrosis of saguaro (*Erwinia* sp.) and wetwood or slime flux. Foliar diseases are rare and insignificant.

Virus diseases, although of great importance in vegetable crops, citrus, and certain ornamentals are less common and less important in urban plantings. Nematode and mistletoe diseases, because of their widespread occurrence, will be covered. The emphasis in this publication is to discuss primarily the major parasitic and nonparasitic diseases that affect the most important landscape plants grown in Arizona.

PARASITIC DISEASES

Fungi

Phymatotrichopsis Root Rot

The most important disease of woody, dicotyledonous plants including perennial ornamentals, perennial vines and perennial shrubs and trees in Arizona is *Phymatotrichopsis* root rot (Cotton or Texas root rot) caused by a unique and widely distributed soil-borne fungus, *Phymatotrichopsis omnivora*.

The fungus is indigenous to and occurs in the alkaline, low-organic matter soils of the southwestern United States and central and northern Mexico. Of the thousands of fungi that cause disease in plants, *P. omnivora* is unique in certain biological characteristics. The fungus has one of the largest host ranges of any known fungal pathogen. Over 2300 species of unrelated plants are susceptible to the disease. Isolates of the fungus are non-specific in their pathogenicity. For example, isolates that kill hundreds of deep rooted dicotyledonous, urban plants are also pathogenic to important crop plants in Arizona such as cotton, alfalfa, stone fruits, and grapes. Isolates from these crop plants are in turn pathogenic to urban plants. Thus, home sites established in old cotton or alfalfa fields, or other areas with a history of *Phymatotrichopsis* root rot can become disaster areas for urban landscapers.

The fungus has almost no method of dissemination but has the unusual capability of surviving in soil in the absence of hosts for very long periods of time. The disease symptoms usually appear during the summer. The fungus only infects roots of mature plants. Seedlings are not susceptible to this disease.

Distribution of the Disease in Arizona

Heavily infested areas of *Phymatotrichopsis* root rot include the flood plains and certain tributaries of the Gila River (Safford, Duncan, Solomon, Thatcher, Fort Thomas, Pima, Eden, Florence, Sacaton, Buckeye, Gila Bend, Agua Caliente, Growler, Roll, Mohawk, and Dome Valley); the Santa Cruz River (Sahuarita, Tucson, Cortaro, Avra Valley, Rillito, Marana, Red Rock, and Eloy); the San Pedro River (Hereford, St. David, Benson, Pomerene, Redington, Mammoth, and Winkelman); Colorado River (Parker, Poston, Ehrenberg, Yuma, Somerton, and Gadsden) and certain locations of the Salt River and Queen Creek. Other infested areas include Chandler, Aguila, San Simon, Bowie, McNeal, Douglas, and Duncan.

The "mesa" (land at elevations above the influence of the Colorado River) in Yuma County seems to be free of the disease, whereas many "valley" sites are infested. *Phymatotrichopsis* root rot occurs at elevations as high as 4,700 feet in the Elgin and Sonoita areas of Santa Cruz County, in the Nogales area and Sierra Vista. Disease has never been detected in the Bonita area north of Willcox to Kansas Settlement, but in the Sulphur Springs Valley, the disease is found near Elfrida, McNeal, and Douglas.

The fungus is not uniformly distributed in local situations. Two distribution patterns are common. In one situation the fungus may occur in many small scattered circular areas, a "shot-gun" scenario. In other situations the infested areas are large and few in number. This explains why the disease may occur in one small area of a landscape throughout the property.

Symptoms

Infected plants suddenly wilt during the summer when temperatures are high. Dead or dying foliage remains attached to the infected plant. The roots of the infected plants are rotted and brown in color. Most of the plants discussed in this publication when planted into areas infested with *P. omnivora* show no symptoms during the first few years after planting. This is in contrast with certain tap rooted crop plants such as cotton and alfalfa that become infected and die the first summer after spring planting.

The fungus is deep seated in the soil, and it may simply be that roots of many susceptible plants do not grow into the deeper, infested areas for a number of years. In grapes, for example, symptoms usually first appear two to four years after planting. Some trees show no symptoms for five or more years after planting. Symptom development and fungal activity is different in plantings in low elevations in Arizona as compared to plantings above 3,600 feet. Symptoms at low elevations consist primarily of initial stress, wilting of foliage and death of the entire plant within a few days after initial symptoms. This death usually occurs from late May through September. At higher elevations, plants may not wilt suddenly, but die more slowly.

Because plants may die during the summer for reasons other than *Phymatotrichopsis* root rot, it is necessary to examine root tissue for the presence of the fungus. The only positive proof of death caused by *P. omnivora* is to examine the cortical tissue of rotted, decayed roots and to identify the characteristic mycelial strands that are produced by the fungus on the surface of cortical tissue from decayed roots.

This examination can be made by an experienced person with the use of a hand lens. However, these strands, masses of vegetative mycelial growth that are unique to this pathogen, can be more easily identified in the laboratory under a dissecting or compound microscope. *Phymatotrichopsis omnivora* may produce fungal spore mats on the surface of soil during the monsoon rain period.

The spore mats are occasionally seen in shaded areas at the base of infected plants during hot, rainy periods in July and August. They are not seen at other times. The usual size of the spore mat is 4 to 8 inches in diameter and about 1/4 inch thick. The spore mats appear, almost mystically, overnight. The mats are initially white in color but become brownish in color after two or three days of growth. The powdery mass of spores produced on the surface of the mat are non-functional. They have never been germinated, and they seem to play no role in dissemination of the pathogen.

Biology of *P. omnivora*

The fungus appears to occur deep in the soil in localized patterns. *P. omnivora* has no effective method of dissemination since there are no aerial or soil-borne spores that spread the fungus. The pathogen produces two important structures, sclerotia and strands. Sclerotia enable *P. omnivora* to survive in soil for many years. The sclerotia are small (up to ¼ inch in diameter), roundish masses of hyphae. When mature, they have a thick outer rind. Sclerotia have been found in soil at depths up to 12 feet. Mycelial growth from germinating sclerotia initiate root infection. The fungus then produces interwoven masses of hyphae known as strands. The strands grow and colonize root tissue. Extensive root infection results in wilting and plant death. Strands, utilizing infected root tissue as an energy source, grow short distances through the soil to infect healthy roots.

Growth of strands from one host to another is probably the only available method of spread for the fungus and explains a typical pattern of kill in home landscaping situations where susceptible trees or shrubs are planted adjacent to each other. The fungus may kill one plant 2 or 3 years after the initial planting. Spread occurs in later years by strand growth from infected to healthy root tissue. Eventually, the entire group of plants may succumb to the disease.

It should be emphasized that the fungus is only a pathogen of mature roots of dicotyledonous plants. All monocotyledonous plants are immune to this disease. Winter annuals escape the disease because *P. omnivora* is not active in cold soils.

Control

A positive identification of the pathogen on roots is essential. In a disease situation not all roots are infected. Select roots with discolored, rotted outer bark. The diseased roots should be about 3/4 inch thick and 6 to 9 inches in length. Microscopic examination will reveal the unique strands of the fungus on the outer bark. Strands can be most easily identified on fresh material. However, they can also be seen on the surface of old, dead roots.

The only real effective method of control is to plant immune or highly resistant species in infested areas. Diocotyledonous plants grown as summer or winter annuals normally escape infection by *P. omnivora*. All monocotyledonous plants, either annuals or perennials, are immune to the disease. This includes large numbers of ornamentals in the Amaryllidaceae, Liliaceae, Iridaceae, Palmaceae, and the large grass family, Gramineae. Important immune plants from these plant families that are commonly grown in Arizona include palms in the genera *Washingtonia* (fan palms), *Phoenix* (date palms), and *Arecastrum* spp. (Queen palms), *Agave* and *Yucca* sp., bamboos and many perennial ornamental grasses.

Other dicotyledonous desert plants, although not immune to the disease, are tolerant and usually grow normally in infested areas. They include species in the genus *Cercidium*, *C. floridum* (blue palo verde), *C. microphyllum* (foothills palo verde), *C. praecox* (Sonoran palo verde); the genus *Prosopis, P. velutina* (honey mesquite), *P. chilensis* (Chilean mesquite); *Simmondsia chinensis* (jojoba); *Parkinsonia aculeata* (Parkinsonia), *Condalia lycioides* (gray thorn) and *Chilopsis linearus* (desert willow). Other plants include *Amorpha fruiticosa* (false indigo), *Celtus* sp. (hackberry), *A. greggi* (catclaw), *Larrea tridentata* (Creosote), *Fouquieria splendens* (ocotillo).

There are probably many other native plants in this category. As interest increases in the use of drought and heat tolerant native plants for landscaping purposes, our list of resistant plants may increase. We do know that some commonly planted non-native dicotyledonous trees and shrubs such as mulberry, Aleppo pine, and citrus are rarely affected by the disease. The list of susceptible plants is more reliable than plants in the resistant list. This, of course, is due to the fact that plants that succumb to the disease can be easily catalogued whereas plants that appear resistant may appear so simply because they have not been exposed to the pathogen. Susceptible plants grown in Arizona include: *Prunus* sp. including almonds, apricots, cherry, sweet cherry, sour cherry, nectarines, plums, peaches; *Fraxinus* spp. including Arizona ash (*F. velutina*); cottonwood, (*Populus deltoides*), *Ulmus* sp. including chinese elm (*U. parvifolia*) and siberian ulm (*U. pumula*); *Ficus* spp. (figs); honey locust (*Gleditsia* spp.); magnolia (*Magnolia grandiflora*); pear (*Pyrus communis*); pecan (*Hicoria pecan*); pistachio (*Pistacia* spp.); pomegranate (*Punica granatum*); sycamore, american and london plane (*Platanus occidentalis* and *P. acerifolia*); chinaberry tree (*Melia azedarach*); willow, weeping and golden (*Salix babylonica* and *S. alba*), bottle tree (*Brachychiton populneum*), silk oak (*Grevillea robusta*); pepper tree, Brazilian and California (*Schinus terebinthifolia* and *S. molle*); Japanese privet (*Ligustrum japonicum*); African sumac (*Rhus lancea*), xylosma (*Xylosma congestum*), oleander (*Nerium oleander*), carob (*Ceratonia siliqua*) and *Cassia*. Other genera with susceptible species include: *Vitis* spp. (grape), *Ilex* spp. (holly), *Cotoneaster* spp. (cotoneaster), *Malus sylvestris* (apple), *Juglans* spp. (walnut), *Buddleia* spp. (butterflybush), *Syringa* spp. (lilac), *Pittosporum* spp. (Pittosporum), Wistaria spp. (wisteria), *Rosa* spp. (roses), *Rubus* spp. (berries), and *Spiraea* spp. (spirea).

Phytophora Diseases

The genus *Phytophthora* contains approximately 35 species of highly pathogenic and destructive plant pathogens. All species are pathogenic. They attack hundreds of species of higher plants throughout the world causing unusually diverse types of plant diseases including leaf and shoot blights, flower, fruit and bud rots, crown rots, stem and trunk cankers of woody and herbaceous plants, seedling damping-off, necrosis of feeder roots and collar and root rots.

In Arizona, because of our desert climate, fungus diseases that affect above ground plant parts (foliage, flowers, fruit, etc.) are rare. Thus, infections by species of *Phytophthora* most commonly occur below ground or at the soil line. Typically, these diseases include seedling damping-off, necrosis of feeder roots, rots of mature roots, and crown and collar rots of woody and herbaceous plants. The identification of a *Phytophthora* as the cause of a root or crown disease is difficult because below ground infections usually cause non-specific above ground symptoms. Also, the fungus is microscopic and difficult to isolate and identify from infected below ground tissues.

Most studies in Arizona concerning diseases caused by *Phytophthora* species have involved commercial crops and not plants used in urban situations. These diseases include root rot of alfalfa (*P. megasperma*), safflower (*P. drechsleri*), citrus (*P. parasitica* and *P. citrophthora*), root and crown rot of apple (*P. cactorum* and *P. cambivora*), crown, stem, and fruit rot of pepper (*P. capsici*), fruit rot of pumpkin (*P. capsici*) and boll rot of cotton (*P. capsici*). The last three diseases occur only during the summer rainy season at elevations above 4000 feet in southeast Arizona.

Several of these species have very wide host ranges. For example, *P. parasitica*, which is the major pathogen causing root disease in citrus grown in Arizona, causes root and crown diseases of the following commonly grown landscape plants in Arizona; *Grevillea robusta* (silk oak), *Leucophyllum frutescens* (Texas ranger), *Hibiscus* spp., *Petunia* spp., *Rosmarinus officinalis* (rosemary), *Simmondsia chinensis* (jojoba), *Verbena* spp., and *Vinca* spp. (periwinkle).

Other diseases in Arizona where a species of *Phytophthora* has been isolated include root and crown rot disease of *Matthiola* spp. (stock), *Antirrhinum majus* (snapdragon), *Aster* spp., *Lilium* spp. (lily), *Paeonia* spp. (peony), foliage plants including *Peperomia* spp., *Hedera* spp. (ivy), and *Dieffenbachia* spp. Other *Phytophthora* root and crown diseases occur in *Juglans* spp. (walnut), *Pinus* spp. (pines), *Prunus* spp. (peach, apricot, cherry), *Pyrus communis* (pear), *Quercus* spp. (oaks), *Salix* spp. (willows), *Ilex* spp. (holly), *Juniperus* spp. (junipers), *Cerotonia siliqua* (carob tree), *Bougainvillae* spp., and *Hicoria pecan* (pecan). No foliar diseases caused by *Phytophthora* spp. have been described from landscape plants in Arizona. *Phytophthora* bud rot of palms, caused by *P. palmivora*, is a serious disease in the wet tropics. During our monsoon, rainy season this disease has been occasionally seen in Arizona.

Symptoms

A number of *Phytophthora* spp., including *P. parasitica* and *P cactorum* infect roots and crown tissue of host plants ranging from herbaceous annuals to woody perennials. Symptoms, however, resulting from these infections are basically similar. As an example, symptoms of two diseases, *Phytophthora* crown and root rot of petunia (an herbaceous annual) caused by *P. parasitica* and collar rot of apple (a deciduous woody perennial) caused by *P. cactorum* have much in common. Symptoms, although obviously developing in different time frames, are similar and consist of overall plant stress, stunting, change in leaf colour, wilting, and eventual plant death.

Phytophthora parasitica infects the lower stem of petunia at or slightly below the soil line. The fungus grows into and kills stem tissue. Infected tissue rots and becomes dark in color. As the disease progresses, the entire plant wilts and dies. The disease is most common in seedlings transplanted during hot weather in September and October.

Optimum temperature for fungal activity is about 85°F. Crown rot of apple has many similarities to this disease. The main pathogen, *P. cactorum*, infects the trunk at or below the soil line. Initially, during the summer, leaves of infected trees may appear light green to yellow in color.

Fruit may be small and color prematurely. The tree may be stunted. The optimum time to survey for collar rot of apples is during September, October, and November. During this period, infected trees appear stressed with stunted and dead terminal growth. Leaves are reddish-yellow in appearance. A dark brown canker at or below the soil line is a characteristic symptom.

If no cankers are found on trees, then factors other that *Phytophthora* are involved. Active cankers are moist in appearance. An exudate may occur at the margins of the canker. Infections are most common and canker development most active during cool-cold weather. This is because the optimum temperature for growth of *P. cactorum* is approximately 50 to 60°F. Disease development is inhibited at soil temperatures above 80°F.

The symptoms described for the petunia and apple diseases are essentially identical for the *Phytophthora* diseases that affect the other herbaceous and woody plants described in the previous section.

Biology

The basic biology of *Phytophthora* spp. that occur in Arizona is very similar. All species survive and live indefinitely in soil. Thick-walled, microscopic survival structures, oospores and chlamydospores, are produced in infected host tissue. There is variation between species as to the presence or absence of these spores and also to their size and shape. The most reliable method of identifying *Phytophthora* spp. is the finding of the sporangial stage. They are commonly produced on infected tissue and can be seen on microscopic examination of isolations made on specific media.

Oospores and chlamydospores germinate under saturated soil conditions to produce characteristic, microscopic, lemon shaped sporangia. Each sporangium liberates swimming spores called zoospores. They swim through water and contact roots or the lower trunk tissue of potential hosts where they germinate and infect these tissues.

The fungus grows into host tissue, girdling the infected root or trunk and eventually killing the tree. As the host dies the fungus produces the survival structures in decaying tissue. If the tree is removed these spores are returned via rotted host tissue to the soil where they enable the fungus to survive in the absence of a host. Few studies have been made on the natural occurrence of *Phytophthora* spp. in Arizona soils. However, studies in Arizona support the thesis that *Phytophthora* pathogens of urban plants are commonly introduced into Arizona on imported nursery stock.

Control Herbaceous Plants

The control of *Phytophthora* diseases in bedding plants and other herbaceous plants starts with the purchase of disease-free plants. For the homeowner this is sometimes difficult. Young seedlings, petunias, for example, may be infected but show no symptoms. The shock of transplanting, and overwatering coupled with high temperature triggers disease development. All *Phytophthora* diseases occur primarily in overwatered, heavy, poorly drained soils. Any technique that improves soil percolation is helpful in disease control. There are a number of fungicides available as drenches that are highly active against *Phytophthora* spp.

Woody Plants

Avoid planting into heavy, poorly drained sites. Break open any caliche area that prevents water percolation. Avoid overwatering. Once collar rot has been identified there are few options available for control. A systemic fungicide is applied as a drench around the trunk of infected trees. Severely infected trees cannot be saved.

The fungicide is effective in controlling the spread of the disease and also for treatment of early infections. Certain citrus are susceptible to *Phytophthora* foot and root rot and others are highly resistant. For example, susceptible varieties include lemons (*Citrus limon*), sweet orange (*C. sinensis*), limes (*C. aurantifolia*), grapefruit (*C. paradisi*), and Troyer and Carrizo citranges. Resistant citrus commonly planted in Arizona is sour orange (*C. aurantium*).

Pythium Diseases

It is appropriate, for a number of reasons, to compare the genus *Pythium* with the previously described genus, *Phytophthora*. First, although the two genera are closely related, they differ in certain biological characteristics. For example, all described species in the genus *Phytophthora* are plant pathogens. The isolation of or even observation of a species of *Phytophthora* in diseased plant tissue is sufficient evidence implicating the fungus as the cause of the disease.

Pythium spp., however are ubiquitous in soil and aquatic environments. Most of the 100 species described infect seeds, roots, or aerial parts of a wide range of plants. Some species, however, do not cause disease and are saprophytic on decaying plant debris. Species of *Phytophthora* often invade woody, mature plant tissue. Pathogenic *Pythium* spp. invade and cause disease primarily in young meristematic, herbaceous tissue.

Species in both genera survive indefinitely in the soil and, under desert conditions, cause diseases primarily of below ground tissues. *Phytophthora* spp. have limited soil saprophytic capabilities. They are slow growing and isolated with difficulty from infected tissue. Specialized, specific media are necessary for isolation. *Pythium* spp., in contrast, are easily isolated from infected host tissue on water agar or other simple media.

There is also, in general, less host specificity in *Pythium* than in *Phytophthora*. The two most important *Pythium* spp. in Arizona, *P. aphanidermatum* and *P. ultimum* are aggressive, rapidly growing soil saprophytes.

They readily colonize soil organic matter. Infection of below ground plant tissue occurs, as with species of *Phytophthora*, under saturated soil conditions. The two species differ primarily in their response to soil temperature. *Pythium ultimum* is pathogenic primarily in soils that are near or below 60°F whereas *P. aphanidermatum* has optimum temperature requirements for pathogenicity above 85°F.

Symptoms

Pythium ultimum and *P. aphanidermatum* are primarily involved in seedling diseases of bedding and ornamental plants. They are both indigenous in Arizona soils. Both species are known pathogens of a number of agricultural crops grown in Arizona including several vegetable and field crops.

In landscape plants, however, these two species are important as causal organisms in seed decay, pre and post emergence damping off of seedlings and root rot of immature or herbaceous plants. Seeds or seedlings rot before or after their emergence from the soil. Post emergence damping off can occur several weeks after emergence. Seedlings become less susceptible with increasing age.

Pythium root rot is also a common disease in many foliage plants including *Philodendron, Peperomia, Scindapsus,* and *Syngonium*. A wide range of young greenhouse, bedding, and garden and landscape plants are susceptible to *Pythium* root rot. For diagnosis, affected plants should be carefully removed from the soil and roots washed in water. Roots and lower stems are often brown or black. The stem slightly above or below the soil line may be smaller in diameter at the infection site than healthy stem tissue. Damping off in flats of bedding plants often starts in the corner or center of the flat. The fungus, after introduction into pasteurized soil, spreads rapidly from diseased to healthy seedlings. Temperatures that adversely affect seed germination and seedling growth increase disease incidence. Wet and poorly drained soils also are factors in increased incidence of disease.

In greenhouse situations, *P. aphanidermatum* is a serious problem only when air and soil temperatures are above approximately 85°F. *Pythium ultimum,* is not pathogenic at these temperatures and becomes active in cold (below 65°F), wet soils.

Biology

Both species produce oospores. *Pythium aphanidermatum* produces sporangia and zoospores. *Pythium ultimum* produces sporangia. These sporangia, however, germinate with the production of mycelia and no zoospores are produced. They both have very wide host ranges and both are non-specific in their host specificity. In other words, an isolate of *P. aphanidermatum* that causes seedling disease in tomatoes will also cause disease in petunia seedlings. Because of the production of oospores both species survive indefinitely in soil.

Control

Garden crops that are seeded directly in the soil are best protected against seed and seedling disease by treating seeds with a fungicide. Most commercial seed bought by landscapers has been treated with fungicides. Any factor that aids in quick germination and rapid seedling growth reduces the chance of *Pythium* seedling diseases. These factors include proper planting period, careful preparation of the seed bed to increase drainage, no overwatering, use of high quality seed, and proper fertilization.

Rhizoctonia Diseases

Although there are several species of *Rhizoctonia* described as plant pathogens, *R. solani,* is the most important species in the genus.

Rhizoctonia solani, a soil borne fungus, combines aggressive saprophytic activity with almost unlimited pathogenic capabilities. The fungus is a worldwide pathogen of hundreds of unrelated plants grown in climates as diverse as our irrigated desert to the humid tropics. In Arizona, *R. solani* is an important pathogen of many of our agricultural crops including cotton, potatoes, lettuce and many other vegetables and field crops.

The fungus causes primarily seed decay, pre- and postemergence damping off of seedlings, bulb rots, root rots, crown blights, neck rots and lower stem rots. Almost any plant tissue in contact with the soil is susceptible to infection. Diseases of aerial plant tissue, including upper stems, leaves, flowers, and fruit, caused by *R. solani*, are common in humid areas but are rare in our desert environment. *Rhizoctonia solani* does not invade and cause disease, under our conditions, in woody plant tissue. Established woody plants including trees, shrubs and vines are not affected by *Rhizoctonia*. The fungus, as with *Pythium* spp., is a pathogen primarily of young, succulent, immature tissue.

Symptoms

During seedling germination and emergence, the fungus causes partial or complete girdling of emerged seedlings at or near the soil surface. The lesions on lower stems are sunken and dark in color. When the soil is moist the fungus grows as weblike mycelium on the soil surface and in the lesions. Mycelial growth is easily visible with a hand lens. Most infections of seedlings and cuttings occur at or just below the soil surface. Infected seedlings wilt and die. Cuttings never root, and they eventually collapse. In plants like dichondra (*Dicondra repens*), the fungus invades and causes brown lesions on the lower stems.

The lesions are sunken and dark in color. Mycelial growth is evident in the infected areas. Similar infections occur in periwinkle (*Vinca major*) and foliage plants such as *Peperomia*. *Rhizoctonia solani* may blight a large stand of turfgrass within a 24 to 48 hour period. The fungus invades young leaf tissue and grows rapidly under warm temperatures (75 to 85°F) and the high humidities that can exist with excessive watering and high mowing of the turf. With cuttings of carnation, a soft, wet rot occurs at the point of callus formation. Infected plants wilt rapidly and die.

Hosts

Rhizoctonia solani has one of the largest host ranges of any fungal plant pathogen. The fungus causes disease in species in 530 genera of higher plants, including both dicots and monocots, from *Abelia* to *Zoysia* grass. The fungus causes seedling diseases and lower stem and root diseases of a large number of plants used in urban plantings in Arizona including aloe (*Aloe* spp.), ageratum (*Ageratum* spp.), aster (*Aster* spp.), coleus (*Coleus* spp.), chrysanthemum (*Chrysanthemum* spp.), carnation (*Dianthus* spp.), dichondra (*Dichondra* spp.), geranium (*Geranium* and *Pelargonium* spp.), iris (*Iris* spp.), lantana (*Lantana* spp.), lilies (*Lilium* spp.), marigold (*Tagetes* spp.), narcissus (*Narcissus* spp.), opuntia (*Opuntia* spp.), periwinkle (*Vinca* spp.), rose (*Rosa* spp.), snapdragon (*Antirrhinum* spp.), sweet alyssum (*Lobularia maritima*), sweet peas (*Lathyrus odoratus*), tulips (*Tulipa* spp.), violets (*Viola* spp.), and zinnia (*Zinnia* spp.). Many house plants such as African violets (*Saintpaulia* spp.), *Dieffenbachia, Syngonium, Peperomia,* and others are affected with basal stem rots caused by *R. solani*. Several lawn grasses are susceptible to damage caused by *R. solani*. They include bent grass (*Agrostis* spp.), bermuda grass (*Cynodon dactylon*), fescue (*Festuca* spp.), ryegrass (*Lolium* spp.), bluegrass (*Poa* spp.), zoysia (*Zoysia* spp.), and St. Augustine (*Stenotaphrum secundatum*).

Biology

R. solani commonly lives in the soil (soil borne) as a saprophyte. Quantitative estimations of soil populations of *R. solani* are based on sieving organic debris from the soil and determining the per cent of debris that has been colonized by *R. solani*. This technique is based on the biological fact that *R. solani* aggressively grows as mycelium in soil and colonizes organic debris. The fungus survives in the debris by the production of thick walled mycelium (resting mycelium) or by the production of hard resting structures called sclerotia. Plant exudates stimulate mycelial growth from the resting mycelium or from the sclerotia.

The mycelium then invades host tissue and causes lesions and girdling typical of the disease. This simple life cycle is complicated by the production, under certain conditions, of the perfect stage of the fungus which has been named *Thanatephorus cucumeris*. Basidia, specialized structures produced on host tissue under humid conditions, produce air-borne spores called basidiospores. The basidia and basidiospores are minute and are only observable under a microscope. In our desert conditions, this aerial, infective stage is rarely seen and is not important in the epidemiology of the disease. In humid areas of the world the basidiospores may initiate infection of leaves, flowers and fruit. All isolates of *R. solani* are identified by their typical mycelial growth characteristics. Also, all isolates have many nuclei in each cell of the mycelium and are considered to be the imperfect state of *Thanatephorus cucumeris*. The species exists in several non-interbreeding populations that vary in their host range. No studies have been made in Arizona on the host ranges of isolates recovered from urban landscape plants.

Rhizoctonia solani is a rapidly growing fungus that is easily isolated from infected tissue on simple media such as water agar.

Control

Urban plants are bought primarily from nurseries and other commercial suppliers. Pathogens may be introduced on planting material purchased from these facilities. The first step for control is the selection of vigorous, healthy plants at the time of purchase. Nurseries have a strict management programme to produce healthy plants. The programmes are based on fungicide treatment of seed (*Rhizoctonia* can be seed-borne), heat treatment of soil (30 minutes at a minimum of 140°F), fumigation of soil and sanitation of containers, benches, and tools.

Verticillium and Fusarium Wilts

There are two unrelated soilborne pathogenic fungi that infect host plants through root tissue and become systemic in vascular (xylem) tissue. The plugging, enzyme and toxin production by growth of these fungi in water conducting tissue causes typical symptoms and often death of infected plants. These two fungi, both worldwide pathogens of hundreds of unrelated plants, are *Verticillium dahliae* and *Fusarium oxysporum*.

Both fungi are persistent in the soil for many years in the absence of any host. *Fusarium oxysporum* consists of many specialized forms which are specific to one host. *Verticillium dahliae* consists of several groups, some of which parasitize many hosts, and others which seem to be very host selective.

Both fungi invade and infect only the vascular tissue of host plants. Overlapping non-specific symptoms occur in plants infected by both pathogens. In general there is yellowing and drying of leaves, overall plant stress, wilting and death of branches, and varying degrees of vascular discoloration. The only method to prove the cause of the disease is to isolate and identify the pathogen from infected vascular tissue.

Hosts of *Verticillium dahliae* include over 120 species in unrelated plant families including many woody and herbaceous ornamentals. Forms of *Fusarium oxysporum* cause disease in many food, fiber and ornamental plants. The species is one of the most important worldwide plant pathogens. Isolates are host specific. For example, an isolate from carnations is only pathogenic to certain cultivars in that species.

Interestingly, although both fungi occur naturally in Arizona soils only *V. dahliae* is an important plant pathogen. The lack of importance of *Fusarium* wilts (caused by biotypes of *F. oxysporum*) in Arizona is thought to be due to our alkaline soils which are not favorable for activity of the fungus. *Verticillium dahliae*, however, is an important plant pathogen of several of our important agricultural crops, including upland cotton (*Gossypium hirsutum*), peppers (*Capsicum* spp.), tomato (*Lycopersicon esculentum*), eggplant (*Solanum melongena*), okra (*Hibiscus esculentus*), and safflower (*Carthamus tinctorius*). Susceptible woody-landscape plants include olive (*Olea europaea*), pistachio (*Pistacia chinensis, P. vera*), ash (*Fraxinus* spp.), maple (*Acer* spp.), pecan (*Carya illinoensis*), carob (*Ceratonia siliqua*), almond, apricot, cherry, peach (*Prunus* spp.), California pepper tree (*Schinus molle*), elm (*Ulmus* spp.), rose (*Rosa* spp.), and privet (*Ligustrum* spp.).

Ornamental plants susceptible to *Verticillium* wilt among others include; asters (*Aster* spp.), chrysanthemums (*Chrysanthemum* spp.), dahlia (*Dahlia* spp.), geranium and pelargonium (*Pelargonium* spp.), petunia (*Petunia* spp.), phlox (*Phlox* spp.), stock (*Matthiola* spp.), snaps (*Antirrhinum majus*), and sweet peas (*Lathyrus odoratus*). The list of resistant or immune plants is very large and includes all cacti; all monocots such as grasses, palms, iris and lilies; and all gymnosperms such as junipers, pines, and cypress.

Some other commonly planted shrubs and trees in Arizona that are resistant or immune to *Verticillium* wilt include: apples, citrus, eucalyptus, Pyracantha, mulberry, oak, oleander, sycamore, poplar, walnuts, and willows.

Although *Verticillium* wilt is common in several agricultural crops, the disease is less important in landscape plants. *Verticillium* wilt diseases of urban plants in Arizona seem to most commonly occur in plantings made in old agricultural land with a history of *Verticillium* wilt. This is because the fungus combines a wide host range with long term survival in the soil.

Biology of *V. dahliae*

One has to have great respect for the biological characteristics that make *V. dahliae* one of the most widespread and destructive soilborne fungal plant pathogens. These characteristics are: rapid host colonization via xylem (water conducting elements), production of large numbers of reproductive spores (condidia and microsclerotia), effective asexual mechanisms of variation, long term survival of microsclerotia in soil (up to 14 years in non-cropped field soils), wide host range, and effective dissemination mechanisms (microsclerotia are carried in air, dust, water, soil, plant residues, and in leaves, stems, and seed).

Another factor contributing to the success of *V. dahliae* as a plant pathogen in arid desert areas is the lack of dependence of the fungus on rain and high humidity for infection and host colonization (the fungus is internal in the host). Also, there are many plants (especially weeds) that, although susceptible to *Verticillium* wilt, show no symptoms when they are infected (symptomless carriers).

The fungus has a simple life cycle and produces only two types of reproductive structures: conidia and microsclerotia. The microscopic conidia are short lived but are factors in rapid internal host colonization. The microsclerotia are black, heavily walled, microscopic aggregates of fungal hyphae. The fungus can be identified under the microscope by noting the whorled arrangement of conidiophore branches and the typical clumped masses of the black microslerotia.

Microsclerotia

Microsclerotia are produced in large numbers in infected host tissue during cool weather. They are returned to the soil on death of the host plant. They germinate in the soil to initiate root infection.

Symptoms and Biology of *Verticillium* Wilt of Olive

Because of the importance of this disease in Arizona, it will be used as an example to discuss symptoms and biology of a typical *Verticillium* disease.

Verticillium initially invades the root system of olives when soil temperatures are cool. The fungus is relatively inactive at temperatures above 85°F. After penetrating the roots, the fungus grows and moves through the plant in the water-conducting (vascular) tissues and eventually invades branches and twigs. This systemic invasion usually occurs from February to June. With the onset of high summer temperatures the fungus is inactivated.

By then, unfortunately, the damage has been done and the trees begin to exhibit symptoms. The presence of the fungus in the vascular system interrupts and reduces the water movement from the roots to the leaves. Wilt symptoms are attributable to impeded internal water flow.

Symptoms usually first appear in the spring near flowering time. Newer leaves roll inward and lose their deep-green, waxy luster and become dull gray and brown. Leaf-drop and twig die-back may follow, depending upon the severity of the infection and the effect of the environment on the water demand of leaves and fruit. Flower clusters on affected branches may die and remain attached. Individual branches, portions of trees or the entire crown may die in one season. Tree death, however, rarely occurs. New growth may develop from unaffected portions of the trees. Suckering from the crown may be prolific.

In Arizona, a slight vascular discoloration of affected twigs and branches may develop. This discoloration can be observed by removing the outside layer of bark from affected branches and exposing the vascular tissue.

When cool weather returns, the fungus again becomes active. In this way branches can be re-invaded each year during the spring season.

Control

Control of *Verticillium* wilt diseases is based primarily on the use of resistant cultivars or immune species. Many resistant cultivars of ornamental plants are available from nurseries and seed companies.

Powdery Mildew

Powdery mildew diseases occur on hundreds of plants grown in urban landscapes. The diseases primarily affect leaves, green stems, flower buds, and immature fruit of a wide range of plants including ornamental flowers, broad leaved shade trees, cereals, weeds, vegetables, fruit trees, and native plants.

All of the powdery mildew fungi are obligate parasites and reproduce on living host tissue. They do not grow saprophytically. This is in contrast to the previously described fungi which combine saprophytic and parasitic stage in their life cycles. The powdery mildew fungi grow primarily on leaf surfaces and aerial plant parts. They are not systemic in plants, and they do not infect roots.

The mycelium is superficial on host tissue in most genera, but in some such as *Oidiopsis*, the mycelium is internal. Chains of asexual colorless conidia are produced from conidiophores that grow from the mycelium. The name *powdery mildew* accurately describes the appearance of the fungus on host tissue. Nutrients are obtained from host tissue by means of microscopic, rootlike organs called haustoria. These specialized fungal structures are produced only in epidermal cells.

Symptoms

Plants infected with powdery mildew fungi typically have a whitish, powdery covering over infected leaves, stems, and other aerial plant parts. Infected leaves are often curled or twisted. Severe leaf infection may cause leaf yellowing, reduced leaf size and defoliation. These symptoms are general. They are influenced by climate, host location (shade effects), host and the causal species of mildew.

The only real method of identification of a powdery mildew disease is to identify the host and the fungus. The fungus is easily identified under the microscope by the characteristic growth habit of the conidial (asexual stage) and by the architecture of the sexual fruiting body (cleistothecium). The conidial stage is always present. The sexual stage of the fungus may or may not be present.

Biology

Under mild winter conditions in the desert areas of Arizona, the powdery mildew fungi occur primarily in their asexual, conidial stage. The sexual stage is not important for survival. Thus, the life cycle is very simple. Conidia are wind carried to host tissue where they germinate and infect host tissue.

Conidia

The conidia germinate on dry leaf surfaces even when atmospheric humidity is low. Spore germination and penetration of tissue usually occurs in 6 hours or less. Many species can produce a new generation of spores in 4 to 6 days under favorable conditions.

Some species of the powdery mildew fungi have very large host ranges. One of the most common species in Arizona is *Erysiphe cichoracearum*. This fungus causes powdery mildew diseases in species in over 160 genera of unrelated plants from *Ageratum* and *Antirrhinum* (snapdragons) to *Verbena* and *Zinnia*. Another species, *E. polygoni* attacks species in many genera of plants from *Acacia* to *Vicia* and *Vigna*. *Erysiphe graminis* causes powdery mildew of grasses.

Some powdery mildews of deciduous plants overwinter as dormant mycelium in leaf buds and in bark. In the spring the fungus becomes active and the conidial stage is produced. Powdery mildews that produce a sexual stage survive as cleistothecia. Sexual spores called ascospores are produced in the cleistothecia and are the primary source of infection during plant growth in the spring.

Control

Powdery mildews are controlled by the use of resistant varieties and also by a number of fungicides, including different formulations of sulfur. These chemicals are used as protective sprays, and it is very important to apply them at the first sign of disease since powdery mildew is extremely difficult to control once established.

Rust Diseases

Rusts are an amazing group of fungi belonging to a single order of basidiomycetes, the Uredinales. Throughout history these fungi have been responsible for catastrophic diseases of many of the world's most important plants including grain crops such as barley, corn, oats, rye, sorghum, and wheat; vegetables such as asparagus and beans; field crops such as cotton, safflower, soybeans, and sunflower; trees such as apple, peaches, pines, firs, junipers, and oaks; and many ornamentals.

Many plants found in urban environments in Arizona including asters, carnations, chrysanthemums, dichondra, geraniums, hollyhock, iris, lily, rose, and snapdragon are affected with rust diseases. Some common woody plants affected with rust diseases in Arizona include firs (*Abies* spp.), *Acacia* spp., cypress (*Cupressus* spp.), ocotillo (*Fouquieria splendens*), fairy duster (*Calliandra* spp.), junipers (*Juniperus* spp.), pines (*Pinus* spp.), aspen (*Populus* spp.), pear (*Pyrus communis*), and oaks (*Quercus* spp.).

Symptoms

Symptoms of rust diseases are almost as diverse as the fungi that cause the diseases. Some rust fungi have unbelievable, complex life cycles.

These life cycles may involve totally unrelated host plants and may include up to four different spore producing stages and five functionally different kinds of spores. Some species complete their entire life cycle on one host (autoecious) whereas other species require two hosts (heteroecious).

In order to understand symptoms caused by infections by the rust fungi, it is necessary to understand the various spore stages of the fungi. Infection by each spore stage causes somewhat different symptoms. Spore stages useful in identification of the disease include aecia, uredia, and telia. The aecia are cup and blister like in appearance. Light yellow to orange wind dispersed aeciospores are produced in the aecia.

Uredia are also blisterlike pustules that produce masses of orange to rust-colored uredospores. Telia are structures that produce masses of teliospores. The telia follow uredia on the same host. The teliospores are usually black in color. Aecia, uredia, and telia can be easily observed on infected host tissue with the use of a hand lens. The spores, produced on each of these structures, however, are microscopic.

Identification of rusts may be complicated because many rusts omit one or more of the above stages. Also, aecia and uredia are somewhat similar in appearance. Symptoms of many rust diseases consist primarily of these small pustules on the underside of leaves.

Although, the rust fungi most frequently attack leaves they also infect flowers, fruit, and stems and branches and trunks of woody flowering plants and conifers. Most rust infections are localized but in some diseases the fungi become locally systemic in host tissue and cause galls, blisters, and cankers in woody tissue.

Biology

The rust fungi, like the powdery mildew fungi, are all obligate parasites. Thus, it is impossible to isolate and grow these fungi in the laboratory. They complete their life cycles only on living host plants.

Variation in the life cycles of rust fungi can be dramatically illustrated by comparing three common rust diseases in Arizona: snapdragon rust

(*Puccinia antirrhini*), hollyhock rust (*P. malvacearum*), and limb rust of Ponderosa pine (*Cronartium arizonicum*). The uredial and the telial stage occur on snapdragons and only the telial stage on hollyhock, respectively.

In contrast to these two simple cycles is the complex cycle of the limb rust pathogen. Aeciospores, produced from aecia on twigs of pine trees infect a totally unrelated host, paintbrush (*Castilleja integra*). Uredia and telia are produced on paintbrush. The urediospores infect only paintbrush. Teliospores, produced from telia on paintbrush, germinate and produce basidiospores that infect twigs of pine in the fall.

Snapdragon rust and hollyhock rust are examples of types of short cycle rusts and limb rust is an example of a long cycle rust. Almost any combination of spore stages is found in nature. The extraordinary biology of these fungi has fascinated plant pathologists throughout history. From an epidemiological consideration, it should be noted that aeciospores in heteroecious rusts always infect the alternate host. Aeciospores may be aerially disseminated for hundreds of miles and remain viable.

Urediospores normally infect the same host on which they develop. They may or may not be aerially disseminated for long distances. Basidiospores, produced from overwintering teliospores, are thin walled and delicate and are not adapted for long range spread. In heteroecious rusts (alternate hosts necessary for completion of life cycle) the basidiospores always infect the alternate host.

Control

The first step in controlling a rust disease, as with all plant diseases, is the identification of the causal fungus. The rust fungi are identified primarily by the anatomy of the aeciospores, urediospores and the teliospores. These spores are microscopic and must be examined with a compound microscope. Also, it is necessary to know the host species. Some hosts are infected by more than one species of rust fungi. Other hosts have only a single rust pathogen. Symptoms of each disease are different and very important in disease identification.

Control of rust disease is as complicated as the biology of the rust fungi. Each disease (there are thousands) may have a different method for control. Leaf diseases, in general, are controlled by the use of preventive foliar fungicides. The use of resistant cultivars, and seed treatments (some rust fungi are seed-borne) for control of certain rust diseases is beneficial. Most rust fungi are host specific.

In the three diseases described, for example, snapdragon rust only attacks certain genetic lines of snapdragons. Hollyhock rust is similar. Limb rust of pine is also host specific. Within each species of rust fungi there are pathogenic races that cause disease in only certain cultivars within the host species.

These pathogenic races may vary from year to year and also be different in other geographical areas. Snapdragons, for example, bred for resistance to rust in one geographical area may be susceptible in other areas.

Cytospora Canker

Cytospora canker is commonly found on a number of fruit and shade trees in Arizona. This disease occurs worldwide on fruit trees, hardwood, forest and shade trees, shrubs and conifers. In Arizona the disease is most common on cottonwood (*Populus fremontii*), lombardy poplar (*P. nigra*), pecan (*Carya illinoinensis*), and willows (*Salix* spp.). A number of *Prunus* spp. including apricot (*P. armeniaca*), peach (*P. persica*), plums (*P. salicina*), prunes (*P. domestica*) and cherry (*P. avium*) are susceptible. Occasionally the disease has been seen on apples (*Malus communis*). Over 40 pathogenic species of *Cytospora* have been described worldwide.

The ascomycetous sexual stage has been named *Valsa* or *Leucostoma*. There is some confusion among authorities on the nomenclature of the causal fungus. The asexual, pycnidial stage, *Cytospora*, is the most common stage seen in Arizona.

Symptoms

Infections take place in above ground woody tissue that has been damaged by frost, fire or sunburn, or through wounds caused by pruning injuries and broken twigs and branches.

Typical symptoms of *Cytospora* canker are sunken lesions on infected tissue. The cankers are perennial and continue to enlarge each year. The fungus slowly invades and girdles limbs or trunks. The result is a dead limb above the infection site. Black pycnidia of *Cytospora* can easily be seen emerging from infected bark with use of a hand lens. The pycnidia are roundish and pinhead in size. They are scattered in the cankered area.

During wet weather, sticky masses of orange-yellow conidia are extended in long tendrils. These conidia are wind disseminated to injured tissue where they germinate and infect host tissue. *Cytospora* is active during spring and summer. The extruded conidial stage is most commonly seen during our summer monsoon season. Inoculum can be found on cankered trunks and branches throughout the year.

Control

Sun damage may be reduced by shading or application of a white interior latex paint to woody tissue. Trees that are properly fertilized and watered are not normally susceptible to infection. Avoid severe pruning. Disinfect pruning cuts with a 1/10 dilution of a household bleach. Cut out infected branches as they are a continual source of infection. Remove and burn where feasible. There are no chemicals recommended for control. Removal of heavily infected cottonwoods near commercial pecan groves has reduced disease incidence in some situations.

Sooty Canker

Sooty canker, also known as branch or limb wilt, is caused by the fungus, *Hendersonula toruloidea*. This wound pathogen invades only sunburned bark or areas that have been mechanically injured, such as pruning wounds on smooth or thin barked deciduous trees. The fungus does not infect uninjured host tissue.

Disease is found primarily at low elevations where sunburn damage commonly occurs on trunks and branches of unprotected or stressed shrubs and trees in Arizona. The fungus has a wide host range and causes diseases in many unrelated plants.

Symptoms

The most common symptom of sooty canker is the sooty, black canker that develops beneath bark tissue. This black canker is due to the presence of masses of black, fungal spores that appear under the bark and on the surface of the canker. Symptoms on leaves of cankered branches appear during summer. Because the fungus grows into and kills sapwood, the leaves on branches with cankers, wilt, turn brown and die. Branches die back to the cankered area. Scattered branches are usually affected. Most cankers develop on unshaded trunks or limbs that face toward the sun. Sunburned trunks and limbs are highly susceptible to infection.

Biology of the Pathogen

The fungus, under our conditions, produces only conidia and thus has a very simple life cycle. The small conidia, produced in black, powdery masses under bark, are easily wind disseminated. These spores, which arise from segmented hyphae, are carried to damaged bark tissue where they germinate and initiate infection. Most active fungal growth occurs during the summer. The mycelium grows into living tissue.

Infected sapwood becomes stained gray to black in color. Early research in California simulated sunburn damage on bark of walnut trees with use of a "blow-torch." This fact says something about our summer conditions.

Common susceptible hosts in Arizona include: almond (*Prunus amygdalus*), apple (*Malus sylbestris*), apricot (*Prunus armeniaca*), ash (*Fraxinus* spp.), carob (*Ceratonia siliqua*), *Citrus* spp. (oranges, grapefruit, lemon, lime), cottonwood (*Populus* spp.), fig (*Ficus cariaca*), mimosa (*Albizia julibrissin*), mulberry (*Morus* spp.), peaches (*Prunus persica*), pecan (*Carya pecan*), plum (*Prunus domestica*), sycamore (*Platanus occidentalis*), walnut (*Juglans* spp.), and wisteria (*Wisteria* spp.)

Control

Sooty canker can be controlled when infections are confined to limbs and upper branches. Smaller infected branches should be removed when symptoms appear. Since sunburned bark is the primary infection site, large limbs should be pruned only when trees are dormant.

When removing infected limbs, cut back to at least 1 foot below the canker. The cut area and pruning tools should be treated with a solution of one part household bleach and nine parts water. Pruning wounds should be painted with a copper fungicide to prevent infection. Reapply the copper compound to the wound each spring to insure adequate protection against infection. Control becomes increasingly difficult as the disease progresses into the scaffold branches and is virtually impossible once the main trunk is infected.

Tree vigour should be maintained through proper fertilization and deep watering on a regular schedule. Severe pruning of larger branches and limbs of trees susceptible to sooty canker should be avoided. Whitewash, applied to exposed lower trunk areas, will reduce the possibilities of infection. This material reflects radiation and reduces bark temperature.

Wood Rots and Decays

Wood-rotting basidiomycete fungi are occasional problems in desert plants including cliff rose (*Cowania* spp.), canotia (*Canotia holacantha*), palo verde (*Cercidium* spp.), creosote bush (*Larrea tridentata*) and junipers. Also, some cacti such as saguaro and cholla which have a large amount of solid, woody tissue may be invaded and decayed by wood-rotting Basidiomycetes as well as a number of landscape trees, including mulberry (*Morus* spp.), cottonwood and poplars (*Populus* spp.), and chinaberry (*Melia* spp.).

Wood-rotting Basidiomycetes are common disease fungi in a large number of conifers, deciduous trees, shrubs, and hardwoods throughout the forest areas of Arizona. Large losses of timber on living and harvested trees are caused annually by these fungi. Weakening of limbs and the subsequent hazard from breakage of large limbs and trunks, especially on windy days or during wind storms, is a serious consequence of these infections.

Symptoms

In living trees and shrubs most rotting is confined to the older, central wood of stems and branches. The conks of these fungi appear near the infection site. These shelf-shaped fungal structures are most commonly seen along the main trunk and on infected branches. Cross sections of infected wood reveals the dark, discolored heartwood where the rot fungus is active. The fungus may be isolated from these tissues.

The fungi enter through wounds. Shelf-shaped or bracket-like structures usually occur after decay has been active for long periods of time. The disease progresses slowly and generally is not noticed until the fungus has destroyed heartwood.

Control

Control consists of removal of infected tissue and prevention of wounds to woody tissue. A specialist is necessary to identify these diseases and to give advice on specific control measures. In any case, affected limbs should be pruned away to avoid damage or injury if they fall.

Ganoderma Root Rot

Another basidiomycete, *Ganoderma lucidum,* causes root rot in native and landscape trees such as olive, African sumac, mulberry, hackberry, and oak. Another Ganoderma species causes root rot in mesquite and Acacia.

Biology and Symptoms

Spores of these *Ganoderma* species infect the roots of susceptible hosts, and as the fungus grows in host tissue, it causes root rot. Infected trees decline rapidly and die. The entire crown is affected as leaves fail to emerge. These fungi seem to be limited to the roots and lower crown. They are soil borne, and spread from plant to plant by root contact.

The creamy colored mycelium of the fungus can be seen if the bark is pulled away from the root. During summer rains, the reproductive structures of these fungi may form on the base of the tree. These are white to reddish-orange fleshy growths on the bark that become hardened when they mature. Brownish-red spore deposits may be visible around the structures. These reproductive spores are easily carried in the wind.

Control

There is no control for *Ganoderma* root rot once the plant is infected. The best way to prevent infection is to prevent wounding. Cutting roots during construction or landscape maintenance should be avoided wherever possible.

Bacteria

The desert environment of Arizona is not conducive to bacterial plant diseases. Foliar and above ground diseases that are of great importance in the wet, humid areas of the world, are rare and insignificant. There are some exceptions, however. Two gall diseases, crown gall and oleander gall are common.

Crown Gall

Crown gall is caused by the soil-borne bacterium, *Agrobacterium tumefaciens*. This disease is one of the most widely studied of all plant diseases. This gall inducing bacterium enters plants through wounds primarily on lower stems and trunks and roots. Cellular growth is stimulated and galls of varying sizes and shapes are produced in infected plant tissue. *Agrobacterium tumefaciens* has the largest host range of any bacterial plant pathogen. More than 600 plant species in over 90 plant families are susceptible.

Symptoms

Galls form on stems and roots, especially at the root crown, the area where roots and stem come together. Galls enlarge with host plant growth. Gall formation does not occur in dormant plants. The galls range in size from less than half inch in diameter to over 8 inches in susceptible, older plants. The size of the galls is influenced by plant species and size and growth rate of the infected plant part. Galls on woody plants are spongy and light colored when young but with age become rough, hard and fissured. Old galls are often sloughed off.

Plants affected most commonly include almonds, apples, apricots, cherry, cottonwood, figs, grapes, nectarine, peaches, pears, pecans, plums, privet, pyracantha, roses, and willows.

Biology

Strains of *Agrobacterium* can be isolated from soil, galls, and root surfaces. Crown gall bacteria are disseminated in soil, water and on or in plants. In grapes, for example, the bacterium becomes systemic in xylem tissue. The most serious cases of crown gall have occurred where early spring growth is followed by freezing temperatures. This is more common at elevations above 3000 feet.

This occurs because the bacterium is a wound pathogen. *Agrobacterium tumefaciens* survives in the soil as a root colonizer of many plants without regard to their susceptibility to infection and gall formation. When susceptible hosts are planted into infested areas the bacteria infect through wounds and galls are produced. The bacteria are returned to the soil when galls disintegrate, thus completing the simple life cycle.

Control

It is very difficult to purchase disease-free plants because early galls are often too small to see or have not formed. Once the bacterium is introduced into your landscaping area for all practical purposes it is there indefinitely. The greatest economic losses caused by crown gall occur in nurseries that produce stone and pome fruit trees such as almond, apple, cherry, peach, and plum because regulations prohibit their shipment and sale.

The damage caused by crown gall may have been historically exaggerated. Recent studies in grapes, for example, suggest that only very extensive galling causes reduced growth and yield loss. There is no practical method, although several have been suggested, to eradicate the galls. If crown gall has been a problem in the past, replant with resistant species such as palms, grasses or conifers. No chemical methods are recommended. Avoid injuries during planting of bare rooted and other ornamental plants.

A biological control may be available to prevent entry of the pathogen. A strain of bacterium that attaches to a wound site but does not cause disease can be used as a root dip or wound paint for preplant prevention. Development of resistance of the pathogen to this strain has been a problem.

Oleander Gall

Oleander (*Nerium oleander*) is one of the most popular evergreen shrubs in Arizona. The gall disease is widespread.

Symptoms and Biology

Oleander gall is caused by the bacterium *Pseudomonas syringae* pv. *savastanoi*. Galls occur on twigs, branches, leaves, flowers, and seedpods. Initially galls appear as small protuberances that subsequently develop into wart-like growths with roughened, fissured surfaces. Galls vary in size but average about ½ to 1 inch in diameter.

Large galls are usually made up of several small galls that have grown together. Galls are the result of the growth and multi-plication of the bacterium. The bacteria enter and infect oleanders through leaf and blossom scars, wounds produced by pruning, frost injury, and natural openings. Rain, sprinkler water, and pruning tools can spread bacteria from diseased to healthy plants.

Control

When purchasing oleanders, examine them carefully to be sure they are free of galls. The vast majority of nursery stock is free from disease but prevention is always the most effective method of disease control. For diseased oleanders, prune out infected plant parts and apply disinfection solution (a 10% solution of household bleach) to each cut surface.

Always dip pruning tools in the disinfectant solution between cuts to reduce the possibility of spreading the bacteria. Pruning operations should be conducted during the dry seasons to avoid infection of wounds. Avoid sprinkler irrigation.

Severe infection of large shrubs is difficult to control by selective pruning. If the entire shrub is cut down, the new succulent growth is extremely susceptible to infection. In certain situations, removal of the diseased plant and replanting may be the best method of control.

Fire Blight

Fire blight, caused by the bacterium *Erwinia amylovora*, is one of the oldest known and most serious bacterial plant diseases. Interestingly all susceptible plants are in the rose family (*Rosaceae*). The most important groups include apples (*Malus* spp.), pear (*Pyrus* spp.), cotoneaster (*Cotoneaster* spp.), hawthorn (*Crataegus* spp.), quince (*Cydonia* spp.), loquat (*Eriobotrya japonica*), *Prunus* spp. (including apricot, cherry, plum, prunes), pyracantha (*Pyracantha* spp.), mountain ash (*Sorbus* spp.), and spirea (*Spiraea* spp.). In Arizona most reports of fire blight relate to apples, pears, and pyracantha.

The causal bacterium, *E. amylovora*, is thought to be indigenous to North America. The disease was first reported on apples, pears, and quinces in the Hudson River Valley of New York in 1780. In 1878, an American plant pathologist, Thomas Burrill, working at the University of Illinois, concluded that the disease was caused by a bacterium. The disease was not described in Europe for another 100 years.

Symptoms

Extensive studies on symptom development, basic biology and control have been made on apples and pears. Fewer studies have been made on other hosts including ornamentals and native plants. In Arizona, fire blight is a problem in Cochise and Graham counties on pears and apples. The disease is occasionally a problem on loquat, cotoneaster, and pyracantha in urban situations. Our desert environment does not favor this disease in normal rainfall seasons.

Disease symptoms first appear when trees or shrubs are blooming. Blossom blight, an early symptom, occurs because the bacteria first invade flowers. The pathogen enters hosts through blossoms, wounds, and natural openings such as stomata, hydathodes, lenticels and nectaries.

If high humidity, high rainfall and warm cloudy weather occurs during the flowering cycle the pathogen can cause extensive damage. Infected blossoms of pear, apple, loquat or pyracantha develop a water-soaked appearance, shrivel, and turn brown to black. Affected flowers may or may not drop. Affected apple blossoms tend to cling to the spurs. Young, rapidly growing apple shoots and twigs also are quite susceptible. In the early stages of disease, reddish-brown streaking can be seen in the tissues below visible infections. Affected apple shoots eventually turn light to dark brown, while pear shoots turn dark brown to black. Affected leaves appear light to dark brown.

Blackening of petioles and the central main vein of leaves is common. Margins of advancing infections of pear fruitlets often have a dark green (water-soaked) appearance, while those of apples are reddish.

The pathogen also can invade major branches and trunks of trees, causing visible cankers. Cankers initially may have no obvious margins, or the margins may be raised or appear as blisters. If a canker girdles a trunk, branch, or twig, the portion above usually dies.

Under warm, humid conditions the bacteria can multiply so rapidly that they will ooze from infected peduncles, shoots, leaves, fruits, and even cankers. Sticky and light to amber colored, such ooze may appear as droplets, tendrils, or discolored streaks. This is not a common phenomenon under Arizona conditions.

Disease Cycle

Erwinia amylovora survives between season within and on host tissues. The bacteria do not survive in soil.

Temperatures between approximately 60° and 85°F, humidity above 60 per cent, and the frequent occurrence of free moisture (dews, rain, fog, sprinkler irrigation) favor the multiplication and spread of the pathogen. Bacteria are transferred from cankers to flower buds, new leaves, succulent shoots, and fruits by splashing water and insects. The bacteria penetrate plant parts via natural openings, including nectaries in flowers and stomata in new leaves and shoots. Penetration also can occur through fresh injuries such as those caused by hail or chewing insects.

Bacteria are secondarily distributed from newly infected flowers and from ooze associated with infections to non-infected flowers, and leaves by insects and splashing water. Pruning tools also can be important in transferring bacteria from infected to non-infected branches. Once infection of flowers or leaves occurs, bacteria can move into shoots, and then upward and downward in the shoots without causing any external evidence of disease. In fact, bacteria have been recovered approximately 35 inches beyond the margins of visible lesions.

Control

Resistant varieties: Of the apple varieties commonly grown in Arizona, Arkansas Black and Red Astrachan are currently considered resistant. Golden Delicious, Red Delicious, Granny Smith, Jonagold, and Gravenstein are moderately resistant to fire blight. Rome Beauty, Jonathon, and Lodi are susceptible to the disease, as are most flowering crab apples. The predominant apple rootstocks used are rated for fire blight susceptibility as follows: MM111, light; MM106, moderate; M9, severe; and M26, very severe.

Currently, Bartley and Bosc pear varieties are considered highly susceptible, Seckel moderately resistant, and Surcrop resistant to the disease.

Chemical Control

Chemical control of fire blight is based on protective sprays. Initiate spraying during the bud/bloom period when the average of daily maximum and minimum temperatures reaches 60°F. Follow label recommendations for mixing and applying sprays, including the timing for repeat sprays (usually at five day intervals) during the blooming period, particularly when rain or hail has occurred since the last application. Since any unprotected, open blossom is a potential infection site, sprays should be continued throughout the bloom period when environmental conditions exist which are favorable for blight.

Two groups of chemicals have traditionally been used for blight control. These are:

Copper Compounds

Copper compounds can be effective in reducing fire blight. They are easy to apply and relatively inexpensive. Although bordeaux (copper sulphate plus lime) probably has been the most frequently used formulation, fixed coppers such as kocide (copper hydroxide) and copper oxychloride sulphate (COCS) are much easier to prepare and use as dormant and blossom sprays. However, copper can cause russet-ting of fruit which can decrease their fresh market value.

Antibiotics

Streptomycin has been the antibiotic of choice in protective sprays. Although more expensive than copper compounds, streptomycin normally does not cause russetting. However, resistant strains of *E. amylovora* have developed in areas where streptomycin has been exclusively and repeatedly used.

Pruning/Sanitation

In the spring, remove infected shoots and flowers. Prune them off at least 15 inches below any visible symptoms. Pruning equipment should be decontaminated after every cut by treating the blades with 10 per cent household bleach. Because of their susceptibility to *E. amylovora*, promptly remove unwanted suckers from trunks, roots, and scaffold branches. During the dormant period, remove all remaining blighted plant parts. All infected prunings (summer and winter) should be burned.

Bacterial Necrosis of Saguaro

This disease is caused by soft-rotting species of *Erwinia*. The pathogen has also been recovered from a number of indigenous cacti including cholla, prickly pear, barrel, and organ-pipe cacti.

Symptoms

Symptoms appear at one or more positions on the trunk or branches of saguaros. The first indicator of bacterial necrosis is a circular darkening and softening of the plant tissues. The infected area enlarges, becoming purplish-black, and splits open. A dark odorous material will frequently "leak" from the plant.

At other times, the soft areas dry and crack, revealing the dark, dry remains of diseased tissues. If conditions are favorable, the plant can confine the disease to a "pocket" by forming a barrier of protective tissue (callus) around the infected area. If this tissue does not rapidly form, the bacteria will spread.

Bacteria occur in the diseased plant tissue of living cacti, and in the exudate associated with the infected areas. Infection begins when the pathogen is introduced into the cactus through wounds or natural openings. Presumably, insects and small animals which are associated with diseased or decaying saguaros serve as the principle carriers.

Control

Removal of diseased tissue is "the most practical way to control the spread of the infection within the plant. If the affected area is small, remove all the rotting material and about one-half inch of the surrounding healthy tissues. Slope the bottom of the excavation so that water will drain out.

The wall of the cleaned rot pocket should be smooth. In removing the rotting material, be careful not to make "puncture-type" cuts into the remaining healthy tissue since the pathogen can survive in such sites. Thoroughly wash the cleansed pocket with a 10 per cent household bleach solution (one part household bleach and 9 parts of water; also include about one teaspoon of liquid detergent per gallon of solution) and then allow the pocket to stand open to hasten healing.

If the lesion is so large as to nearly girdle or weaken an arm or plant, serious consideration should be given to removal of the affected structure. Otherwise, damage might result should the branch or plant unexpectedly fall.

Wetwood or Slime Flux

These two diseases are described under bacterial diseases because a number of diverse bacteria, including *Erwinia* spp., are thought to be the cause of these poorly understood diseases. In the literature the disease is referred to as slime flux and/or wetwood.

Symptoms

Symptoms of Slime Flux consist of water-soaked, discolored areas at or below branch crotches and trunk wounds with chronic bleeding of sap. Wilting and die back of branches may occur. Water-soaked wood with large numbers of bacteria is discolored and dead. Liquid may seep out of cracks and wounds and run down the bark. The liquid, because of contamination with microorganisms, becomes dark in color, sticky and odiferous. Fermentation of tree tissues may cause increases of pressure and toxin production within the infected tree. Normally, the disease is not found in young trees. This is probably due to the fact that in the sapwood and heartwood of normal, young actively growing trees, bacteria and fungi are rare. Susceptible hosts in Arizona include: ash (*Fraxinus* spp.), elms (*Ulmus* spp.), cottonwood (*Populus fremontii*), mulberry (*Morus* spp.) and mesquite, common and chilean (*Prosopis juliflora* and *P. chilensis*).

Control

There are no preventative methods for Slime Flux except good tree health care practices, proper watering, feeding and pruning. There are no controls for the disease. The practice of installing tubes to drain liquid is no longer recommended since it does not alleviate the problem and the holes are a good infection site for many pathogenic organisms. Trees with Slime Flux will usually live for many years, but any weakened limb should be removed if it is a safety risk. If the dripping causes stains on patios or walkways, a hard water spray, applied routinely, may prevent staining.

Plant-parasitic Nematodes

There are hundreds of species that parasitize plants. Most plant-parasitic nematodes attack only roots. Symptoms on roots cover the range from swelling, lesions, galls, and suppression of root elongation. Above ground symptoms are non-specific and consist of slow growth, chlorosis and all symptoms associated with root damage and nutrient deficiencies. Specific diagnosis requires the analysis of root and soil tissue to determine qualitative and quantitative populations of nematodes.

Root-Knot Nematodes (Meloidogyne spp.)

These nematodes are the most common and important group. They cause disease in hundreds of plants including ornamentals, vegetables and the following commonly planted landscape trees: Acacia (*Acacia* spp.), almonds (*Prunus* spp.), apricots (*Prunus* spp.), Arizona ash (*Fraxinus velutina*), Chinese elm (*Ulmus parvifolia*), fig (*Ficus carica*), peach (*Pyrus* spp.), pear (*Pyrus communis*), plum (*Prunus* spp.), pomegranate (*Punica granatum*), weeping willow (*Salix babylonica*), golden willow (*Salix alba 'Tristis'*), bottle tree (*Brachychiton populneus*), olive (*Oleaeuropaea*), palm (*Phoenix canariensis* and *P. dactylifera, Washingtonia filifera* and *W. robusta, Chamaerops humilis, Arecastrum romanzoffianum, Trachycarpus fortunei*), and Japanese privet (*Ligustrum japonicum*).

Symptoms

Plants are stunted with small, pale green or chlorotic foliage that tends to wilt and partially defoliate in warm weather. Flower production and fruit set are reduced. Irregular, spherical swellings (knots) are found on the roots at the point of nematode feeding.

Control

Control is based on first identifying the nematode. Then it is possible to implement certain cultural techniques such as the use of resistant plants and varieties, rotation, and fallow. Purchase plants from reputable nurseries and producers.

Parasitic Higher Plants

Over 2500 species of higher plants live parasitically only on other living plants. The most important genera worldwide include dwarf mistletoes of conifers (*Arceuthobium* spp.), mistletoes on broadleafed trees (*Phoradendron* spp.), the European true mistletoes (*Viscum* spp.), broomrape (*Orobanche* spp.), witchweed (*Striga* spp.), and dodder (*Cuscuta* spp.). All of these parasitic plants produce leaves, stems, flowers, and seeds but no true roots. The mistletoes have chlorophyll but depend on their hosts for water and nutrients. Others, like dodder, have little or no chlorophyll and no true roots. The dodders are totally dependant on their hosts for completion of their life cycles.

Mistletoes

Although dodder and broomrape are occasionally seen on a number of broad-leafed plants, the most important and common parasitic plants in this group are the mistletoes in Arizona. Two groups are important, the dwarf mistletoes of conifers and the true mistletoes of broadleafed trees and shrubs. Dwarf mistletoes are common problems in our conifer forests.

In urban plantings in the desert areas of Arizona the only significant mistletoes are the true mistletoes caused by *Phoradendron* spp. Several *Phoradendron* spp. have been described in Arizona including P. *californicum* (parasitic on leguminous shrubs and trees such as acacia (*Acacia* spp.), blue palo verde (*Cercidium floridum*), foothill palo verde (*Cercidium microphyllum*), Mexican palo verde (*Parkinsonia aculeata*), ironwood (*Olneya tesota*) and mesquite (Prosopis spp.). Other *Phoradendron* spp. occur on juniper (*Juniperus* spp.) and oak (*Quercus* spp.).

The most conspicuous and largest leaved mistletoe in Arizona is *P. tomentosum* which parasitizes cottonwood (*Populus fremontii*), sycamore (*Platanus wrightii*), ash (*Fraxinus* spp.), hackberry (*Celtis* spp.), walnut (*Juglans* spp.), and willow (*Salix* spp.). It is often a serious problem along rivers and streams, washes and in parks and golf courses with large cottonwood trees.

Symptoms

One of the most common sights in areas where these hosts grow is the green, straggly, bushy growth of mistletoe hanging from infected branches. The true mistletoes are spread by birds that eat the berries and deposit the viable seeds with their feces. Seeds germinate on the host plant and cause new infections.

Often the mistletoe completely takes over the plant and death occurs. This is a long process. Heavily infected desert shrubs and trees have been infected for many years. Mistletoe plants are often so numerous as to obscure the host plant. *Phoradendron* spp. are perennial evergreens. Thus, deciduous trees, like cottonwoods, appear almost as evergreens during the winter if infection is heavy.

Infected branches and stems become swollen. The mistletoe itself grows into the plant well beyond the visible its growth on the plant. Slow, progressive decline and death of branches may occur. Infections on lower trunks, which are fairly common in desert legumes, are more damaging to the tree than infections that occur on upper branches. Dead or dying branches are weakened and become susceptible to breakage.

Control

Mistletoes are very difficult to control. The only practical method of control is to prune out infected branches approximately one foot below the infected sites. Also, the mistletoe plant should be physically removed at least annually in situations where pruning (lower trunk infection) may not be feasible.

NON-PARASITIC DISEASES

Many plant diseases that occur in our diverse climate zones are not caused by parasitic micro-organisms but are non-parasitic in nature. Soil conditions where these nonparasitic diseases are common include high pH (alkaline soils), saline soils (salt contents with electrical conductivity measurements of 4 mmhos per cm or greater from a saturated soil extract, ECe), sodic soils (exchangeable sodium percentages, ESP of 15 or greater), low soil organic matter content, poor soil moisture holding characteristics, shallow soils, poor soil structure, and caliche deposits.

Weather conditions contributing to these diseases include intense summer heat, low humidities, drying winds, low rainfall and unpredictable freezes. Other factors include inappropriate plant selection, poor pre-plant soil preparation, inadequate or excessive fertilization, improper watering techniques (particularly in drip irrigation systems) and damage caused by herbicides.

Some of the most common non-parasitic diseases are:

Alepppo Pine Blight

Symptoms

This physiological disease only occurs on the commonly planted Aleppo pine (*Pinus halepenis*). Death of needles, twigs, and branches occurs usually in trees over 5 years of age. Most symptoms develop in the upper part of the tree. Blighted needles take on a gray-green color that later turns reddish-brown. These needles may persist on the tree until their seasonal summer defoliation. Some twig and small-branch death may follow needle blight.

Conditions Favoring Disease

Aleppo pines planted in shallow or poorly draining soils are particularly subject to drought stress. Poor soil drainage caused by underlying hard-pan contributes to blight by hampering root development. Drying winds and low relative humidity during fall and spring are commonly associated with the onset of symptoms.

Control

Maintain a uniform deep water supply to the tree throughout the year. Irrigate so that water is available to a depth of at least 5 feet for mature trees. Apply about ¼ cup of nitrogen fertilizer per inch of the trunk in diameter. Apply one-half the fertilizer in March and the other half in July.

Scorch

Symptoms

This disease occurs during hot, dry, windy weather. It is characterized by marginal browning and drying of foliage. The roots of the plant fail to take up sufficient moisture to make up for the heavy amounts of moisture lost during the dry, hot period. Deep, thorough irrigations at 2 to 3 week intervals may help prevent this problem. This symptom, caused by water stress during our hot, dry summer period is common to many trees, shrubs and ornamentals.

Arizona Ash Decline *(Fraxinus velutina)*

Symptoms

Branches may exhibit symptoms of leaf tip and edge burning. These symptoms are similar to those associated with drought or excess salts. Leaves are usually small, and elongation of internodes is reduced, causing a tufted or rosette appearance. Dead leaves often remain attached to the affected limbs. Dieback becomes noticeable beginning about July. As the decline progresses entire branches and limbs die until the whole tree is killed.

Conditions Favouring the Disease

The disease has been observed throughout the state wherever ash trees are cultivated (at elevations ranging from 1,300 to 5,700 feet). As a native of southwestern Arizona, Arizona ash is relatively tolerant of drought and alkali. Well fertilized, deeply irrigated ash trees appear more able to compensate for the dieback and remain lush in spite of being affected.

Control

Maintaining trees in a vigorous condition will help reduce the rate and severity of decline. Frequent (weekly to bi-weekly for mature trees), deep irrigations during the hot summer months and at least monthly irrigations in the cool seasons are recommended.

Mulberry Tree Decline *(Morus* spp.*)*

Symptoms

Symptoms consist primarily of small leaves and dieback of the upper twigs and branches. The disease usually appears in trees that are 15 to 20 years of age. The overall tree decline is slow, but death may occur two or three years after the initial symptoms.

Causes of Disease

There are many possible factors involved in any tree decline disease. One of the major factors, however, is insufficient watering, particularly in trees that are in lawn situations.

Control

The mulberry tree needs infrequent (once a month) deep (4 feet) irrigations particularly during the summer months. Tree wells should extend to the drip line of the tree.

Oleander Decline *(Nerium spp.)*

Symptoms

Because of the stiff, leathery leaves and woody stems and branches, wilting is not commonly observed in oleander. Instead, in response to water stress, foliage turns dull gray-green in appearance and becomes brittle. Lower leaves turn yellow, dry, and drop off.

Control

If a watering basin is used, it should be three to four inches deep and extend out from the base of the plant to the drip line. Basins should be filled at each irrigation in order to saturate soil to a depth of at least three feet.

These five diseases are examples of water stress conditions. The symptoms are similar in most of the non native, introduced shrubs and trees. This disease is often noticed in poorly designed drip irrigation systems. Superficial sprinkling, instead of deep basin waterings, are a major factor in these problems.

Salt Problems

The most common non-parasitic disease in our desert areas is damage caused by excessive soil salts. Factors that increase salt accumulation in our desert soils include: poor drainage caused by dense subsoil layers and caliche deposits, inadequate leaching which allows salt accumulation in the rooting area, excessive salt in irrigation water, low rainfall and high temperatures, and excessive applications of fertilizer and manure. Symptoms of salt damage include plant stunting, marginal burning of leaves, and premature defoliation. Salt tolerance of urban plants to salt damage varies greatly. Symptoms of salt damage are nonspecific.

There are many causes of the above described symptoms including root diseases, insects, mineral deficiencies and excesses, and herbicide damage. Diagnosis of salt problems requires the taking of a soil sample in the root area of the affected plant. Tissue analysis may also be necessary.

Miscellaneous Problems

Other non-parasitic problems include a wide range of conditions from lightening damage, frost and freezing damage, sun scald, nutrient deficiencies, pesticide damage and air pollution. Professional help is necessary to determine the cause of many of these problems. Some, however, like lightening damage, frost damage, extreme water stress, and pesticide damage, can be diagnosed with only the use of a little common sense. Nutrient problems, salt damage, and air pollution require professional help for diagnosis and control.

Another common problem in Arizona is the planting of shrubs, trees, and ornamentals that are not adapted to our climates and soils. Local horticulturists and landscapers should be consulted before attempting to landscape a specific location.

Sugarcane and Its Diseases

Sugarcane is an industrial crop with acreage of about four million hectares and production to the tune of 300 million tonnes in India. It provides employment to over a million people directly or indirectly besides contributing significantly to the national exchequer. In commercial agriculture, cane is subjected to various weather conditions and stresses. In the Indian subtropics erratic availability of moisture and frequent occurrence of red rot disease severely impair the productivity of cane. In addition to this, acute water scarcity in many areas would need the development of drought tolerant/ water use efficient cane genotypes to sustain the cane industry.The commercial sugarcane is no longer pure *Saccharum officinarum* but a species hybrid, complex polyploid with a large number of chromosomes.

This does not offer a clean system for genetic manipulation through conventional means. As a result, inheritance of most of the characters of interest for varietal breeding is not thoroughly worked out, so much so that neither the number of genes nor the nature of gene action governing the expression of these traits is fully known. Thus sugarcane has remained geneticists' nightmare.With the advancement of molecular biology, newer techniques have become available to unravel the sugarcane genome.

Monitoring of differential tissue-specific gene expression in genotypes of contrasting genetic potential for traits under study by expressed sequence tagging may be used as a technique to get an access to the complexity of gene function in sugarcane. Development of ESTs in sugarcane is already in progress in some cane growing countries (in fact in a big way in Brazil) It is expected that the proposed work would reinforce this international endeavour and provide specific benefits to Indian sugarcane cultivation. Identification of genes in sugarcane against various stresses may help better understanding of the underlying physiological mechanisms of resistance/ tolerance and facilitate genetic manipulation to tailor the sugarcane plant to cope with these stresses.

Sugarcane, owing to its vegetative propagation and genetic complexity, is easily amenable to biotechnological applications like the production of transgencis and the DNA analysis of segregating population to effect early selection for the trait of interest (marker assisted selection). The proposed EST approach shall identify and make available genes for stress endurance and allow their incorporation in the reigning sugarcane varieties through genetic transformation.

Matching with long diversity of conditions under which sugarcane is grown in the world, there is wide spectrum of pests and diseases which have come to acquire a place of priority for control on regional or inter-regional basis due to the agro-climatic management conditions associated with the area.

In addition the susceptibility of the variety to the diseases and pests aggravates the situation and creates additive problems. Below herein is given a brief account of symptoms of important pests and diseases occurring in several parts of the world.

Early Shoot Borer (*Chilo infescatellus*)

Symptoms

- Attacks the crop during the early part of cane growth, before internode formation. It also attacks the cane stalks in the years of scanty rainfall.
- Larvae enter the cane laterally through one or more holes in the stalks (shoot) and bores downwards as well as upwards killing the growing point. Thus it cuts of the central leaf spindle, which eventually dries forming a dead heart. The dead heart can be easily pulled out. It emits an offensive odour.
- Borer infestation during the germination phase kills the mother shoots resulting in the drying up of the entire clump. This leads to gaps in the field.

Causes heavy yield losses as it affects the plant stand/unit area. It also leads to canes of different age, which will be poor in juice quality, with less cane weight. When borer infects cane stalks, both yield and quality are reduced.

Internode Borer (*Chilo Saccharifagus Indicus*)

Symptoms

- Damages the crop soon after internode formation and its activity continues till hatvest.
- Lodging, high dosage of nitrogen, waterlogged condition and presence of water shoots favour buildup of pest.
- Fresh borer attack is mostly found in the top five immature internodes.
- Caterpillars bore at the nodal region and enter the stem and tunnel up-wards in a characteristic spiral fashion. Entrance hole is usually plugged with excreta.
- Larvae feed and multiply in water shoots. One larvae found in a single cane damages one-three internodes. The length and girth of the infected internodes get reduced.
- Yield loss and juice quality deterioration occurs when the infestation is severe.

Top Borer (*Scirpophaga excerptalis*)

- Waterlogging favours moth attack
- Larva first tunnels into the midrib of the leaves and causes a white streak which later turns reddish brown usually in the second to fifth leaf from the top. As a result of biting across the spindle, a number of shot holes are formed in the leaf. As larva nibbles into the central core of the cane a portion of the internal tissue is eaten resulting in dead heart formation. Dead heart when formed is reddish brown, appears charred, and cannot be easily pulled out. In tillering phase of the crop, the attacked shoots die, side shoots (tillers) develop producing a bunchy top appearance.
- In the grand growth period, the crop growth is arrested, and the crown with dead heart dries and may be blown off leaving the stump.
- Severe yield loss and quality deterioration occurs due to top borer. Depending upon the incidence level yield loss may be up to 20-30 per cent.

Scale Insect (*Melanaspis glomerata*)

- Waterlogging, high temperature and humidity favour buildup of scale insect population. Rainwater and high wind velocity facilitate dispersal of the pest. It spreads to new areas through seed material. Men and animals passing through the infested fields also lead to spread of the pest to the adjoining areas.

- Scales usually establish on internodes covered with leaf sheath. The leaves of infested canes show signs of tip drying and unhealthy pale green colour and with continued infestation turn yellow. Desapping leads to non-opening of leaves also, which also turn yellow and finally dry out. Nodal region is more infested than internodal region.
- Infested crop losses its vigour, canes shrivel, growth is stunted and the internodal length is reduced drastically. Ultimately cane dries up. Such canes when slit open appear brownish red. Thus yield and quality suffer. The yield loss could range from negligible to total crop failure.

Pyrilla (*Pyrilla purpusilla* Walker)

- Pyrilla is the most destructive foliage-sucking pest of sugarcane.
- Heavy rainfall followed by 75-80 per cent humidity, intermittent drought periods, high temperature (26-30°C) and wind movement favour rapid buildup of pyrilla. Other factors favouring pyrilla buildup are dense and luxuriant crop, excess nitrogen application, water logging, lodging of cane and varieties with broad and succulent leaves.
- Adults and the nymps suck leaf sap from the under surface of the lower leaves. When the infestation is heavy, leaves turn yellowish white and wither away. Due to continuous desapping by large number of hoppers top leaves in the affected canes dry up and lateral buds germinate.
- The hoppers exude a sweet sticky fluid known as honeydew, which promotes quick and luxuriant growth of the fungus, capanodium species and as a result the leaves are completely covered by the sooty mould. This affects photosynthesis.
- The loss in cane yield due to pyrilla have been estimated to be around 28 per cent with about 1.6 per cent unit loss in sugar.
- Termites (*Coptotermes heimi* Wasmann; *Odontotermes Assmuthi* Holmgr; *O. obesus* Rambur; *O. wallonensis* Wasmann; *Microtermes obesi* Holmgr; *Trinervitermes biformis* Wasmann).
- Polyphagous and found throughout the world. More serious under prolonged drought conditions and in light textured soils viz., sandy and sandy loam soils.

- The termites attack setts, shoots, canes and also stubbles
- The termites gain entry through the cut ends or through buds of the setts and feed on the soft tissue. The tunnel excavated is filled with the soil. This affects germination and thus the initial crop stand and ultimately the cane yield. The germination failure could be up to 60 per cent.
- In the stalks the termites feed on the inner tissues leaving the rind intact. The cavity formed is filled up with moist soil, having galleries, in which, they move about. The affected canes die.

Whitefly (*Aleurolobus barodensis* Mask)

- Waterlogging and nitrogen starvation cause severe out break of whiteflies. Summer droughts and dry spells during monsoon season also favour buildup of this pest.
- Varieties with broad and long leaves are more susceptible to this pest.
- The nymphs of white flies suck the sap from the under surface of leaves which turn yellow and pinkish in severe cases and gradually dry up.
- Heavy infested leaves are covered by the sooty mould caused by the fungus, which adversely affects photosynthesis. The whitefly infestation retards cane growth and reduces sugar content.
- Considerable loss on yield and sugar recovery has been observed. At 80 per cent leaf infestation 23.4 per cent loss in cane yield and 2.9 per cent units loss in sucrose has been reported.

Red Rot (*Colletotrichum falcatum*)

- It is the most dreaded disease of sugarcane which has caused the elimination of several important sugarcane varieties from cultivation.
- Yellowing and drying of leaves from margin to midrib, drying of the entire top including the crown, loss of natural colour and considerable shrinkage of the stalk, appearance of reddish lesions on the rind are some of the external symptoms of red rot disease.
- Most characteristic and diagnostic symptom of the disease is the presence of reddish discoloured patches or lesions interspersed with white horizontal patches on the internal tissue. As the diseases progresses the internal tissues become dark in colour and dry resulting in longitudinal pith cavities.

Smut (*Ustilago scitaminea*)

- Primary spread of the disease is through infected setts and the secondary spread is through wind borne teliospore.
- Stunting of infected stools, profuse sprouting of lateral shoots i.e., tillers, reduction in internodal length, formation of thin stalks and narrow erect leaves are certain symptoms of smut.
- Characteristic symptom is the production of long whip like structure from the terminal bud of the stalk, which is black in colour covered by thin silvery membrane. This silvery membrane ruptures releasing millions of reproductive spores of smut fungus, which are present in the form of powdery mass.
- Losses due to smut in sugarcane depend on various factors viz., primary or secondary infection, plant or ratoon crop that is affected and early or late infection and have been reported to range from 30-40 per cent in plant crops and even up to 70 per cent in ratoons. Sucrose content of infected cane is reduced to 3-7 per cent.

Pineapple Disease (*Ceratocystis paradoxa*)

- Essentially a disease of seed material i.e., setts. Typical disease symptoms are detected in setts after 2-3 weeks of planting.
- Pathogen enters the sett mainly through the cut ends and destroy the central soft portion i.e., parachymatous tissues of the internode and then damages the buds.
- Affected tissues first develop a reddish colour, which turns to brownish black in the later stages. Cavities are formed inside the severely affected internodes. The presence of the fungus inside the sett prevents their rooting. In most cases setts decay before bud sprouts or the shoots grown to an height of 6-12cm. Thus causing germination failure leading to reduced initial crop stand per unit area.
- Occasionally, the disease occurs in standing crop too due to the entry of the pathogen through stalk damaged by borers, rat damage or any such injuries. Drought accelerates the damage. Pathogen spreads rapidly throughout the canes, foliage turns yellow, and ultimately plant withers. The diseased stalk when cut open smells like mature pineapple. The pineapple odour is due to production of ethyl acetate by the fungus.

Wilt (*Cephalosporium sacchari*)

- Disease spreads through infected setts. The fungi gain entry mainly through injuries.

- Biotic stresses like nematode, root borer, termite, scales, mealy bugs etc and abiotic stresses like drought, water logging etc predispose the plants for wilt infection
- Moisture stress coupled with high temperature and low humidity reduces plant resistance to wilt.
- Typical wilt symptoms appear during monsoon and post monsoon periods.
- Affected plant appears wilted and conspicuously stunted. The crown leaves turn yellow, loose turgor and eventually withers.
- Wilt-affected canes loose their normal colour and are light in weight. The most characteristic symptom during the early stage of infection is the presence of diffused reddish brown patches on the internal tissue. Later canes become light and hallow and shrink.
- Disease reduces germination and in severe cases total cane yield losses occur due to drying up of shoots and wilting of the stalks.

Ratoon Stunting Disease

- Ratoon stunting disease has been considered as the most important cause for sugarcane varietal degeneration
- Primary spread of the disease is through infected setts.
- Also spreads through harvesting implements contaminated with the juice of diseased canes.
- Expression of disease is more under adverse conditions.
- Progressive yield decline takes place due to the disease. Ratoon crop suffers more damage due to RSD than the plant crop.
- Disease is known to reduce germination and yield
- Most characteristic symptom of the infected stalks is the presence of pin head like orange coloured dots of bacteria on the internal soft tissue in the nodal region.
- Other symptoms include stunted growth, thin stalks with short internodes, pale yellowish foliage and rapid tapering of the stem towards the top.

Leaf Scald (*Xanthomonas albileneans*)

- It is a bacterial disease, widely spread in many countries.
- Disease is favoured by wet seasons, water stress due to drought, water logging and low temperatures.

- Disease symptoms appear in two phases, the chronic and acute phases.
- In the chronic phase, "white pencil line" extending entire length of lamina reaching the margin of young leaves and stripes diffuse later resulting in leaf etiolation. Drying from tip onwards presents a scalded appearance and hence the name. Different degrees of chlorosis from total albinism to interveinal chlorosis in young leaves during summer, germination of buds in acropetal manner with bushy appearance in standing cane, cut open stalks showing dark red vascular strands, prominent streaks at node invariably in the side shoots, are other prominent symptoms of chronic phase.
- In the acute phase the symptoms appear suddenly and die without any major leaf symptoms. The masking of symptoms is more common during monsoon and symptoms may appear suddenly any time during crop growth.

Yellow Leaf Spoot (*Cercospora koepkei*)

- Prolonged rain with intermittent sunshine, waterlogged conditions and higher nitrogen doses are congenial for disease development.
- Warm humid weather favours rapid and abundant production of conidia by the pathogen and sopread of the disease.
- Characteristic symptoms are presence of small, yellow coloured, irregularly shaped spots over the leaf surface. Density of spots is minimum in the lower surface, moderate in the middle and maximum towards the tip of the leaf. Spots coalesce at late stages and cause drying of leaves. Badly affected foliage looks reddish-brown when viewed from a distance.

Eye Spot (*Helminthosporium sacchari*)

- Usually a crop of 6-7 months is more susceptible to the disease.
- Fungus penetrates the host tissue either through stomota, bulliform cells or directly through the cuticle.
- Cloudy weather, high humidity with drizzle coupled with low night temperatures, wetting of leaves either through precipitation or dew greatly enhance disease development.
- Likewise water logging, high fertility status and excess nitrogen fertilization also favour the spread of the disease.
- Lesions first appear as small water soaked spots, darker than the surrounding tissues. The spot becomes more elongated and turns

straw coloured within a few days. Finally the central portion becomes reddish brown surrounded by straw coloured tissues. Then reddish brown streaks of develop extending from the lesions towards the leaf tip along the veins. Later the spots and streaks coalesce to form large patches and causes drying of leaves.

Sugarcane Grassy Shoot Disease

- It is a mycoplasamal disease.
- Primary transmission of disease is through disease infected setts
- Profuse tillering with narrow chlorotic leaves giving a grass like appearance is characteristic symptom of GSD incidence
- Very few tillers of GSD infected plants develop into canes, which are thin and produce white shoots from the side buds.

Sugarcane grassy shoot disease (SCGS), caused by small, parasitic bacteria, contributes to losses of 5% to 20% in the main crop of sugarcane, and these losses are higher in the ratoon crop. A higher incidence of SCGS has been recorded in some parts of Southeast Asia and India, resulting in 100% loss in cane yield and sugar production.

Causal Organism and Transmission

Causal Organism

- SCGS disease is caused by a phytoplasma (*Candidatus phytoplasma*), which is one of the destructive pathogens of sugarcane (*Saccharum officinarum L*). In India, SCGS phytoplasmas are spreading at an alarming rate, adversely affecting yield of the sugarcane crop.
- Phytoplasmas, formerly called mycoplasma-like organisms (MLOs), are a large group of obligate, intracellular, cell wallless parasites classified within the class Mollicutes.
- Phytoplasmas are associated with plant diseases and are known to cause more than 600 diseases in several hundred plant species, including gramineous weeds and cereals. The symptoms shown by infected plants include: whitening or yellowing of the leaves, shortening of the internodes (leading to stunted growth), smaller leaves and excessive proliferation of shoots, resulting in a broom phenotype and loss of apical dominance .

Transmission

Sugarcane is a vegetatively propagated crop, so the pathogen is transmitted via seed material and by phloem-feeding leafhopper vectors.

Saccharosydne saccharivora, *Matsumuratettix hiroglyphicus*, *Deltocephalus vulgaris* and *Yamatotettix flavovittatus* have been confirmed as vectors for phytoplasma transmission in sugarcane. Unconfirmed reports also suggest a spread through the steel blades (machetes) used for sugarcane harvesting.

SCGS Disease Symptoms

Phytoplasma-infected sugarcane plants show a proliferation of tillers, which give it typical grassy appearance, hence the name grassy shoot disease. The leaves of infected plants do not produce chlorophyll, and therefore appear white or creamy yellow. The leaf veins turn white first as the phytoplasma resides in leaf phloem tissue. Symptoms at the early stage of the plant life cycle include leaf chlorosis, mainly at the central leaf whorl. Infected plants do not have the capacity to produce food in the absence of chlorophyll, which results into no cane formation. These symptoms can be seen prominently in thestubble crop.

The eye or lateral buds sprout before the normal time on growing cane. A survey of various fields of western Maharashtra showed grassy shoot with chlorotic or creamy white leaves was the most prevalent phenotype in sugarcane plants infected with SCGS.

Symptoms of iron deficiency (interveinal chlorosis) are very similar to those of SCGS. It shows creamy leaves, but no chlorosis occurs in leaf veins, and they remain green. In the case of severe iron deficiency, veins may lose chlorophyll in the absence of iron and appear similar to SCGS disease. Iron deficiency is caused by a lack of iron nutrients in the soil; therefore, one may observe several plants showing symptoms of iron deficiency in localized patches in a field.

Phytoplasma-infected plants, though, may occur anywhere in the field in a more random distribution. Treatment with 0.1% ferrous sulfate, either by spraying or supplying it through fertilizer cures iron deficiency, but phytoplasma-infected sugarcane does not respond to any treatment. Phytoplasma-infected plants growing *in vitro* show sensitivity to tetracycline.

Detection Methods

Based on Symptoms

- Phytoplasma-infected sugarcane can be recognized by visual symptoms, but there are limitations.
- Visual symptoms occur only after considerable growth, normally two to three weeks after planting.
- If not observed keenly, confusion may occur on differences between symptoms of SCGS disease and iron deficiency.

- In addition to above points, the poor relationship between symptoms and phytoplasma presence has been confirmed by earlier findings that symptoms alone are not reliable indicators of infection or identity. This highlights the importance of employing tests, such as the molecular tests, to verify associations between phytoplasma and putative disease symptoms. Also it suggests the inability to recognize a symptomless sugarcane harboring a phytoplasma could result in inadvertent exposure of sugarcane to a potential disease source.
- Precise diagnosis is therefore necessary for effective disease identification and control. Though reliable, DNA hybridization, electron microscopy and PCR techniques require specialized equipment and trained human resources. Among these, PCR is an accurate, economical and convenient method, which allows analysis of samples in a short time.

Polymerase Chain Reaction

In recent years, regions of the rRNA operon of the prokaryotic and eukaryotic organisms have been sequenced and are being used to develop PCR-based detection assays. These sequences are highly specific to the infecting organism.

Phytoplasma rRNA Operon

- The ribosomal DNA contains one transcriptional unit with a cluster of genes coding for the 18S, 5.8S and 28S rRNAs and two internal transcribed spacer regions, ITS1 and ITS2 in eukaryotes, and for 16S, 5S and 23S in prokaryotes . Previous studies have demonstrated the complex ITS regions are useful in measuring close genealogical relationships, because they exhibit greater interspecies differences than the smaller and larger subunits of rRNA genes.
- The use of specific probes as selective PCR primers offers an impressive approach for the rapid identification of a large number of phytoplasma isolates.
- The agarose gel electrophoresis image beside shows amplification of partial, 1.2k b long, 16S rDNA of *Candidatus* phytoplasma, where total genomic DNA from a suspected sugarcane plant has been used as template DNA.

ELISA

ELISA has been used as a diagnostic tool in medicine and plant pathology. Serological detection using a specific antiserum is an economical and convenient method that allows for both analysis of many samples in a short time and immunohistological observation of infected tissues.

A phytoplasma-specific antibody can be prepared using the following steps:

1. Cloning of the phytoplasma gene fragment into an *Escherichia coli* expression vector;
2. Expression in *E. coli* and purification of the protein; and
3. Preparation of antibodies in rabbits.

This technique has been used to develop antibodies to the immunodominant membrane protein of several phytoplasmas. These antibodies represent important tools in the detection, localization, and purification of phytoplasmas and the target antigen.

Preventing Disease

In SCGS disease, the primary concern is to prevent the disease rather than treat it. Large numbers of phytoplasma-infected seed sets used by the farmers usually cause fast SCGS disease spread. Healthy, certified 'disease free' sugarcane sets are suggested as planting material. If disease symptoms are visible within two weeks after planting, such plants can be replaced by healthy plants. Uprooted infected sugarcane plants need to disposed of by burning them.

Moist hot air treatment of sets is suggested to control infection before planting. This reduces percentage of disease incidence, but causes a reduction in the percentage of bud sprouting.

Reports that the disease spreads through steel blades used for sugarcane harvesting are unconfirmed, but treating the knives using a disinfectant (Lysol) or by dipping them in boiling water for some time is suggested as a precaution.

Phytoplasma infection also spreads through insect vectors; it is therefore important to control them.

General field observation reports the ratoon crop has higher percentage of disease incidence than the initial planted (main) crop. When the disease incidence is more than 20%, it is suggested to discontinue that crop cycle.

It is always wise to purchase the certified planting material from authorized seed growers, which assures disease-free planting material.

Chlorosis

In botany, chlorosis is a condition in which leaves produce insufficient chlorophyll. As chlorophyll is responsible for the green colour of leaves, chlorotic leaves are pale, yellow, or yellow-white.

The affected plant has little or no ability to manufacture carbohydrates through photosynthesis and may die unless the cause of its chlorophyll insufficiency is treated, although some chlorotic plants, such as the albino *Arabidopsis thaliana* mutant *ppi2* are viable if supplied with exogenous sucrose. Chlorosis which is caused by lack of light is called etiolation.

Causes

Chlorosis is typically caused when leaves do not have enough nutrients to synthesise all the chlorophyll they need. It can be brought about by a combination of factors including:

- A specific mineral deficiency in the soil, such as iron or magnesium.
- Deficient nitrogen and/or proteins.
- A soil pH at which minerals become unavailable for absorption by the roots.
- Poor drainage (waterlogged roots).
- Damaged and/or compacted roots.
- Pesticides and particularly herbicides may cause chlorosis, both to target weeds and occasionally to the crop being treated.
- Exposure to sulphur dioxide.

Of course, the exact conditions would be different for different plants. For example, Azaleas prefer unusually acidic soil and rice isn't troubled by waterlogged soil.

Treatment

Like many other plants, grape vines are susceptible to chlorosis, and symptoms of iron deficiency tend to be common on soils rich in limestone. In the wake of The Great French Wine Blight, when European *Vitis vinifera* were affected by *Phylloxera*, chlorosis became a greater problem in viticulture. To deal with the Phylloxera blight, *V. vinifera* was grafted onto rootstock based on American species of the *Vitis* genus, such as *Vitis riparia*, *Vitis rupestris*, *Vitis berlandieri*.

However, many of these were less adapted to the lime-rich soils that were common in France's vineyards, in particular many of those that produced wines of top quality. Many grafted vines in lime-rich vineyards therefore showed signs of iron deficiency, and in France this specific form of chlorosis was termed *chlorose calcaire*. The problem was largely overcome by the selection of lime-resistant American vines as basis for hybrid vines used for rootstock material.

However, since such rootstocks may be less than optimal in other respects, it is necessary for the viticulturalist to balance the need for chlorosis resistance against other viticultural needs. This is illustrated by one of the most common lime-resistant rootstocks, 41 B, which is a hybrid between *V. vinifera* cultivar Chasselas and *V. berlandieri*, which generally has a sufficient, but not extremely high, Phylloxera resistance.

Specific nutrient deficiencies (often aggravated by high soil pH) may be corrected by supplemental feedings of iron, in the form of a chelate or sulphate, magnesium or nitrogen compounds in various combinations.

Sugarcane Smut

Sugarcane smut is a fungal disease of sugarcane caused by the fungus *Sporisorium scitamineum*. It is sometimes known as culmicolous, which describes the outgrowth of fungus of the stalk of the cane.

The fungus grows within the meristematic tissue and induces formation of flowering structures which it colonises to produce its teliopores. The flowering structures, usually typical grass arrows, are transformed into a whip like sori that grows out between the leaf sheaths. At first it is covered by a thin silvery peridium (this is the host tissue) which easily peels back when desiccated to expose the sooty black-brown teliospores.

The spores are reddish brown, round and subovoid and may be smooth to moderately echinulate. The size varies from 6.5 to 8 µm. The main mode of dispersal is wind where spores may travel intercontinental.

Wheat Diseases

Cereals are at risk from numerous diseases due to the level of intensification necessary for profitable production since the 1970s. More recently varietal diversification, good plant breeding and the availability of effective fungicides have played a prominent part in cereal disease control. Use of break crops and good rotations are also good cultural control measures. The demise of UK straw burning in the 1980s also increased the importance of good disease control.

Active control measures include use of chemical seed treatments for seed-borne diseases and chemical spray applications for leaf and ear diseases. Development of resistance by diseases to established chemicals has been a problem during the last three decades.

FUNGICIDES

Some cereal fungicide groups and examples of active ingredients:

- Benzimidazoles
  - *(a)* carbendazim
- Ergosterol biosynthesis inhibitors
  - *(a)* prochloraz
  - *(b)* flutriafol
  - *(c)* tetrachonazole

- Morpholines
    (*a*) fenpropimorph
- Strobylurines
    (*a*) kresoxim-methyl
- Phthalonitriles
    (*a*) chlorothalonil

Principal Diseases of Wheat

- Barley yellow dwarf virus, BYDV.
- Brown rust *Puccinia recondita.*
- Common bunt (aka Covered smut) *Tilletia caries.*
- Ergot *Claviceps purpurea.*
- Eyespot *Pseudocercosporella herpitrichoides.*
- Glume blotch *Septoria nodorum* plus *Septoria tritici.*
- Leaf blotch *Septoria tritici.*
- Mildew *Erysiphe graminis.*
- Seedling blight *Fusarium* spp., *Septoria nodorum.*
- Sharp eyespot *Rhizoctonia cerealis.*
- Spot blotch *Biplolaris sorokiana.*
- Take-all *Gaeumannomyces graminis.*
- Tan spot *Pyrenophora tritici-repentis.*
- Yellow rust *Puccinia striiformis.*

UNDERSTANDING WHEAT DISEASES

Wheat is subject to more diseases than other grains, and, in some seasons, especially in wet ones, heavier losses are sustained from those diseases than are in other cereal crops. Wheat may suffer from the attack of insects at the root; from blight, which primarily affects the leaf or straw, and ultimately deprives the grain of sufficient nourishment; from mildew on the ear; and from gum of different shades, which lodges on the chaff or cups in which the grain is deposited.

Examples of Wheat Diseases

Bacterial Diseases

- Bacterial leaf blight *Pseudomonas syringae* subsp. *syringae*

- Bacterial sheath rot *Pseudomonas fuscovaginae*
- Basal glume rot *Pseudomonas syringae pv. atrofaciens*
- Black chaff = bacterial streak *Xanthomonas campestris* pv. *translucens*
- Pink seed *Erwinia rhapontici*

Fungal Diseases

- Alternaria leaf blight *Alternaria triticina*
- Anthracnose *Colletotrichum cereale Manns*
- Ascochyta leaf spot *Ascochyta tritici*
- Black head molds = sooty molds *Alternaria* spp., *Cladosporium* spp.
- Common bunt = stinking smut *T. tritici, T. laevis*
- Downy mildew = crazy top *Sclerophthora macrospora*
- Dwarf bunt *Tilletia controversa*
- Ergot *Claviceps purpurea*
- Foot rot = dryland foot rot *Fusarium* spp.
- Leaf rust = brown rust *Puccinia triticina*
- Leaf and glume blotch, *Stagonospora nodorum* or *Phaeosphaeria nodorum*
- Pink snow mold = Fusarium patch *Microdochium nivale*
- Powdery mildew = *Blumeria graminis*
- Scab = head blight *Fusarium* spp., *Gibberella zeae,*
- Septoria blotch *Septoria tritici = Mycospharella graminicola,*
- Smut = Ustilaginomycotina clade of the class Teliomycetae, subphylum Basidiomycota
- Storage moulds *Aspergillus* spp., *Penicillium* spp.
- Wheat mildew
- Wheat leaf rust
- Wheat stem rust

Nematodes, Parasitic

- Grass cyst nematode *Punctodera punctata*
- Root gall nematode *Subanguina* spp.

Viral Diseases and Viruslike Agents

- Agropyron mosaic genus *Rymovirus*, Agropyron mosaic virus (AgMV)

- Barley stripe mosaic genus *Hordeivirus,* Barley stripe mosaic virus (BSMV)
- Oat sterile dwarf genus *Fijivirus,* Oat sterile dwarf virus (OSDV)
- Tobacco mosaic genus *Tobamovirus,* Tobacco mosaic virus (TMV)
- Wheat dwarf genus *Monogeminivirus,* Wheat dwarf virus (WDV)
- Wheat yellow mosaic Wheat yellow mosaic bymovirus

Phytoplasmal Diseases

- Aster yellows phytoplasma

AIR POLLUTION AND SEPTORIA BLOTCH

A team of researchers examined a library of British wheat samples dating back to 1843. For each year, they determined the levels of *Phaeosphaeria nodorum* and *Mycospharella graminicola* DNA in the samples. After accounting for influences such as growing and harvesting methods and weather conditions, they compared the DNA data with estimates of emissions of air pollutants.

The effect of sulfur dioxide correlated with the abundance of the two fungi. *P. nodrum* grew more successful with the dawn of the industrial revolution. *M. graminicola* was more abundant before 1870 and since the 1970s. The success since the 1970s may be linked to reductions in sulfur dioxide emissions due to environmental regulations.

Pseudomonas Syringae

It is a rod shaped, Gram-negative bacterium with polar flagella. It is a plant pathogen which can infect a wide range of plant species, and exists as over different-different pathovars, all of which are available to legitimate researches via international culture collections such as the NCPPB, ICMP, and others. Many of these pathovars were once considered to be individual species within the *Pseudomonas* genus, but molecular biology techniques such as DNA hybridization have shown these to in fact all be part of the *P. syringae* species.

It is a member of the *Pseudomonas* genus, and based on 16S rRNA analysis, it has been placed in the *P. syringae* group. It is named after the lilac tree (*Syringa vulgaris*), from which it was first isolated.

It tests negative for arginine dihydrolase and oxidase activity, and forms the polymer levan on sucrose nutrient agar. Many but not all strains secrete the lipodepsinonapeptide plant toxin syringomycin, and it owes its yellow fluorescent appearance when cultured *in vitro* on King's B medium to production of the siderophore pyoverdin.

It also produce Ina proteins which cause water to freeze at fairly high temperatures, resulting in injury to plants. Since the 1970s, *P. syringae* has been implicated as an atmospheric "biological ice nucleator", with airborne bacteria serving as cloud condensation nuclei. Recent evidence has suggested that the species plays a larger role than previously thought in producing rain and snow. They have also been found in the cores of hailstones, aiding in bioprecipitation. These Ina proteins are also used in making artificial snow.

It pathogenesis is dependent on effector proteins secreted into the plant cell by the bacterial type III secretion system. Nearly sixty different type III effector families encoded by *hop* genes have been identified in *P. syringae*. Type III effectors contribute to pathogenesis chiefly through their role in suppressing plant defense.

Owing to early availability of the genome sequence for three *P. syringae* strains and the ability of selected strains to cause disease on well-characterized host plants including *Arabidopsis thaliana, Nicotiana benthemiana*, and tomato, *P. syringae* has come to represent an important model system for experimental characterization of the molecular dynamics of plant-pathogen interactions.

Frost Damage in Plants

P. syringae, more than any mineral or other organism, is responsible for the surface frost damage in plants, exposed to the environment. *P. syringae* can cause water to freeze at temperatures as high as "1.8 °C (28.8°F), but strains causing ice nucleation at lower temperatures (down to "8°C) are more common. The freezing causes injuries in the epithelia and makes the nutrients in the underlying plant tissues available to the bacteria.

P. syringae have *ina* (ice nucleation-active) genes that make Ina proteins which translocate to the outer bacterial cell wall on the surface of the bacteria where the Ina proteins act as nuclei for ice formation. Artificial strains of *P. syringae* known as ice-minus bacteria have been created to reduce frost damage.

It has been found in the center of hailstones, suggesting that the bacterium may play a role in Earth's hydrological cycle.

Favourable Conditions for Diseases

Disease by *P. syringae* tends to be favoured by wet, cool conditions—optimum temperatures for disease tend to be around 12–25°C, although this can vary according to the pathovar involved. The bacteria tend to be seed-borne, and are dispersed between plants via rain splash.

Although it is a plant pathogen, it can also live as a saprotroph in the phyllosphere when conditions are not favourable for disease. Some saprotrophic strains of *P. syringae* have been used as biocontrol agents against post-harvest rots.

Pathogenesis

A large number of *P. syringae* genes contribute to bacterial survival on and within the host plant, including those involved in bacterial attachment and nutrient uptake. This latter category may include siderophores, which are required for iron acquisition. The primary virulence factors produced by *P. syringae* are type III effectors and toxins.

Type III Effectors

P. syringae Type III effectors, also known as Hop proteins, are coordinately synthesized by the bacterium in response to conditions inside the plant apoplast. Induction of the *hop* genes (also referred to by the older gene designation *avr*) is mediated by the ECF sigma factor HrpL. The effectors are injected into the plant cell by the bacterial type III secretion system. The first *P. syringae* type III effectors to be characterized were identified by their ability to cause a plant-type hypersensitive response upon recognition by plant resistance or R genes.

With the public release of complete genome sequences for three *P. syringae* strains it was possible to identify novel effector genes using conserved properties in the sequence. Useful properties for effector identification include the DNA motif to which HrpL binds, located upstream of the effector genes, as well as conserved elements in the amino acid sequences of the effector proteins involved in targeting them through the type III secretion system. Nearly sixty different type III effector families have been identified in *P. syringae* with selected individual strains encoding 30 or more. Gene names are assigned according to a nomenclature system that relies on both sequence and experimental characterization.

Type III effectors contribute to pathogenesis chiefly through interference with diverse aspects of plant defense including formation of receptor complexes, MAP kinase signaling, vesicle transport, and RNA binding. A comprehensive listing of effector action in host plants can be found in the Gene Ontology-based *P. syringae*-Plant Interaction Resource. Ongoing sequencing of additional *P. syringae* strains is directed in large part to identifying correlations between effector repertoire and host range.

Toxins

Toxins contribute significantly to virulence in pathovars where they occur. The toxin coronatine suppresses salicylic acid-mediated defense as well as activating the jasmonic acid signaling pathway through mimicry of jasmonate.

An important impact of coronatine action is to induce opening of the plant stoma to permit entry of the pathogen. Additional toxins characterized in *P. syringae* strains include syringomycin and syringopeptin, associated with attachment and surfactant activity and phaseolotoxin, tabtoxin, and mangotoxin which target metabolic pathways in the host.

Pathovars

Following ribotypical analysis, incorporation of several pathovars of *Pseudomonas syringae* into other species was proposed (see *P. amygdali*, *'P. tomato'*, *P. coronafaciens*, *P. avellanae*, *'P. helianthi'*, *P. tremae*, *P. cannabina*, and *P. viridiflava*). According to this schema, the remaining pathovars are as follows:

- *Pseudomonas syringae* pv. *aceris* attacks maple *Acer* species.
- *Pseudomonas syringae* pv. *aptata* attacks beets *Beta vulgaris*.
- *Pseudomonas syringae* pv. *atrofaciens* attacks wheat *Triticum aestivum*.
- *Pseudomonas syringae* pv. *dysoxylis* attacks the kohekohe tree *Dysoxylum spectabile*.
- *Pseudomonas syringae* pv. *japonica* attacks barley *Hordeum vulgare*.
- *Pseudomonas syringae* pv. *lapsa* attacks wheat *Triticum aestivum*.
- *Pseudomonas syringae* pv. *panici* attacks *Panicum* grass species.
- *Pseudomonas syringae* pv. *papulans* attacks crabapple *Malus sylvestris* species.
- *Pseudomonas syringae* pv. *pisi* attacks peas *Pisum sativum*.
- *Pseudomonas syringae* pv. *syringae* attacks *Syringa*, *Prunus* and *Phaseolus* species.
- *Pseudomonas syringae* pv. *aesculi* attacks horse chestnut *Aesculus hippocastanum*, causing Bleeding Canker of Horse Chestnut.
- *Pseudomonas syringae* pv. *actinidiae* attacks kiwifruit *Actinidia deliciosa*.

However, many of the strains for which new species groupings were proposed continue to be referred to in the scientific literature as pathovars of *P. syringae*, including pathovars tomato, phaseolicola, and maculicola. Note that *Pseudomonas savastanoi* was once considered a pathovar or sub-species of *P. syringae*, and in many places continues to be referred to as *Pseudomonas syringae* pv. *savastanoi*, although as a result of DNA-relatedness studies it has been instated as a new species. It itself has three host-specific pathovars: *fraxini* (which causes ash canker), *nerii* (which attacks oleander), and *oleae* (which causes olive knot).

Genome Sequencing Projects

The following table lists some of the genomes of strains of *P. syringae* that have been sequenced so far (or are in the process of being sequenced):

Pathovar	Strain	Disease	Hosts
Tomato	DC3000 (NCPPB 4369)	Bacterial speck	Tomato, Arabidopsis
Syringae	B728A	Brown spot	Bean
Phaseolicola	1448A (NCPPB 4478)	Halo blight	Bean
Savastanoi	NCPPB 3335	Olive knot	Olive
Tomato	T1	Bacterial speck	Tomato
Tomato	NCPPB1108	–	Tomato
Tomato	Max13	–	Tomato
Tomato	K40	–	Tomato
Tabaci	ATCC11528	Wildlife	Tobacco
Aesculi	2250	Bleeding canker	European horse chestnut
Aesculi	NCPPB 3681	Leaf spot	Indian horse chestnut
Oryzae	1_6	–	Rice
Syringae	FF5	–	–
Syringae	642	–	–
Glycinea	Race 4	Bacterial blight	Soybean
Glycinea	B076	Bacterial blight	Soybean

Pseudomonas syringae pv. *tomato* DC3000 (Donors reference DC52) is a mutant generated from NCPPB 1106. The difference between 1106 and DC3000 is rifampicin resistance (it was generated as a spontaneous mutant). Both DC3000 (NCPPB 4369) and NCPPB 1106 are available from the National Collection of Plant Pathogenic Bacteria.

Pseudomonas Syringae as a Model System

Owing to early availability of genome sequences for *Pseudomonas syringae* pv tomato strain DC3000, *P. syringae pv. syringae* strain B728a, and *P. syringae pv phaseolicola* strain 1448A, together with the ability of selected strains to cause disease on well-characterized host plants such as *Arabidopsis thaliana, Nicotiana benthemiana*, and tomato, *P. syringae* has come to represent an important model system for experimental characterization of the molecular dynamics of plant-pathogen interactions. The *P. syringae* experimental system has been a source of pioneering evidence for the important role of pathogen gene products in suppressing plant defense. The nomenclature system developed for *P. syringae* effectors has been adopted by researchers characterizing effector repertoires in other bacteria, and methods used for bioinformatic effector identification have been adapted for other organisms.

In addition, researchers working with *P. syringae* have played an integral role in the Plant-Associated Microbe Gene Ontology (PAMGO) working group, aimed at developing Gene Ontology terms that capture biological processes occurring during the interactions between organisms, and using the terms for annotation of gene products.

P. syringae *pv tomato strain DC 3000* and Arabidopsis thaliana

As mentioned above, the genome of *P. syringae pv tomato* DC3000 has been sequenced, and approximately 40 Hop (Hrp Outer Protein) effectors, pathogenic proteins that attenuate the host cell, have been identified. These forty effectors are not recognized by *A. thaliana* thus making *P. syringae pv tomato* DC3000 virulent, that is, *P. syringae pv tomato* DC3000 is able to infect *A. thaliana* which is susceptible to this pathogen.

Many Gene-for-Gene relationships have been identified utilizing the two model organisms, *P. syringae pv tomato* strain DC3000 and *Arabidopsis*. The Gene-for-Gene relationship describes the recognition of pathogenic avirulence (avr) genes by host Resistance genes (R-genes). *P. syringae pv tomato* DC3000 is a useful tool for studying avr: R-gene interactions in *A. thaliana* because it can be transformed with aver genes from other bacterial pathogens, and furthermore, because none of the endogenous Hops are recognized by *A. thaliana*, thus any observed aver recognition identified utilizing this model can be attributed to recognition of the introduced aver by *A. thaliana*. The transformation of *P. syringae pv tomato* DC3000 with effectors from other pathogens have led to the identification of many R-genes in *Arabidopsis* to further advance knowledge of plant pathogen interactions.

Pseudomonas Fuscovaginae

Pseudomonas fuscovaginae is a fluorescent, Gram-negative soil bacterium that is pathogenic to rice, causing brown sheath rot. The type strain is CCUG 32780.

Alternaria Triticina

Alternaria triticina is a plant pathogen that causes leaf blight on wheat. It was first identified in India in 1962 and still causes significant yield loss to wheat crops on the Indian subcontinent. The disease causes necrotic leaf lesions and in severe cases seeds will become shriveled.

CANKER

Canker and anthracnose are general terms for a large number of different plant diseases, characterised by broadly similar symptoms including the appearance of small areas of dead tissue, which grow slowly, often over a period of years. Some are of only minor consequence, but others are ultimately lethal, and of major economic importance in agriculture and horticulture.

Different cankers and anthracnoses are caused by a wide range of organisms, including fungi, bacteria, mycoplasmas and viruses. The majority of canker-causing organisms are tied obligately to a single host species or genus, but a few will attack a wider range of plants. Canker can be spread by weather and animals, making an area that even has a slight amount of canker hazardous.

Some cankers are treatable with fungicides or bactericides, but many are not; often the only treatment available is to destroy the infected plant to prevent the disease from spreading to other plants.

Examples :

- Apple canker, caused by the fungus Nectria galligena
- Ash bacterial canker, caused by the bacterium Pseudomonas syringae.
- Butternut canker, caused by the fungus Sirococcus clavigignenti-juglandacearum.
- Bleeding Canker of Horse Chestnut, caused by the bacterium Pseudomonas syringae pv. aesculi.
- Citrus canker, caused by the bacterium Xanthomonas axonopodis.
- Cypress canker, caused by the fungus Seiridium cardinale.
- Dogwood anthracnose, caused by the fungus Discula destructiva.
- Grape canker, caused by the water mould Eutypa lata.
- Honey locust canker, caused by the fungus Thyronectria austro-americana.
- Mulberry canker, caused by the fungus Gibberella baccata.
- Oak canker, caused by the fungus Diplodia quercina.
- Pine pitch canker, caused by the fungus Fusarium pini.
- Plane anthracnose, caused by the fungus Apiognomonia veneta.
- Poplar canker, caused by the bacterium Xanthomonas populi.
- Rapeseed stem canker, caused by the blackleg fungus Leptosphaeria maculans.
- Rose cankers, caused by the fungus Leptosphaeria coniothyrium and Cryptosporella umbrina.

- Scleroderris canker, caused by the fungus Gremmeniella abietina.
- Willow anthracnose, caused by the fungus Marssonina salicicola.

POWDERY MILDEW

It is a fungal disease that affects a wide range of plants. Powdery mildew diseases are caused by many different species of fungi in the order Erysiphales. It is one of the easier diseases to spot, as its symptoms are quite distinctive. Infected plants display white powdery spots on the leaves and stems.

The lower leaves are the most affected, but the mildew can appear on any above-ground part of the plant. As the disease progresses, the spots get larger and denser as large numbers of asexual spores are formed, and the mildew may spread up and down the length of the plant.

Powdery Mildew of Grape

Erysiphe necator (or *Uncinula necator*) causes powdery mildew of grapes. It produces common odors such as 1-octen-3-one and (Z)-1, 5-octadien-3-one.

Powdery Mildew of Wheat

Blumeria graminis forma specialis (f. sp.) tritici, causes powdery mildew of wheat. It can persist between seasons most likely as ascospores in wheat debris left in the field. Wheat mildew thrives in cool humid conditions. Though present throughout wheat growing regions it especially favors the eastern seaboard of the United States as well as coastal regions of the United Kingdom.

Controlling the disease involves eliminating conducive conditions as much as possible by altering planting density and carefully timing applications and rates of nitrogen. Since nitrogen fertilizers encourage dense leafy growth, nitrogen should be applied at precise rates to control decrease severity.

Crop rotation with non-host plants is another way to keep mildew infection to a minimum, however the aerial nature of conidia and ascospore dispersal makes it of limited use. Chemical control is possible with fungicides such as triademefon and propiconazole. In addition, control of powdery mildews is possible using cultivars containing R genes (resistance genes) to prevent infection.

Powdery Mildew of Onions

The fungus causing powdery mildew of onions is Leveillula taurica (also known by its anamorph name, Oidiopsis taurica). It also infects the artichoke.

Powdery Mildew of Apples and pears

Podosphaera leucotricha is a fungus that can cause powdery mildew of apples and pears.

Powdery Mildew of Gourds and Melons

Podosphaera fusca is a fungus that can cause powdery mildew of Curcurbits: cucumbers, squashes including pumpkins, luffas, melons and watermelons.

Powdery Mildew in Lilacs

Microsphaera syringae is a fungus that can cause powdery mildew in lilac.

Powdery Mildew in Strawberry

Podosphaera aphanis is the cause of powdery mildew in strawberries and other Rosaceae like Geum rivale (the Water Avens)

Powdery Mildew on Tree Leaves

Sawadaea tulasnei is a fungus that causes powdery mildew on tree leaves. This fungus attacks the leaves of the Acer platanoides (Norway Maple) in North America, and in Great Britain and/or Ireland, Acer palmatum (also known as the Japanese Maple or Smooth Japanese Maple).

Reproduction

Powdery mildew fungi reproduce both sexually and asexually. Sexual reproduction is via chasmothecia (formerly cleistothecium), a type of ascocarp. Within each ascocarp are several asci. Over time, ascospores mature and are released to initiate new infections. Conditions necessary for spore maturation differ among species.

STEM RUST

The stem, black or cereal rusts are caused by the fungus Puccinia graminis and are a significant disease affecting cereal crops. An epidemic of stem rust on wheat caused by race Ug99 is currently spreading across Africa, Asia and most recently into Middle East and is causing major concern due to the large numbers of people dependent on wheat for sustenance. The strain was named after the country where it was identified (Uganda) and the year of its discovery (1999).

It spread to Kenya, then Ethiopia, Sudan and Yemen, and is becoming more virulent as it spreads. Scientists are working on breeding strains of wheat that are resistant to UG99. However, wheat is grown in a broad range of environments. This means that breeding programmes would have extensive work remaining to get resistance into regionally adapted germplasms even after resistance is identified.

There is considerable genetic diversity within the species *P. graminis* and several special forms, forma specialis, which vary in host range have been identified.

- *Puccinia graminis* f. sp. avenae, oat
- *Puccinia graminis* f. sp. dactylis
- *Puccinia graminis* f. sp. lolii
- *Puccinia graminis* f. sp. poae
- *Puccinia graminis* f. sp. secalis, rye, barley
- *Puccinia graminis* f. sp. tritici, wheat, barley

Like other *Puccinia species, P. graminis* has a complex life cycle featuring alternation of generations, the fungus is also heteroecious which means that its various life cycle stages require alternate host species. The complete life cycle of P. graminis requires barberry as well as a cereal species.

In the spring and summer, stem rust infections on cereal plants produce dikaryotic urediniospores, which are spread by the wind to nearby cereal plants, where they germinate and infect cereals by penetrating through the stomata. This polycyclic asexual phase can rapidly spread the infection over a wide area.

Towards the end of the growing season, the rust converts to producing teliospores, which again contain these two haploid nuclei of opposite mating types. Before the winter, the nucleii fuse to form a diploid cell, which remains dormant until the next spring when it undergoes meiosis to produce four haploid cells known as basidiospores, borne on a structure called a basidium.

The basidiospores then undergo a mitotic nuclear division to produce the mature basidiospore which contains two haploid nuclei of the same mating type. Basidiospores cannot infect cereal plants, but are instead, carried in the wind, and infect young leaves of common barberry (*Berberis vulgaris*) or other susceptible Berberis, Mahonia, or Mahoberberis species or cultivars. On barberry, the basidiospore penetrates the leaf epidermis directly, and the resulting infections produce specialized infection structures called 'pycnia' (or spermagonia).

Pycnia (or spermagonia), which result from infection on young barberry leaves by basidiospores, are the sexual stage of the fungus life cycle. When a receptive hypha from one pycnium has been fertilized by pycniospores (or spermatia) from a mating type compatible pycnium, its haploid cells become dikaryotic. The fertilized hypha forms an aecium, on the underside of the barberry leaf, which produces chains of aeciospores surrounded by a bell-like enclosure of fungal cells.

Like the urediniospores and like the cells of the aecium, each aeciospore contains two nuclei. Aeciospores are carried by the wind, and infect cereals by penetrating through stomata. After infecting a cereal plant, the aecispores develop and form uredia under the plants epidermis, these produce the dikaryotic urediniospores. These uredia eventually rupture the plant's epidermis and again spread by the wind to nearby cereal plants, continuing the lifecycle.

The stem rust fungus attacks the parts of the plant which are above ground. Spores that land on green wheat plants form a pustule that invades the outer layers of the stalk. The site of infection is a visible symptom of the disease. Where infection has occurred on the stem or leaf, elliptical blisters or pustules called uredia develop. Infected plants produce fewer tillers and set fewer seed, and in cases of severe infection the plant may die.

Pycnia typically form on the upper side of barberry leaves, and aecia form within five to seven days after fertilization on the lower side of the leaf directly below each fertilized pycnium.

Ug99, which has the designation of TTKS, is a race of black stem rust (Puccinia graminis tritici). It is virulent to the great majority of wheat varieties. Unlike other rusts, which only partially affect crop yields, UG99 can bring 100 per cent crop loss. Up to 80 per cent yield losses were recently recorded in Kenya.

The blight was first noted in Uganda in 1999 and has spread throughout the highlands of East Africa. In January 2007, spores blew across to Yemen, and north into Sudan. In March 2007, FAO announced its concern regarding the spread through Iran-based on Iranian authorities report.

The fungal ancestors of stem rust have infected grasses for millions of years and wheat crops for as long as they have been grown. According to Jim Peterson, professor of wheat breeding and genetics at Oregon State University, "Stem rust destroyed more than 20 per cent of U.S. wheat crops several times between 1917 and 1935, and losses reached 9 per cent twice in the 1950s," with the last U.S. outbreak in 1962 destroying 5.2 per cent of the crop.

WHEAT LEAF RUST: A FUNGAL DISEASE

Wheat leaf rust, is fungal disease that effects wheat, barley and rye stems, leaves and grains. In temperate zones it is destructive on winter wheat because the pathogen overwinters. Infections can lead up to 20 per cent yield loss—exacerbated by dying leaves which fertilize the fungus. The pathogen is Puccinia rust fungus. *Puccinia triticina* causes 'black rust', *P. recondita* causes 'brown rust' and *P. sriiformis* causes 'Yellow rust'.

It is the most prevalent of all the wheat rust diseases, occurring in most wheat growing regions. It causes serious epidemics in North America, Mexico and South America and is a devastating seasonal disease in India. All three types of Puccinia are heteroecious requiring two distinct and distantly related hosts (alternate hosts). Rust and the similar smut are members of the class Teliomycetes but rust is not normally a black powdery mass.

Wheat leaf rust is spreads via airborne spores. Five types of spores are formed in the life cycle. Uredospores, teleutospores and basidiospores develop on wheat plants and pycnidiospores and aeciospores develop on the alternate hosts. The germination process requires moisture, and works best at 100 per cent humidity. Optimum temperature for germination is between 15-20 °C. Before sporulation, wheat plants appear completely asymptomatic.

In the Asian subcontinent, the spores cannot survive the hot dry weather but are re-introduced every year from the Himalayas or surrounding hills, possibly coming from *Berberis* spp, *Thalictrum flavum* and *Muehlenbergia huglet* or even some grasses. Wheat rust pathogens are biotrophic and require living plant cells to survive.

P. triticina has an asexual and sexual life cycle. In order to complete its sexual life cycle *P. triticina* requires a second host *Thalictrum* spp. which it will overwinter on. In places where *Thalictrum* does not grow, such as Australia, the pathogen will only undergo its asexual life cycle and will overwinter as mycelium or uredinia. The germination process requires moisture and temperatures between 15-20 °C. After around ten to fourteen days of infection, the fungi will begin to sporulate and the symptoms will become visible on the wheat leaves.

The pathogen has an asexual and sexual cycle. In North America, South America and Australia the pathogen only undergoes its asexual cycle. However this does not seem to be a disadvantage to it, and wheat leaf rust has many races with different virulence. The sexual life cycle of wheat leaf rust requires a different host species, *Thalictrumn* spp.

Symptoms and Control

Small brown pustules develop on the leaf blades in a random scatter distribution. They may group into patches in serious cases. Infectious spores are transmitted via the soil. Onset of the disease is slow but accelerated in temperatures above 15°C, making it a disease of the mature cereal plant in summer, usually too late to cause significant damage in temperate areas. Losses of between 5 and 20 per cent are normal but may reach 50 per cent in severe cases.

Varietal resistance is important. Chemical control with triazole fungicides may be useful for control of infections up to ear emergence but is difficult to justify economically in attacks after this stage.

WHEAT MILDEW

It is a wheat disease that affects the ear, and is brought on by causes somewhat similar to those that cause blight, though at a more advanced period of the season. If this disorder comes on immediately after the first appearance of the ear, the straw is also affected—but if the grain is nearly or fully formed, injury to the straw is less discernible. Wheat may mildew where the straw is perfectly fresh, but only rarely.

A severe mildew, however, retards further grain and straw maturation and leads to death. Something akin to mildew is the gum, which, in all warm moist seasons, attaches itself to the ear, and often causes considerable damage.

All these different disorders are generally accompanied by insects, and by minute parasitic vegetable growths, considered by many to be the cause of the damage. Their appearance, however, may justly be attributed to the diseased state of the plant; for wherever putrefaction takes place, either in animal or vegetable substances, the presence of these parasites will never be wanting.

Another disorder that affects wheat, which several people consider the real rust, is brought on by excessive heat, which makes the plants suffer from malnutrition, and become sickly and feeble. In this atrophic state a kind of dust gathers on the stalks and leaves, which increases with the disease, till the plant is in a great measure worn out and exhausted.

The only remedy in this case, and it is one that cannot easily be administered by the hand of man, is a plentiful supply of moisture, by which, if it is received before consumption is too far advanced, the crop is benefited in a degree proportional to the extent of nourishment received, and the stage at which the disease has arrived.

Some people have recommended using blighted and mildewed wheat for seed. This, however may be hazardous. Light or defective wheat does vegetate and produce a plant, but the plant may be of poor quality and inapable of withstanding winter blasts.

What are Septoria?

Septoria are Ascomycete fungi that causes numerous leaf spot diseases on field crops, forages and many vegetables, and is responsible for yield losses. The genus is widespread, and estimated to contain 1072 species.

Septoria leaf blotch is a fungal disease due to Septoria tritici, anamorph Mycosphaerella graminicola, that affects wheat and occasionally other grasses including barley. It is the major disease of wheat in the UK.

Septoria apiicola is the cause of late blight of celery. it is characterized by the production of conidia within pycnidia. The symptoms include chlorotic spots that turn brown and necrotic. Septoria apiicola can survive on seeds.

Several species of passion flower are infected by several species of Septoria, and a fungus, which has been going by the name Septoria passiflorae but which is probably an undescribed species, has been used to control the invasive Passiflora tarminiana in Hawai.

Fusarium and Nematodes on Cotton

Fusarium wilt of cotton, caused by *Fusarium oxysporum* f.sp. vasinfectum (Fov) has become a significant constraint to cotton production in Australia, since it was first recognised on the Darling Downs in Queensland in 1993. The estimated loss in crop production from fusarium wilt is estimated at \$100 million per year while flow-on losses to cotton-ginners, contractors and consultants, machinery and chemical suppliers is estimated to be several hundred million dollars per year.

Currently, most of the high yielding varieties are susceptible to Fusarium wilt. Disease control measures rely heavily on the use of varieties with enhanced resistance to the fungus and disease prevention strategies to limit the spread of the pathogen in cotton production areas. Early detection and identification of the disease in clean areas is critical, as the available disease prevention strategies must be implemented as soon as possible to be effective.

Fusarium wilt is a cotton disease caused by the soil-inhabiting fungus *Fusarium oxysporum* f.sp. vasinfectum (Fov). The disease was first identified in Australian cotton crops in the Brookstead/Cecil Plains district of the Darling Downs in March 1993.

Australian isolates of Fov are different to Fov found in other cotton-producing countries. Initially, Vegetative Compatibility Group analyses were used to identify two strains of the pathogen VCG01111 and VCG001112. Both strains appear to be equally capable of causing the disease in all currently available Australian commercial cotton varieties.

At the time of writing, Fusarium wilt has been identified in most Australian cotton-producing districts, except Queensland's Emerald region, Hilston and Tandau in New South Wales, and the Ord Irrigation Area of Western Australia.

Real-time polymerase chain reaction (PCR) assays were developed to detect and differentiate the two Australian genotypes. The assay was recently used to prove that an outbreak of Fov in cotton growing regions around Athens (Greece) did not originate from clean seed imported from Australia. While the usefulness of the assay in soil testing to differentiate strains is in question, the assay is a highly effective tool for differentiating strains of Fov in pure culture and from plant extracts.

The diagnostic test developed in this project will help cotton growers to detect the pathogen in soil and, in turn, help Australia to safeguard its US market for cottonseed exports. The net benefits afforded from the availability of this test have been calculated at around $17 million – a twelve-fold return on the Centre's investment in this project.

Plants can be affected by Fov at any stage. Disease incidence in seedlings can be high in cold soils, but mean temperatures about 23°C favour the disease. Higher temperatures above 28°C reduce symptom expression. Fusarium wilt is a stress-related pathogen, meaning plants are often able to resist attack until they become stressed by other factors. The fungus can then rapidly colonise the stressed plants.

The fungus has a resting phase in the soil. Once the fungal spores become established, they can survive in the soil for at least a decade, even in the absence of cotton plants.

There is no commercially viable way to eradicate this disease from the soil, and it can spread across fields, farms and regions. Spores are effectively spread over long distances in infected soil attached to boots, vehicles, farm equipment and in water (irrigation and overland flows). It can also be transferred in infected plant material, including seed.

The incidence of Fusarium wilt in Australian cotton crops is increasing. On some severely affected properties, disease levels have caused whole fields to be ploughed out.

Fusarium wilt is considered by many growers and other industry representatives as the most important constraint to sustainable cotton production to have developed in Australia in recent years.

A major research effort has been mounted to counter the threat of this disease. Researchers from many agencies are collaborating in the effort. These include the Queensland Department of Employment, Economic Development and Innovation (DEEDI), CSIRO, the Cotton Catchment Communities CRC (CCC CRC), New South Wales Department of Primary Industries (NSWDPI), Cotton Seed Distributors (CSD) and Deltapine Australia. Management of this disease will be most effective if approached on an industry-wide basis.

Symptoms

Areas of reduced or patchy plant stand can be seen in affected fields, usually spreading in the direction of irrigation flows. Plant death, wilting, yellowing and defoliated plants are typical of disease symptoms. The vascular tissue of affected plants exhibits a brown/chocolate discolouration through the entire main stem. Some plants affected with the disease show some regrowth.

REDUCING THE IMPACT

Avoiding Crop Stresses

This includes over-irrigation and over-application of nitrogen.

Growing only Resistant Varieties

Cotton varieties with high levels of resistance to Fusarium wilt are the cornerstone for management of this disease. Resistant varieties will slow the build-up of Fusarium in the soil, in contrast to susceptible varieties. However, when weather conditions are particularly conducive to disease development, disease incidence may increase substantially even in resistant varieties.

A standard ranking scheme has been developed which indicates the resistance performance of commercially available cotton varieties as a percentage of industry nominated benchmark varieties. The Fusarium wilt rank value (F-rank) is detailed in varietial information published annually by Cotton Seed Distributors and Deltapine Australia. The commercial breeding programmes are continuing major efforts to breed cotton varieties with increased disease resistance.

Managing your Weeds

Isolates of fusarium have been found in the vascular systems of *Amaranthus macrocarpus* (dwarf amaranth), *Hibiscus trionum* (bladder ketmia), *Sesbania cannabini* (sesbania), *Ipomoea plebeia* (bellvine) and *Citrullus lanatus* (wild melon). Other weeds may also be symptomless hosts of the disease. Hence, weeds should be controlled in fallows and in-crop.

Crop Rotation Options

Results from trials conducted on the Darling Downs from 2001 to 2005 highlight the importance of a fallow preceding a cotton crop grown on

Fusarium wilt infected soils. Significantly more cotton plants survived until maturity following a bare fallow rotation compared to cotton following either maize, cotton or sorghum crops.

The greatest plant death and severity of disease occurred where soybean and mungbean crops had been grown immediately prior to cotton. Residue and organic matter levels may influence field pathogen survival and disease incidence.

Growers are urged to grow only the most resistant cotton varieties available in fields known to be infected with Fusarium wilt. Field inspection for early detection and containment of isolated outbreaks.

In regions or fields where the disease has only just been found, it is extremely important to detect all outbreaks as soon as possible and to maximise efforts to contain the spread.

With Small Patches

Pull out affected plants and burn them on the spot. Consider soil solarisation. Raking and burning the whole field at this stage is not an option, and raking is likely to spread the disease.

With Large Patches

Kill affected plants, preferably by spraying with herbicide and leaving them to die in place (including regrowth and volunteer plants)

Sow a persistent ground cover in the fallow (such a cereal) to stabilise the soil in the affected area and to prevent erosion after the cotton plants have died. Clean down any gear used for establishment and maintenance of the crop and do not allow irrigation tail water to leave the strip.

Such areas may be suitable for the establishment of lucerne strips for IPM, as long as traffic in and out of the area is minimised and agricultural practices are not conducted under wet conditions.

With Any Patch

Festroy 1-2 m of plants in the healthy crop area surrounding the patch, taking particular care to minimise the transfer of affected soil from the area. Reduce traffic to zero in the affected patches. Minimise traffic in adjacent areas and restrict it to dry conditions only.

Stop irrigating affected patches. Use bunding to divert rainwater around the affected patch and, if possible, to contain rainwater that falls on it. Collect the trash from the tailwater of infested fields and burn it on-site to minimise movement of trash to other fields.

Farm Hygiene

Practise good farm hygiene to maintain disease-free farms (including vehicle wash-down facilities, footbaths, use of Farmcleanse) and ensure that all farm traffic adheres to the Come Clean-Go Clean industry hygiene strategy. Commonsense practices of farm hygiene also reduce the rate of spread, especially in relation to mud and trash. Some regions have hygiene protocols for particular weeds and diseases.

Hygiene Measures Include

- Ensuring machinery and vehicles are free of mud or crop debris.
- Keeping irrigation tailwater and runoff water on-farm.
- Controlling weeds.
- Using a crop-rotation strategy.
- Maintaining good soil nutrition levels.
- Mulching infected cotton stubble and leaving it on the soil surface a month before incorporating. Pull mulchers are preferred as more infected plant material would be left on the surface to be subjected to sunlight.
- Minimising spillage and loss when transporting modules, hulls, cotton seed or gin trash.

Managing Fusarium Wilt of Cotton

Early detection and containment of new outbreaks are the key strategies for managing Fusarium wilt of cotton. All farm staff and contractors should be advised of the symptoms of the disease and encouraged to be on the lookout for suspect plant systems in-crop.

Growers are encouraged to send stem sections from suspect plants for examination at DEEDI's Plant Pathology Laboratories in Toowoomba or Indooroopilly. Early detection of disease outbreaks will enable management strategies to be implemented quickly to minimise the spread of the disease.

A moderate amount of root knot resistance is associated with fusarium resistance in varieties developed in the Southeast and selected on wilt- and nematode-infested soils. In the process of selecting for fusarium resistance and high yield in segregating progenies; moderate resistance to root knot is obtained without specific effort on the part of the breeder. This resistance contributes to the fusarium resistance and to the yield of such lines. High resistance to root knot is not present in any upland varieties.

However, there are considerable differences between the most susceptible and the most resistant ones. Varieties combining both fusarium resistance and moderate root knot resistance are Stonewilt, Coker too wilt, and Plains. Several varieties considered susceptible to root knot are Rowden, Miller, Deltapine, Bobshaw, Stoneville, Empire, and Pandora.

A search for high resistance to root knot was made at the Alabama Agricultural Experiment Station in 1951. A number of the world cotton species and many types and varieties were planted, and the roots were later examined for size and abundance of galls. Several sources of resistance were found, the most promising of which were *Gossypium barbadense* var. darwinii and two wild cottons from Mexico. The latter two introductions from Mexico are much like upland (*G. hirsutum*) but are not productive.

These three were crossed and back-crossed to productive upland varieties. The segregating progenies will be selected for root knot resistance and further backcrossed. Eventually high root knot resistance in combination with desirable agronomic characters will be obtained. Improved root knot resistance will increase the yields of varieties grown on infested soils and should also improve the resistance to fusarium wilt.

The use of balanced fertilizers to maintain a vigorous growth of cotton plants is an important cultural practice to prevent losses from cotton Wilt. Potash tends to reduce wilt losses.

Nitrogen and phosphorus tend to increase wilt within certain limits. The proper balance of nitrogen, phosphorus, and potash gives the maximum yields and best control of wilt when no one of the three elements is deficient. Cotton rust, or potash deficiency, was early confused with cotton wilt. George F. Atkinson discovered that ample application of potash prevented the occurrence of rust. Rust on cotton continued to cause serious losses and increased the losses from wilt until 1926, when American sources of potash were developed, which provided ample supplies at a reasonable cost.

Nematocides can control fusarium wilt and nematodes and thereby can double yields of resistant varieties and triple and quadruple the yields of susceptible varieties grown on soils heavily infested by both pathogens. In experiments in Alabama in 1947, I learned that wilt is controlled indirectly by destroying the nematodes. The yields are increased as a result of control of both the wilt and nematodes. On treated plots better stands are maintained, the plants grow off more rapidly, grow larger, and produce greater yields.

Most economical control is obtained by applying the material in the row at the rate of six to eight gallons an acre a few days before planting.

Materials giving satisfactory control are ethylene dibromide and a mixture of dichloropropene and dichloropropane. Their trade names are Dowfume W-40 and D D. Row application gives control of nematodes in a zone near the young plants. Once the plants are established and growing rapidly, later nematode infections do little damage to the crop. Annual applications are necessary if only the row application is made.

Rotating Cotton with crops that reduce the amount of root knot is a cultural practice of value in reducing wilt losses and increasing yields. Crops that reduce root knot nematodes are grasses, sorghum, small grains, corn, peanuts, crotalaria, velvetbeans, alfalfa, and nematode-resistant cowpeas.

Several crops that are particularly susceptible to root knot tend to intensify wilt and nematode losses. Among them are cowpeas susceptible to root knot, annual lespedezas, sweet-potatoes and tobacco.

Crops grown during mild winters for green manure sometimes increase populations of root knot to the extent of causing increased losses in the cotton crop that follows them. Blue lupine, Austrian winter peas, and vetch are examples. On the contrary, increased organic matter is beneficial in improving yields and reducing wilt losses.

Rotations help to control other diseases of cotton. An example is ascochyta blight of young plants, which sometimes becomes epidemic. Rotation is likewise of value against bacterial blight infections in the Southwest and irrigated valleys, where plant refuse is not decayed over winter.

The rotation of cotton with other crops has not become a widely used practice. Farmers are reluctant to follow some other crops with cotton, particularly peanuts and hay crops, which exhaust the soils of some minerals to the extent that yields of cotton may be reduced. Other reasons may have to do with the accessibility of the land to the house, weeds, and the tendency to select the most productive land for cotton.

ROTYLENCHULUS RENIFORMIS

It is a plant parasite nematode with a worldwide distribution in the tropical and subtropical regions. This nematode has a wide host range infecting plants in many species around the word. It belongs to the Family Hoplolaimidae; it was first observed on the roots of cowpea in Hawaii.

The reniform nematode was described as new species in 1940 by Linford and Oliver after four years of investigations . It is called the reniform nematode because of the distinct kidney-shaped appearance of the mature female. *R. reniformis* is the only species of major economic importance to agriculture of the ten *Rotylenchulus* species described.

Distribution and Host Range

R. reniformis has been found associated with hundreds of species of plants in tropical and subtropical areas. It has been reported in thousands of localities in South America, Central America, North America, the Caribbean Basin, Africa, Europe, India, Southeast Asia, Australia, China, Japan and the Philippines.

Its wide distribution is due to the wide range of host it infects; including fruit trees, lentil, cotton, cowpea, pigeonpea, tea, tobacco, soybean, pineapple, bananas, okra, coconut, cabbage, sweet potato, alfalfa, corn, asparagus, palm, cucumber, tomato, pumpkin, squash, cassava, radish, eggplant, guava, melon and ginger.

Certain species of plants such as wild barley, mustard, oats, barnyard grass, pangola grass, red-hot and sweet pepper, spinach have been reported as non-host to reniform nematode.

Morphology

Reniform nematodes have esophageal glands overlapping the intestine, short stylet, a strongly developed framework; the dorsal esophageal gland orifice is located posterior to the stylet knobs. Immature females are slender, free in the soil. The body often assumes an open spiral or 'C' shape when killed by heat.

Mature females have a swollen kidney-shaped body with a short tail, slender and short stylet, rounded knobs; with a three-part esophagus, a long and narrow isthmus, and well-developed metacarpus. The vulva is just behind the mid-portion of the body. Males are vermiform; they have a weak stylet and knobs, curved spicules and pointed tail; the esophagus is degenerate, with a reduced median bulb.

Life Cycle

R. reniformis is sedentary semi-endoparasite on roots of many plants. Mature females penetrate partly into roots, leaving the posterior portion of their bodies projecting at the surface. Juveniles, males and immature females are found in soil. The immature female is the infective stage penetrating roots. Males are not parasites, they do not feed but they are important for reproduction. Under drought conditions, R. reniformis can survives one to two years without host by entering an anhydrobiotic state.

R. reniformis is sexually dimorphic; its life cycle is completed in seventeen to twenty three days under favourable temperatures. The developing juvenile (J1) molt once while still inside the egg shell; the eggs hatch in eight to ten days, then a J2 develops molting three times (J3 and J4) in the soil to become immature males and females. The anterior one-third of the young female body penetrates roots and forms a feeding site (syncytium) in the endodermis. The female continue to develop, swelling and becoming kidney-shaped. The female deposits eggs in a gelatinous matrix containing about fifty eggs on surface of the root after seven to ten days.

HOST-PARASITE RELATIONSHIP

Infective stage penetrates the epidermis and cortical parenchyma of the host root, only the anterior part of the body is embedded within root tissue. Penetration is stopped when lips reach the endodermis, resulting in formation of a trophic site that consist of a syncytium structure, which forms from an endodermal cell and enlarge by incorporation of adjacent parenchyma cells of the pericycle and vascular parenchyma. A feeding tube forms from stylet secretions.

R. reniformis can induce symptoms resembling those of moisture and nutrient deficiencies on above ground plant parts. Reniform nematode can causes hypertrophy in the pericycle cells of root seedlings and in the periderm cells of the roots of four to five week old plants. Generally root growth is reduced with limited secondary root development. It can produce root necrosis in pineapple and banana. Shoot growth suppression is observed and reduction of fruit quality in infected crops such as pineapple.

Infected plants can become severely stunted and chlorotic, and may wilt. Wilting is often caused by opportunistic parasites such as the *Fusarium* and *Verticillium* wilts on cotton . Root decay can be caused by secondary fungi infection. Damage from *R. reniformis* is directly related to the number of nematodes present when the crop is planted. Variation among nematode populations, host, environmental conditions and soil types may alter the threshold or economic injury level across the geographic distribution of this nematode.

MANAGEMENT

Genetic resistance to reniform nematode has not been found in pineapple and cotton. Certain soybean and tomato cultivars are resistant to this nematode. Chemical control is one of the most common management practices against reniform nematode; nematicides prior and post-planting are effective and increase yield.

Inter-cropping cover crops and crop rotation with resistant or non-host plants is used as a cultural practices to enhance soil physical characteristics, increase antagonistic micro-organism, and reduce nematode populations to low levels prior to planting because some of them have allelopathic effects towards nematode.

Rotations with species such as French marigold (*Tagetes patula*), Sunn hemp (*Crotalaria juncea*), are recommended. Moist fallow with weed control is also recommended to declines reniform nematode in crops like pineapple. Use of *Paecilomyces lilacinus* as a biocontrol agent, has been reported in Chickpea.

On 26th March 2002 in-spite of inadequate tests of biosafety and viability, Monsanto managed to get clearance for commercial planting of three varieties of genetically engineered *Bt* cotton from Genetic Engineering Approval Committee (GEAC) under Ministry of Environment and Forests (MoEF).

Ironically, this permission was granted in spite of an ongoing Supreme Court case, filed by RFSTE, challenging the 1998 field trials and stating that there were numerous irregularities and violations of biosafety laws and guidelines in previous year field trials. Even then the GEAC have cleared *Bt* cotton for commercial release by Monsanto-Mahyco.

The Research Foundation for Science, Technology and Ecology (RFSTE), Navdanya, farmers unions and public interests groups in India had warned the government that this irresponsible, rushed clearance would have high cost for farmers in terms of the economic sovereignty and seed sovereignty. What we have had predicted has come true.

In three major states, Bt cotton has been wiped out completely leaving farmers in great economic and livelihood crisis. Not only the new pests and diseases emerged, the *Bt* cotton has failed to even prevent bollworm attack for which it has been designed. While *Bt* cotton is sold as pest resistant seed in India, it has proved to be more vulnerable to pest and diseases than the traditional and conventional varieties.

Madhya Pradesh, the heart of the cotton-growing belt in India, witnessed total failure of genetically engineered Bt cotton. The farmers of Khargoan district where *Bt* is a 100 per cent failure are up in arms against Monsanto-Mahyco that supplied these GM seeds and are demanding compensation from the company for the failure of their crop. The failure of the *Bt* cotton has devastated the farmers since they have spent five to six times to buy seeds of *Bt* than the normal seed. The economics that was worked out by the Indian Council of Agricultural Research (ICAR), Genetic Engineering Approval Committee and Monsanto-Mahyco to promote this unsustainable technology has turned out to be untrue.

Bt cotton has been afflicted with the 'leaf curl virus' in the whole of northern States of India. Dr. Venugopal, ex-project coordinator of the Central Institute for Cotton Research (CICR), Coimbatore told Business Line that while some of the private hybrids and varieties released earlier were resistant to LCV, *Bt* cotton was found susceptible to LCV.

In Maharashtra, the adjoining state of Madhya Pradesh, the same story has been repeated. In Vidarbha, primarily cotton growing area in Maharashtra, *Bt* cotton crop has failed miserably. The first GE crop has been failed in 30,000 hectares in this district alone, completely devastating the already poor farming community. The farmers of the area are demanding a compensation of Rs. 5000 million (500 crores rupees) to meet their economic loss lest they would take a legal action against the Government of Maharashtra and Monsanto-Mahyco for allowing sale of inadequately tested GM seeds.

The *Bt* cotton crop in Vidarbha has been badly affected by the root-rot disease, a disease of roots. It is believed that this disease is caused due to wrong selection of Bt genes developed in America and brought to India. Many farmers have recorded only upto 50 per cent germination of seeds and many others had poor germination, which is suspected to be caused by both, drought and poor seed quality. While other cotton varieties have also been adversely affected by the drought, they report a failure rate of only around 20 per cent.

The main idea behind approving genetically engineered Bt cotton as a commercial crop was that this would increase farmers' income by reducing expenditure on chemical pesticides, which accounts for 70-80 per cent of the total expenditure on hybrid cotton due to the heavy infestation of pest, mainly American Bollworm in last 3-4 years and the increased evolution of resistance to the chemical pesticides.

However, in Gujarat there is a heavy infestation of bollworm on the *Bt* cotton in the districts of Bhavanagar, Surendranagar and Rajkot. Initially *Bt* Cotton was found resistant to Bollworms in the early phase of plant growth, but as soon as the formation of boll has started, the worms started attacking them.

The Department of Agriculture, Government of Gujarat has written to the Gujarat Agricultural University to submit a status report providing detailed information about the kind and intensity of the damage. It has also been found that Gujarat is growing 18,000 hectares of the *Bt* cotton more than the permitted 12,000 hectares by the Government of India.

Failure of BT Cotton Case

The failure of Bt cotton case in India reaffirms RFSTE's stand of safety first-commercial release of any new genetically engineered crops (e.g. transgenic mustard) and organisms must be frozen till a proper independent tests are conducted, the proper biosafety structure are put in place and capacity is built at the multiple level of governments as well as farmers to deal with biosafety issues.

It is not just in the case of *Bt* cotton that corporation like Monsanto are deceiving poor farmers. Monsanto is pushing the farmers of drought stricken and famine-ridden Udaipur and neighbouring districts of Rajasthan to take to industrial farming of maize, and to use its Roundup, no doubt as a prelude to introducing the genetically engineered Roundup Ready varieties once farmers are further pushed on to this ecologically genocidal herbicide trap. But Monsanto is introducing hybrid corn and Roundup (herbicide) with false claims to deceive poor and innocent farmers of Rajasthan.

Monsanto claims that as a result of the *Humsafar programme*, the yield of maize rose from 25 quintals per hectare to 50 quintals per hectare and the profitability of the farmers also doubled form Rs. 7500 per hectare to Rs. 15000 per hectare, whereas its publicity brochures distributed among the farmers is claiming even much higher yields i.e. 50-90 quintals per acre (125-225/ hectare).

However, a study conducted by RFSTE shows that Monsanto claims are based on utter lies. Monsanto's own field staff at Wana and Menar villages in Udaipur reported that their varieties have achieved maize productivity of only 12 quintals/acre (30 quintal/ha.).

Corn Seedling Diseases

This growing season has started out cool with slow heat unit accumulation with frequent precipitation events across the state keeping soils wet. Although some are still out planting corn, there are some fields where corn is at growth stage V2. Reports of seedling blights are beginning to filter in.

As you start to assess plant stands, remember also to check below ground growth, specifically general root and mesocotyl health. Wet and cool soil conditions (less than 50-55° F) predispose seedlings to infection by a number of fungi which cause disease that may result in seedling death. Remember too, that while uneven emergence and stunted seedlings may indicate seedling disease, insect feeding and herbicide damage may be factors.

Survival of young corn seedlings depends on a healthy kernel and mesocotyl which should remain firm and white through at least growth stage V6. Damage to the kernel or mesocotyl prior to establishment of the nodal root system can result in stunted, weak or dead seedlings. A developing corn seedling relies on the kernel endosperm for nourishment until the nodal root system has fully developed, usually around the six-leaf stage. Thus the mesocotyl acts as the "pipeline" for translocation of nutrients from the kernel and seminal roots to the seedling stalk and leaf tissues.

Seedling diseases of corn (seed rots, seedling blights and/or root rots) are caused by numerous fungi including *Pythium, Fusarium, Rhizoctonia, Aspergillus, Penicillium* and *Trichoderma,* all of which are common inhabitants of soils. In addition, these fungi also can be seed-borne in corn, except Pythium. Seedling susceptibility to infection increases the longer the seed sits in the ground, and the more stress germinating corn undergoes. Corn germinates well at soil temperatures above 68°F. When soil temperatures are below 55° F, germination is greatly retarded. Thus seedling disease often is more severe in early planted or no-till/reduced tillage fields because of cool soil temperatures.

Typical below ground symptoms associated with seedling disease include rotting seed and brown discoloration (rotting) of the mesocotyl and seminal roots. It is sometimes possible to determine in the lab which fungus is the culprit, however this information is not crucial since management options are the same for all seedling disease: plant high quality fungicide-treated seed, plant when soil temperatures are above 50° F, and ensure planting depth is not too deep.

Although crop rotation can be helpful in reducing inoculum levels, some fungi are pathogenic on both corn and soybean. Thus good records of seedling disease problems can be a helpful management tool. For example, fields with a history of seedling blight can be planted later in a planting schedule when soil temperatures are warmer.

Seed treatment fungicides have been standard practice in corn production since the 1930s, but many changes have occurred recently and other changes are on the way. The fungicide combination on most commercial corn seed now includes Maxim XL® / Apron XL® (fludioxonil and mefenoxam) and Dynasty® (azoxystrobin) from Syngenta Crop Protection. Some seed also may be treated with Trilex® (trifloxystrobin, Bayer CropScience) instead of Dynasty, or with Allegiance (Metalaxyl) instead of Apron XL. Stamina® (pyraclostrobin) seed treatment fungicide (BASF Corp.) was approved for use in 2009, and is available on a limited scale this year.

In 2010, we noticed the launch of Monsanto's Acceleron® seed treatment brand on corn, which included the fungicide ipconazole, in combination with other active ingredients. Many seed companies are routinely applying insecticides such as Cruiser® (thiamethoxam, from Syngenta) and Poncho® (clothianidin, Bayer CropScience)) in combination with the fungicide seed treatments.

Earlier this year, the nematicide Avicta® (abamectin) was registered for use on corn. The product will be launched commercially in 2010 in combination with Cruiser® seed treatment insecticide and the seed treatment fungicide Apron XL®, Maxim® XL and Dynasty®. Many other fungicides and insecticides are registered for use on corn, some for onfarm use.

The rapid developments in commercial seed treatment use are strengthening the spectrum and duration of protection, but no amount of seed treatment will eliminate seed and seedling disease under all conditions. It continues to be important to be aware of what's on your seed and the performance that you experience with the products.

HOW TO PLANT CORN SEEDLINGS?

Gardeners in regions with chilly spring temperatures opt to sow corn seeds indoors four to six weeks before the expected last spring frost date. Nurtured by the warmth and sun indoors, the seeds sprout into healthy seedlings in small, individual peat-filled pots.

Seedlings later are transplanted outdoors into the garden. Prepare the garden soil by tilling it 8 to 12 inches deep and add 3 to 4 inches of compost, incorporating it well with a shovel. This crumbly, organic-rich soil is the ideal place to plant the corn seedlings. Ideally, plant the seedlings outdoors once soil temperatures are above 55 to 65° F.

Place the corn seedlings outdoors to harden them off. Hardening seedlings means incrementally exposing indoor-grown seedlings to the cooler temperatures and brighter light outdoors before planting. Put the corn seedlings in a wind-free, bright but shaded place (no direct sun) for a week before you plan to plant them in the permanent garden location in the sun. On the first day of hardening, place them outdoors for one hour, the next day three hours, and so on.

Dig a small planting hole with the hand-held garden trowel. Make it large enough and deep enough to accommodate the corn seedling. You don't want to plant the seedling any deeper than it grew in the peat pot.

Remove the corn seedling carefully from the seedling pot. Invert the plant and gently jostle and slide it out or push the pot base up from the bottom to allow you to grab the soil root ball. You want to keep the soil and roots of the corn seedling intact during the transplanting. Gently grasp or cup the plant by the root ball once it's out of the container to ensure that the root ball remains together.

Place the seedling into the planting hole. Carefully lift out the root ball if you need to make the planting hole slightly larger or shallower to accommodate the seedling's root ball mass. Match the top of the root ball with the top rim of the planting hole.

Pinch the soil in and down around the corn seedling root ball with your fingers spread open. Compact the soft garden soil around the root ball, but don't pack it so firmly that the soil no longer maintains a crumbly texture.

Space additional corn seedlings in the planting row eight to ten inches apart. Additional rows are spaced two to three feet apart to allow you to walk down the corn rows later in the season.

Water the seedlings with a sprinkling can, giving each seedling two to three inches of water. If it's chilly outside, try to wet only the soil, not the leaves. This watering brings soil particles into direct contact with the roots and eliminates air pockets.

SEEDLING DISEASES OF CORN

Soggy soils certainly are favorable for important seed rots and seedling diseases of corn, especially Pythium diseases. However, two things are working in the producers' favour:

1. Pythium species attack stressed corn. Soils in May are generally warm enough that corn is better able to fight off infections than it would be in late March or early April.
2. Common seed-treatment fungicides provide a fair amount of protection against seed and seedling diseases.

It's always a good idea to monitor corn stands for emergence and stand establishment, but I am less worried about widespread seedling problems than I am about leaf diseases. Continued sogginess could eventually result in major delays in planting. Corn crops planted in early to mid-May and beyond are at greater risk from a variety of destructive diseases, especially gray leaf spot, northern leaf blight, and southern rust. We're not at that stage yet, but it is worth being aware of this potential risk.

Disease in Crop

Disease is a condition that can afflict most crops grown through the Farming skill. When a healthy crop ends a growth cycle, there is a chance it may become diseased. While diseased, the crop stops growing and does not advance to the next stage. Crops do not recover from disease on their own. If the disease is not cured, the crop dies at the end of the diseased cycle. Dead crops require use of a spade to dig up their remains before planting another crop in the patch.

Players may treat plants in diseased herb, flower, allotment, hops, belladonna, cactus, and jade vine patches with plant cure to restore the crop to health. Doing so may let the crop advance to the next growth stage normally upon the end of the cycle, although it is possible that it may become diseased again. For diseased trees and bushes, the player may use secateurs on the plant to trim the diseased branch and restore the crop to health.

Alternatively, if a player has access to the Lunar Magic spellbook they may use the Cure Plant spell instead, which is substantially more expensive but may save the player valuable inventory space during a crop run.

Crops grow in real-time, so they may become diseased when a player is offline. In addition, crops that have been cured of disease may become afflicted once again.

Players may purchase plant cure from a Farming shop, but it is usually both more convenient and less expensive to purchase it from the nearest farmer.

REDUCING DISEASE RISK

Treating a farming patch with compost or supercompost before planting a crop reduces the chance of disease during all growth cycles. The general risk of a plant becoming diseased without any treatment remains unknown and may vary depending on the crop and even patch, but supercompost seems to reduce the risk of disease to roughly ten per cent for many types of crops.

If a player forgets to treat a farming patch, the expensive but useful Fertile Soil spell may be used to treat the patch with supercompost both before and after planting a seed or sapling. Remote farm may also be used to view plant status and cure any diseased farming patch, but it must be unlocked from Livid Farm.

While they do not reduce disease risk, when worn an amulet of farming vibrates when a farming patch attuned to it has become diseased. An amulet of nature also alerts a player to disease if worn, and in addition offers the option of being directly teleported to the infected crop. Both amulets may also be rubbed to check whether or not a plant is still healthy.

ELIMINATING DISEASE RISK

A herb that has died from disease during its last growth phase. If the player had timed their crop run or used an amulet of nature, this herb might have survived.

Watering allotment and flower patches with a watering can eliminates the risk of disease occurring at the end of that growth cycle. During the next growth cycle, the plant moves from being watered back to normal and becomes at risk for disease once more, unless it is watered again. Only allotment, flower and hops patches may be watered.

Planting different flowers or a scarecrow provides protection from disease to a variety of crops in allotment patches once the flower is fully grown.

Otherwise, the only way to eliminate disease risk entirely is to pay one of the Group of Advanced Gardener farmers near the farming patch to watch over it and ensure that it grows to completion. Payment must be in the exact form requested. For instance, a farmer does not accept five apples in return of a basket of apples. However, farmers do accept noted payment. Note that farmers require separate payment for each allotment patch.

The belladona, mushroom, and cactus patches do not have farmers available to oversee them. Herb patches cannot be watered, and despite farmers overlooking the allotment patch, they do not accept payment for either the flower or herb patches.

Poison ivy bushes and evil turnip patches are immune from disease. Farmers will not accept payment to watch over a poison ivy bush, and the evil turnip patch does not allow a player to treat or water the patch. The special herb patch received by completing My Arm's Big Adventure is immune from disease, although yields may be increased by treating it with supercompost.

COMPOST: DEFINITION, PROPERTIES AND UTILITIES

Compost is organic matter that has been decomposed and recycled as a fertilizer and soil amendment. Compost is a key ingredient in organic farming. At its most essential, the process of composting requires simply piling up waste outdoors and waiting a year or more. Modern, methodical composting is a multi-step, closely monitored process with measured inputs of water, air and carbon- and nitrogen-rich materials.

The decomposition process is aided by shredding the plant matter, adding water and ensuring proper aeration by regularly turning the mixture. Worms and fungi further break up the material. Aerobic bacteria manage the chemical process by converting the inputs into heat, carbon dioxide and ammonium. The ammonium is further converted by bacteria into plant-nourishing nitrites and nitrates through the process of nitrification.

Compost can be rich in nutrients. It is used in gardens, landscaping, horticulture, and agriculture. The compost itself is beneficial for the land in many ways, including as a soil conditioner, a fertilizer, addition of vital humus or humic acids, and as a natural pesticide for soil. In ecosystems, compost is useful for erosion control, land and stream reclamation, wetland construction, and as landfill cover. Compost can also be used to generate biogas through anaerobic digestion.

Composting as a recognized practice dates to at least the early Roman Empire since Pliny the Elder (AD 23-79). Traditionally, composting was to pile organic materials until the next planting season, at which time the materials would have decayed enough to be ready for use in the soil. The advantage of this method is that little working time or effort is required from the composter and it fits in naturally with agricultural practices in temperate climates. Disadvantages (from the modern perspective) are that space is used for a whole year, some nutrients might be leached due to exposure to rainfall, and disease producing organisms and insects may not be adequately controlled.

Composting was somewhat modernized beginning in the 1920s in Europe as a tool for organic farming. The first industrial station for the transformation of urban organic materials into compost was set up in Wels/ Austria in the year 1921. The early personages most cited for propounding composting within farming are for the German-speaking world Rudolf Steiner, founder of a farming method called biodynamics, and Annie Francé-Harrar, who was appointed on behalf of the government in Mexico and supported the country 1950-1958 to setup a large humus organization in the fight against erosion and soil degradation.

In the English-speaking world it was Sir Albert Howard who worked extensively in India on sustainable practices and Lady Eve Balfour who was a huge proponent of composting. Composting was imported to America by various followers of these early European movements in the form of persons such as J.I. Rodale (founder of Rodale Organic Gardening), E.E. Pfeiffer (who developed scientific practices in biodynamic farming), Paul Keene (founder of Walnut Acres in Pennsylvania), and Scott and Helen Nearing (who inspired the back-to-land movement of the 1960s). Coincidentally, some of these personages met briefly in India—all were quite influential in the U.S. from the 1960s into the 1980s.

There are many modern proponents of rapid composting which attempt to correct some of the perceived problems associated with traditional, slow composting. Many advocate that compost can be made in two to three weeks. Many such short processes involve a few changes to traditional methods, including smaller, more homogenized pieces in the compost, controlling carbon to nitrogen (CN) ratio at 30 to 1 or less, and monitoring the moisture level more carefully.

However, none of these parameters differ significantly from early writings of Howard and Balfour, suggesting that in fact modern composting has not made significant advances over the traditional methods which take a few months to work.

For this reason and others, many modern scientists who deal with carbon transformations are sceptical that there is a "super-charged" way to get nature to make compost rapidly. They also point to the fact that it is the structure of the natural molecules—such as carbohydrates, proteins, and cellulose—that really dictate the rate at which microbial-mediated transformations are possible.

Some cities such as Seattle and San Francisco require food and yard waste to be sorted for composting.

Composting organisms require four equally important things to work effectively:

- Carbon — for energy; the microbial oxidation of carbon produces the heat.
  (*a*) High carbon materials tend to be brown and dry.
- Nitrogen — to grow and reproduce more organisms to oxidize the carbon.
  (*b*) High nitrogen materials tend to be green (or colorful, such as fruits and vegetables) and wet.
- Oxygen — for oxidizing the carbon, the decomposition process.
- Water — in the right amounts to maintain activity without causing anaerobic conditions.

Certain ratios of these materials will provide beneficial bacteria with the nutrients to work at a rate that will heat up the pile. In that process much water will be released as vapour ("steam"), and the oxygen will be quickly depleted, explaining the need to actively manage the pile. The hotter the pile gets, the more often added air and water is necessary; the air/water balance is critical to maintaining high temperatures (135°-160° F) until the materials are broken down. At the same time, too much air or water also slows the process, as does too much carbon (or too little nitrogen).

The most efficient composting occurs with a carbon:nitrogen mix of about thirty to one. Nearly all plant and animal materials have both carbon and nitrogen, but amounts vary widely, with characteristics noted above (dry/wet, brown/green). Fresh grass clippings have an average ratio of about 15 to 1 and dry autumn leaves about 50 to 1 depending on species.

Mixing equal parts by volume approximates the ideal C : N range. Few individual situations will provide the ideal mix of materials at any point in time. Observation of amounts, and consideration of different materials as a pile is built over time, can quickly achieve a workable technique for the individual situation.

Human Urine as Fertilizer

People excrete far more of certain water-soluble plant nutrients (nitrogen, phosphorus, potassium) in urine than in faeces. Human urine can be used directly as fertilizer or it can be put onto compost. Adding a healthy person's urine to compost usually will increase temperatures and therefore increase its ability to destroy pathogens and unwanted seeds. Urine from a person with no obvious symptoms of infection is generally much more sanitary than fresh faeces.

Unlike faeces, urine doesn't attract disease-spreading flies such as house flies or blow flies, and it doesn't contain the most hardy of pathogens, such as parasitic worm eggs. Urine usually does not stink for long, particularly when it is fresh, diluted, or put on sorbents.

Urine is primarily composed of water and urea. Although metabolites of urea are nitrogen fertilizers, it is easy to over-fertilize with urine creating too much ammonia for plants to absorb, acidic conditions, or other phytotoxicity.

Basic Composting Ingredients

On many farms, the basic composting ingredients are manure generated on the farm and bedding. Straw and sawdust are common bedding materials. Non-traditional bedding materials are also used, including newspaper and chopped cardboard. The amount of manure composted on a livestock farm is often determined by cleaning schedules, land availability, and weather conditions. Each type of manure has its own physical, chemical, and biological characteristics.

Cattle and horse manures, when mixed with bedding, possess good qualities for composting. Swine manure, which is very wet and usually not mixed with bedding material, needs to be mixed with straw or similar raw materials. Poultry manure also needs to be blended with carbonaceous materials—preferably those low in nitrogen, such as sawdust or straw.

Micro-organisms

With the proper mixture of water, oxygen, carbon, and nitrogen, micro-organisms are allowed to break down organic matter to produce compost. The composting process is dependant on micro-organisms to break down organic matter into compost. There are many types of microorganisms found in active compost of which the most common are:

- **Bacteria:** The most numerous of all the micro organisms found in compost.
- **Actinomycetes:** Necessary for breaking down paper products such as newspaper, bark, etc.
- **Fungi:** Molds and yeast help break down materials that bacteria cannot, especially lignin in woody material.

- **Protozoa:** Help consume bacteria, fungi and micro organic particulates.
- **Rotifers:** Rotifers help control populations of bacteria and small protozoans.

In addition, earthworms not only ingest partly-composted material, but also continually recreate aeration and drainage tunnels as they move through the compost.

A lack of a healthy microorganism community is the main reason why composting processes are slow in landfills with environmental factors such as lack of oxygen, nutrients or water being the cause of the depleted biological community.

These common items can likely be added to compost with no negative effect:

- Cardboard or clean paper.
- Dried-out egg shells.
- Leaves, yard trimmings.
- Fruits and vegetables.
- Coffee and tea.

Uses

Compost is generally recommended as an additive to soil, or other matrices such as coir and peat, as a tilth improver, supplying humus and nutrients. It provides a rich growing medium, or a porous, absorbent material that holds moisture and soluble minerals, providing the support and nutrients in which plants can flourish, although it is rarely used alone, being primarily mixed with soil, sand, grit, bark chips, vermiculite, perlite, or clay granules to produce loam.

Generally, direct seeding into a compost is not recommended due to the speed with which it may dry and the possible presence of phytotoxins which may inhibit germination, and the possible tie up of nitrogen by incompletely decomposed lignin. It is very common to see blends of 20–30 per cent compost used for transplanting seedlings at cotyledon stage or later.

Destroying Pathogens, Seeds, or Unwanted Plants

Composting can destroy pathogens or unwanted seeds. Unwanted living plants (or weeds) can be discouraged by covering with mulch/compost.

The "microbial pesticides" in compost may include thermophiles and mesophiles, however certain composting detritivores such as black soldier fly larvae and redworms, also reduce many pathogens. Thermophilic (high-temperature) composting is well known to destroy many seeds and nearly all types of pathogens where exceptions may include prions.

However, thermophilic composting requires a fair amount of material, around a cubic meter. Destruction of pathogens would only take place in the high temperature zone in the center and not in the outer fringes—it is therefore a questionable practice if the intent is to kill pathogens.

The sanitizing qualities of (thermophilic) composting are desirable where there is a high likelihood of pathogens, such as with manure. Applications include humanure composting or the deep litter technique.

Types

Bokashi Composting

Bokashi is a method of intensive composting. It can use an aerobic or anaerobic inoculation to produce the compost. Once a starter culture is made, it can be used to extend the culture indefinitely, like yoghurt culture. Since the popular introduction of effective microorganisms (EM), Bokashi is commonly made with only molasses, water, EM, and wheat bran.

In home composting applications, kitchen waste is placed into a container which can be sealed with an air tight lid. These scraps are then inoculated with a Bokashi EM mix. This usually takes the form of a carrier, such as rice hulls, wheat bran or saw dust, that has been inoculated with composting micro-organisms.

The EM are natural lactic acid bacteria, yeast, and phototrophic bacteria that act as a microbe community within the kitchen scraps, fermenting and accelerating breakdown of the organic matter.

The user would place alternating layers of food scraps and Bokashi mix until the container is full. Liquid "compost tea" is drained once or twice a week and can be diluted 1:100 and added to plants as fertilizer, or poured directly down drains to help clean them. Once the container is full, it is left to ferment for an additional two weeks in the container, and then buried under six to eight inches of soil, in ground or in a non-reactive container. After another two weeks buried under soil, the food scraps should be broken down into rich compost.

Compost Tea

Compost tea is a liquid solution or suspension made by steeping compost in water. It is used as both a fertilizer and in attempts to prevent plant diseases. The liquid is applied as a spray to non-edible plant parts such as seedlings, or as a soil-drench (root dip), or as a surface spray to reduce incidence of harmful phytopathogenic fungi in the phyllosphere. Totally green produces the ORCA Green Machine which allows governments, universities and commercial institutions to employ this aerobic method of composting to presorted organic waste.

Hügelkultur

The practice of making raised beds filled with rotting wood. It is in effect creating a Nurse log though covered with dirt. The buried decomposing wood will give off heat, as all compost does, for several years. This effect has been used by Sepp Holzer for one to allow fruit trees to survive at otherwise inhospitable temperatures and altitudes.

How Humanure Prevents Soil Degradation?

"Humanure" is a neologism designating human excrement (faeces and urine) that is recycled via composting for agricultural or other purposes. The term was popularized in a 1994 book by Joseph Jenkins that advocates the use of this organic soil amendment.

Humanure is not traditional sewage that has been processed by waste-treatment facilities, which may include waste from industrial and other sources; rather, it is the combination of faeces and urine with paper and additional carbon material such as sawdust. A humanure system, such as a composting toilet does not require water or electricity, and when properly managed does not smell.

By disposing of faeces and urine through composting, the nutrients contained in them are returned to the soil. This aids in preventing soil degradation. Human faecal matter and urine have high percentages of nitrogen, phosphorus, potassium, carbon, and calcium. It is equal to many fertilizers and manures purchased in garden stores.

Humanure aids in the conservation of fresh water by avoiding the usage of potable water required by the typical flush toilet. It further prevents the pollution of ground water by controlling the faecal matter decomposition before entering the system. When properly managed, there should be no ground contamination from leachate.

As a substitute for a flush water process, it reduces the energy consumption and hence greenhouse gas emissions associated with the transportation and processing of water and waste water.

Humanure may be deemed safe for humans to use on crops if handled in accordance with local health regulations, and composted properly. This means that thermophilic decomposition of the humanure must heat it sufficiently to destroy harmful pathogens, or enough time must have elapsed since fresh material was added that biological activity has killed any pathogens. To be safe for crops, a curing stage is often needed to allow a second mesophilic phase to reduce potential phytotoxins.

Humanure is different from night soil, which is raw human waste spread on crops. While aiding the return of nutrients in faecal matter to the soil, it can carry and spread a vast number of human pathogens. Humanure kills these pathogens both by the extreme heat of the composting and the extended amount of time (1 to 2 years) that it is allowed to decompose.

Vermicompost is the product of composting utilizing various species of worms, usually red wigglers, white worms, and earthworms to create a heterogeneous mixture of decomposing vegetable or food waste (not to include meat, dairy, fats or oils), bedding materials, and vermicast. Vermicast, also known as worm castings, worm humus or worm manure, is the end-product of the breakdown of organic matter by species of earthworm. This type of composting is sometimes suggested as a feasible indoor composting method.

The earthworm species (or composting worms) most often used are Red Wigglers (*Eisenia foetida* or *Eisenia andrei*), though European nightcrawlers (*Eisenia hortensis*) could also be used. Red wigglers are recommended by most vermiculture experts as they have some of the best appetites and breed very quickly. Users refer to European nightcrawlers by a variety of other names, including dendrobaenas, dendras, and Belgian nightcrawlers.

Containing water-soluble nutrients, vermicompost is a nutrient-rich organic fertilizer and soil conditioner. Vermicompost tea has been shown to cause a 173.5 per cent increase in plant growth by mass over plants grown without castings. These results were seen with only 10 per cent addition of castings to produce these results.

ALTERNATIVE TO LAND-FILLING

As concern about landfill space increases, worldwide interest in recycling by means of composting is growing, since composting is a process for converting decomposable organic materials into useful stable products. Industrial scale composting in the form of in-vessel composting, aerated static pile composting, and anaerobic digestion takes place in most western countries now, and in many areas is mandated by law. There are process and product guidelines in Europe that date to the early 1980s (Germany, the Netherlands, Switzerland) and only more recently in the UK and the US.

In both these countries, private trade associations within the industry have established loose standards, some say as a stop-gap measure to discourage independent government agencies from establishing tougher consumer-friendly standards. The USA is the only Western country that does not distinguish sludge-source compost from green-composts, and by default in the USA 50 per cent of states expect composts to comply in some manner with the federal EPA 503 rule promulgated in 1984 for sludge products. Compost is regulated in Canada and Australia as well.

Industrial composting systems are increasingly being installed as a waste management alternative to landfills, along with other advanced waste processing systems. Mechanical sorting of mixed waste streams combined with anaerobic digestion or in-vessel composting, is called mechanical biological treatment, and are increasingly being used in developed countries due to regulations controlling the amount of organic matter allowed in landfills.

Treating biodegradable waste before it enters a landfill reduces global warming from fugitive methane; untreated waste breaks down anaerobically in a landfill, producing landfill gas that contains methane, a potent greenhouse gas.

Large-scale composting systems are used by many urban areas around the world. Co-composting is a technique which combines solid waste with de-watered biosolids, although difficulties controlling inert and plastics contamination from municipal solid waste makes this approach less attractive.

The world's largest MSW co-composter is the Edmonton Composting Facility in Edmonton, Alberta, Canada, which turns 220,000 tonnes of residential solid waste and 22,500 dry tonnes of biosolids per year into 80,000 tonnes of compost. The facility is 38,690 meters^2 (416,500 ft^2), equivalent to four-and-half Canadian football fields, and the operating structure is the largest stainless steel building in North America, the size of 14 NHL rinks.

In 2006, the State of Qatar awarded Keppel Seghers Singapore, a subsidiary of Keppel Corporation to begin construction on a 275,000 tonne/year Anaerobic Digestion and Composting Plant licensed by Kompogas Switzerland. This plant, with fifteen independent anaerobic digestors was be the world's largest composting facility once fully operational in early 2011 and forms part of the Qatar Domestic Solid Waste Management Center, the largest integrated waste management complex in the Middle East.

Sugar Beet
A Hardy Botanical Plant

Sugar beet is a hardy biennial plant that can be grown commercially in a wide variety of temperate climates. During its first growing season, it produces a large i.e. one to two kilogram storage root whose dry mass is 15–20 per cent sucrose by weight. If the plant is not harvested at this time, then during its second growing season, nutrients in the root will be used to produce flowers and seeds and the root will decrease in size. In commercial beet production, the root is harvested after the first growing season.

In most temperate climates, beets are planted in the spring and harvested in the autumn. At the northern end of its range, growing seasons as short as 100 days can produce commercially viable sugarbeet crops. In warmer climates, such as in California's Imperial Valley, sugarbeets are a winter crop, planted in the autumn and harvested in the spring. In recent years, Syngenta has developed the so-called tropical sugar beet. It allows the plant to grow in tropical and subtropical regions. Beets are planted from a small seed; 1 kg of beet seed comprises 100,000 seeds and will plant over a hectare of ground (1 lb will plant about an acre).

Sugar beets are an important cash crop for Michigan farmers and also provides jobs and contributes to the local economy. Sugarbeets are grown mostly in the thumb of Michigan and around Saginaw. Michigan Sugar Company is a grower owned cooperative meaning that the growers own the company. The Michigan Sugar Cooperative has approximately 1250 farmer-members who grow sugarbeets on 175,000 acres of land each year. The sugarbeets are then processed into sugar at factories located in Bay City, Sebewaing, Caro and Croswell.

Sugarbeets are a difficult and expensive crop to grow but can also return more money to the growers than other common crops such as wheat, corn or soybeans. Sugarbeets are planted in the early spring. Farmers prepare the ground for planting by plowing the previous fall and then lightly cultivating the ground (stirring up the dirt) in the spring just before planting. Growers also apply fertilizers before planting to help the sugarbeets grow.

Sugarbeet seeds are small (about the size of a BB) and are planted about one inch deep into the soil. The seeds are spaced about four inches apart in rows. It usually takes a week or two for the sugarbeets to germinate and emerge from the soil.

Young sugarbeet seedlings are called cotyledons (see picture to the right). These cotyledons face many obstacles to their survival. Soil diseases, insects and crusted soil (soil that has hardened) caused by hard rains prevent some seeds from surviving. The seeds are treated with fungicides to help in their battle against soil diseases. If insects such as cutworms which are similar to caterpillars are attacking the young plants, growers can spray an insecticide to kill the insects. Weeds are also a major problem for sugarbeet growers. Many times, there will be more weeds coming up than sugarbeets.

Weeds take away the much needed water and nutrients from the soil and shade small sugarbeets. If not controlled, weeds will choke out (out grow) the sugarbeets. Growers use a combination of herbicides (chemical), cultivation and people (physical labour) to remove the weeds from the sugarbeet rows. The sugarbeet cultivator is a series of sweeps (like little hoes) mounted to a tractor. As the tractor moves through the field, the weeds between the sugarbeet rows are hoed out but the sugarbeets are not damaged.

The weather is very important to sugarbeets. If the soil is too dry, the seeds will not germinate and heavy rains can drown out the sugarbeets. Freezing weather can also kill small seedlings. After planting, the farmer is hoping for some warm weather and soft rains, maybe about one inch of rain per week. Strong winds can cause the sugarbeets to twist and turn and along with blowing soil the sugarbeets can be cut in half by the wind. Sugarbeet growers have learned different ways to help combat the weather, but occasionally the crop can be lost or severely damaged.

After sugarbeets get a little bigger approximately 6 to 12 inches tall and roots look like small carrots they are able to withstand harsh weather and insect problems. By mid-summer, sugarbeets will have leaves that are one to two feet tall and will begin storing sugar in their roots. Several diseases attack sugarbeets throughout the summer and the farmer may need to spray fungicides to fight off the diseases.

The root of the sugarbeet plant is harvested. This harvest usually begins about October 1. First, farmers will defoliate the beets take off the leaves with a machine called a sugarbeet topper or defoliator. The harvester follows closely behind the topper, pops the beets out of the ground, and moves them up into a bin. Dirt is removed from the sugarbeets by shaking the beets using rollers on the way to the bin. The beets are then loaded into trucks, taken to the sugar factory, and put in a very large pile. The piles are 20 feet high, 200 feet wide and over 1,000 feet long.

In the sugar factory, sugarbeets are turned into pure sugar. First, the beets are washed and fed into a machine that slices the beets into long, small pieces called cossettes. The cossettes are dumped into a very large tank filled with hot water called a diffuser. As the cossettes move through the diffuser, the sugar comes out of the cossettes and goes into solution (sugar water). The sugar water is pumped through a series of tanks and filters that then remove the water and the impurities leaving only pure white sugar. The sugar factory calls this processing period their "campaign". It takes the sugar factories about five months to process the 3.7 million tons of sugarbeets into 970 million pounds of pure, white sugar.

Root Knot Nematodes cause distinct knots or galls on the roots of sugar beets. These are generally more numerous on the lighter type soils than on the heavier ones, but may be a serious problem wherever sugar beets are grown. They also are controlled by soil fumigation or by crop rotation, but since no cyst is formed shorter rotation periods can be used. Since several species of root knot nematodes attack sugar beets and these differ in their host relationships, no definite rotation system can be specified. Rotation details must be worked out on a local basis.

Among the minor root diseases is verticillium wilt, caused by *Verticillium alboatrum*. It occurs to a limited extent in Colorado and Nebraska. It is serious in the Yakima Valley of Washington. The foliage becomes yellow and dries. Roots show only slight evidence of small, blackened fibrils here and there in the flesh. The lateral root through which the fungus entered the plant usually can be detected because it becomes black and water-soaked. Probably crop rotations with several years between sugar beet crops would reduce the incidence of the disease.

Crown gall, caused by *Agrobacterium tumefaciens*, is an overgrowth that usually takes the form of a smooth gall or knot on the shoulder or central part of the beet root. It is caused by the same bacterial organism that attacks fruit trees and other plants. Occasional affected plants have been found in nearly all sugar beet districts. The overgrowth excites attention because frequently the gall is as large as the beet root itself. No control measures are necessary as the disease is limited on sugar beets.

Texas root rot, caused by *Phymatotrichum omnivorum*, attacks sugar beets in New Mexico and Arizona, on soil in which Texas root rot, well known as a cotton disease, occurs. The tissue of an affected plant is rotted completely. The fungus produces a thin, feltlike coating of hyaline or yellowing mycelium on the surface of the root. It advances on the root surface as a whitish or yellow fan-shaped growth. Sugar beets are not grown for sugar production to any extent in areas where Texas root rot is common. No loss in the seed-producing areas of Arizona or New Mexico has been reported.

Storage Rots are caused by Phoma betae, *Botrytis cinerea*, *Rhizopus nigricans*, *Rhizoctonia solani*, several species of *Fusarium*, and other fungi. To prevent cold weather from interfering with harvesting, factories in nearly all the beet-growing districts must accept deliveries of sugar beet roots in excess of their capacity for prompt processing so huge tonnages of roots are piled at the factories and their receiving stations.

The roots stored in the huge piles are alive; like all living things, they respire. Respiration involves the oxidation of the sucrose in the root. Temperature influences the rate of respiration;therefore, if the storage piles are kept cold, the loss of sugar from respiration is at a minimum. Because respiration produces heat, if a storage pile contains layers of dirt and masses of leaves and trash, the dissipation of heat by air currents may not take place and a chain of conditions is set-up that leads to the generation of heat in pockets of the pile. First, respiration is accelerated; finally, roots become subject to fungus rots, and the rotting organisms feeding on the rich sugar stores of the roots produce excessive heating in the piles. These manifest themselves as "hot spots". In some years, the losses from storage rots are staggering.

Experiments by Myron Stout and Charles A. Fort a few years ago started active prevention of sugar losses from stored sugar beets by cooling the roots by forced ventilation of the piles with chill night air. Engineers at beet sugar factories promptly capitalized on this finding, and today piles of sugar beets at the factories very commonly have ventilating ducts laid through them. Thermostats are located at critical points to control the operation of blowers. Cold air is forced through the piles by blowers as the temperatures within the piles may require.

Sugar losses still occur with roots in storage piles, and after a period in storage such losses may sharply rise. Studies to reduce losses further are continuing. Beets grown with abundant nutrients, particularly phosphorus and nitrogen, and with adequate soil moisture, are resistant to storage rots, particularly to *Phoma betae*.

Drying in the field before piling has bad effects on keeping qualities. High temperatures have been shown to break down the resistance of roots to the attack of organisms that ordinarily are saprophytes unable to attack a live root. Thus, a period of 60° F is enough to change the character of the sugar beet root so that the bread mold, Rhizopus nigricans, can rot the tissue.

Roots have been exposed to invasion by *Phoma betae* and *Botrytis cinerea*, nerea, chief rotters of roots in storage, and the most resistant roots selected. Progenies from such selections keep better than parents. Sugar beets with good keeping quality may be bred, since apparently this is governed by the genetic make-up of the sugar beet.

Beet Mosaic occurs in Colorado, Nebraska, Utah, Idaho, Oregon, California, and other Western States. This virus disease produces mottling of the young leaves of sugar beet. Sometimes veinlet clearing develops on the youngest leaves of an affected plant. The green peach aphid (*Myzus persicae*) and other aphids transmit the virus from plant to plant.

The disease is apparently limited to the sugar beet, red garden beet, chard, and mangel-wurzels. Spinach and other plants have been artificially inoculated.

Other than in California, mosaic is chiefly to be found close to infected commercial seed fields or near breeding stations where mosaic-affected roots are carried over winter for transplanting in spring. Ordinarily it is not prevalent beyond the flight zones of aphids usually a matter of a few miles. In California, mosaic is very common. Since sugar beet crops overlap from year to year and seed crops of both sugar beet and red garden beet are grown, there is no break in the cycle of development.

Furthermore, the aphid vectors are abundant and have year-round activity. The absence of mosaic in the more eastern beet-growing sections, such as Michigan, Ohio, and Minnesota, is not understood. It is probable that wherever the virus has been introduced, a cycle of development has been broken because affected plants have not been overwintered.

Any damage that sugar beet mosaic may do to sugar beets grown for sugar has not been appraised. It is known that plants affected with mosaic are significantly poorer than healthy plants as seed producers. As yet no control measures are employed against sugar beet mosaic, or its insect vectors.

Savoy, which is a virus disease that is transmitted by the lacewing bug, *Piesma cinerea*, curls and distorts the leaves and dwarfs the root of sugar beet. The disease also affects red garden beet, chard, and mangel-wurzel, but is not known on other hosts. Usually the disease appears as a plant here and there in the field, but 10 to 15 per cent Savoy has been found in fields bordering wood lots or weedy areas where the insect could overwinter. The disease occurs from Maryland and Virginia westward through Wyoming and Montana, but it has not been found in sugar beets west of the Rocky Mountains although the insect vector occurs throughout the United States.

The most definite symptom of Savoy is the swelling and thickening of the veins. Their growth is reduced and they show up as prominent network on the under side of the leaves. The leaves curl and roll downward. The tissue between the veins bulges out; the whole leaf becomes whiplike and distorted. The roots show darkened vascular rings, the flesh between becoming glassy white. Affected plants make very limited growth, and the roots show much reduced sugar storage.

Ordinarily the disease is minor in its effects, the lessened growth being compensated by greater growth of the neighboring plants. No direct control measures are employed against the disease.

Virus Yellows, long known as the most serious disease attacking sugar beets in Europe, was found in 1951 in Michigan, Colorado, Utah, Oregon, and California. It is probably widespread in the United States and may have been here for some time but overlooked. This virus is spread by aphid vectors, of which the green peach aphid, Myzus persicae, is most important. Only the older leaves show the disease symptoms.

They turn a greenish yellow, particularly at their tips. The veins stay greener than the interveinal tissue. The leaf blades become thick and brittle. Apparently the disease does its damage to the sugar beet plants by interfering with the movement to the root of the food elaborated in the leaves. If a plant is attacked early, its root growth is checked and storage of sugar is strongly reduced. With early attack, sugar production may be cut from 40 to 50 per cent. If the attack occurs in August, damage may be much less.

Totally infected fields were found in California in 1951 and 1952. Instead of a normal green color, the fields were canary yellow. The condition has been known for several years in California as "Salinas yellows," but now is identified as virus yellows. Because infection was total, there was no measuring stick of healthy fields for determining effects of the disease. In 1952, the disease was prevalent in Colorado, where it appeared in late August. Early records indicate the disease probably occurred in Colorado as far back as 1940.

Studies in California have shown that the disease may strikingly reduce root weight, and cause strong declines in sucrose percentage. In light of present knowledge, virus yellows may rank with curly top as a serious menace.

Control measures now in use in Europe are not likely to be of particular applicability in the United States. There is some evidence that breeding for resistance to virus yellows may be fruitful, but no resistant varieties have as yet been developed.

SUGARBEET PRODUCTION

Until the latter half of the last century, sugarbeet production was highly labor-intensive, as weed control was managed by densely planting the crop, which then had to be manually thinned two or three times with a hoe during the growing season.

Harvesting also required many workers. Although the roots could be lifted by a plough-like device which could be pulled by a horse team, the rest of the preparation was by hand. One laborer grabbed the beets by their leaves, knocked them together to shake free loose soil, and then laid them in a row, root to one side, greens to the other. A second worker equipped with a beet hook a short-handled tool between a billhook and a sickle followed behind, and would lift the beet and swiftly chop the crown and leaves from the root with a single action. Working this way, he would leave a row of beets that could be forked into the back of a cart.

Sugar beet, a cultivated plant of Beta vulgaris, is a plant whose tuber contains a high concentration of sucrose. It is grown commercially for sugar production. Sugar beets and other B. vulgaris cultivars such as beetroot and chard share a common wild ancestor, the sea beet (Beta vulgaris maritima.)

The European Union, the United States, and Russia are the world's three largest sugar beet producers, although only the European Union and Ukraine are significant exporters of sugar from beets. The U.S. harvested 1,004,600 acres (4,065 km^2) of sugarbeets in 2008. Beet sugar accounts for 30–35% of the world's sugar production.

Today, mechanical sowing, herbicide application for weed control and mechanical harvesting have displaced this reliance on farm workers. Harvesting is now entirely mechanical.

A root beater uses a series of blades to chop the leaf and crown (which is high in non-sugar impurities) from the root. The beet harvester lifts the root, and removes excess soil from the root in a single pass over the field. A modern harvester is typically able to cover six rows at the same time. The beets are dumped into trucks as the harvester rolls down the field, and then delivered to the factory. The conveyor then removes more soil.

If the beets are to be left for later delivery, they are formed into clamps. Straw bales are used to shield the beets from the weather. Provided the clamp is well built with the right amount of ventilation, the beets do not significantly deteriorate. Beets that freeze and then defrost produce complex carbohydrates that cause severe production problems in the factory. In the UK, loads may be hand examined at the factory gate before being accepted.

In the US, the fall harvest begins with the first hard frost, which arrests photosynthesis and the further growth of the root. Depending on the local climate, it may be carried out over the course of a few weeks or be prolonged throughout the winter months. The harvest and processing of the beet is referred to as "the campaign", reflecting the organization required to deliver the crop at a steady rate to processing factories that run 24 hours a day for the duration of the harvest and processing (for the UK the campaign lasts approximately five months).

In the Netherlands this period is known as *"de bieten-campagne"*, a time to be careful when driving on local roads in the area while the beets are being grown. The reason for this is because the naturally high clay content of the soil tends to cause slippery roads when soil falls from the trailers during transport.

Sebewaing in Michigan is known (to Americans) as the sugar beet capital of the world. Sebewaing lies in the Thumb region of Michigan; both the region and state are major sugar beet producers. Sebewaing is home to one of three Michigan Sugar Company factories. The town sponsors an annual "Michigan Sugar Festival".

Arthur Stayner, because of his energetic work in experimenting with the growing of sugar beets in alkali soils, is regarded as the "father and founder of the movement that made the manufacture of sugar in Utah a success."

After they are harvested, beets are hauled to a factory. In the UK, beets are transported by a hauler, or by a tractor and a trailer by local farmers. Railways and boats are no longer used. Some beets were carried by rail in the Republic of Ireland, until the shutdown of sugar beet production in 2006 after the end of the government subsidies.

Each load is weighed and sampled before it gets tipped onto the reception area, typically a "flat pad" of concrete, where it is moved into large heaps. The beet sample is checked for

- soil tare - the amount of non beet delivered
- crown tare - the amount of low sugar beet delivered
- sugar content ("pol") - amount of sucrose in the crop
- nitrogen content - for recommending future fertilizer use to the farmer.

From these elements, the actual sugar content of the load is calculated and the grower's payment determined. The beet is moved from the heaps into a central channel or gulley, where it is washed towards the processing plant. After reception at the processing plant, the beet roots are washed, mechanically sliced into thin strips called cossettes, and passed to a machine called a diffuser to extract the sugar content into a water solution.

Diffusers are long vessels of many metres in which the beet slices go in one direction while hot water goes in the opposite direction. The movement may either be caused by a rotating screw or the whole rotating unit, and the water and cossettes move through internal chambers. There are three common designs of diffuser: the horizontal rotating 'RT' (Raffinerie Tirlemontoise, manufacturer), inclined screw 'DDS' (De Danske Sukkerfabrikker), or vertical screw "Tower". Modern tower extraction plants have a processing capacity of up to 17,000 metric tons per day.

A less common design uses a moving belt of cossettes, with water pumped onto the top of the belt and poured through. In all cases the flow rates of cossettes and water are in the ratio one to two. Typically cossettes take about one and half hour to pass through the diffuser, the water only 45 minutes. These are all countercurrent exchange methods that extract more sugar from the cossettes using less water than if they merely sat in a hot water tank. The liquid exiting the diffuser is called raw juice. The colour of raw juice varies from black to a dark red depending on the amount of oxidation, which is itself dependent on diffuser design.

The used cossettes, or pulp, exit the diffuser at about 95 per cent moisture but low sucrose content. Using screw presses, the wet pulp is then pressed down to 75 per cent moisture. This recovers additional sucrose in the liquid pressed out of the pulp, and reduces the energy needed to dry the pulp. The pressed pulp is dried and sold as animal feed, while the liquid pressed out of the pulp is combined with the raw juice, or more often introduced into the diffuser at the appropriate point in the countercurrent process. The final byproduct, Vinasse, is used as fertilizer or growth substrate for yeast cultures.

During diffusion, there is a degree of breakdown of the sucrose into invert sugars. These can undergo further breakdown into acids. These breakdown products are not only losses of sucrose but also have knock-on effects reducing the final output of processed sugar from the factory. To limit (thermophilic) bacterial action, the feed water may be dosed with formaldehyde and control of the feed water pH is also practiced. There have been attempts at operating diffusion under alkaline conditions, but the process has proven problematic. The improved sucrose extraction in the diffuser is offset by processing problems in the next stages.

Carbonatation

It is a procedure which removes impurities from raw juice before it undergoes crystallization. First, the juice is mixed with hot milk of lime a suspension of calcium hydroxide in water. This treatment precipitates a number of impurities, including multivalent anions such as sulfate, phosphate, citrate and oxalate, which precipitate as their calcium salts and large organic molecules such as proteins, saponins and pectins, which aggregate in the presence of multivalent cations.

In addition, the alkaline conditions convert the simple sugars, glucose and fructose, along with the amino acid glutamine, to chemically stable carboxylic acids. Left untreated, these sugars and amines would eventually frustrate crystallization of the sucrose.

Next, carbon dioxide is bubbled through the alkaline sugar solution, precipitating the lime as calcium carbonate (chalk). The chalk particles entrap some impurities and absorb others. A recycling process builds up the size of chalk particles and a natural flocculation occurs where the heavy particles settle out in tanks (clarifiers). A final addition of more carbon dioxide precipitates more calcium from solution; this is filtered off, leaving a cleaner, golden light-brown sugar solution called thin juice.

Before entering the next stage, the thin juice may receive soda ash to modify the pH and sulphitation with a sulfur-based compound to reduce colour formation due to decomposition of monosaccharides under heat.

Evaporation

The thin juice is concentrated via multiple-effect evaporation to make a thick juice, roughly 60% sucrose by weight and similar in appearance to pancake syrup. Thick juice can be stored in tanks for later processing, reducing load on the crystallization plant.

Crystallization

Thick juice is fed to the crystallizers. Recycled sugar is dissolved into it, and the resulting syrup is called mother liquor. The liquor is concentrated further by boiling under a vacuum in large vessels (the so-called vacuum pans) and seeded with fine sugar crystals. These crystals grow as sugar from the mother liquor forms around them. The resulting sugar crystal and syrup mix is called a *massecuite*, from "cooked mass" in French.

The *massecuite* is passed to a centrifuge where the liquid is removed from the sugar crystals. The remaining syrup is rinsed off with water and the crystals are dried in a granulator using warm air.

The remaining syrup is fed to another crystallizer from which a second batch of sugar is produced. This sugar ("raw") is of lower quality with a lot of color and impurities and is the main source of the sugar that is dissolved again into the mother liquor. The syrup from the raw is also sent to a crystalliser.

From this, a very low-quality sugar crystal is produced (known in some systems as "AP sugar") that is also redissolved. The syrup separated is molasses, which still contains sugar but contains too much impurity to undergo further processing economically.

Actual procedure may vary from the above description, with different recycling and crystallisation processes.

Other Uses

Beverages

In a number of countries, most notably the Czech Republic, sugar from sugar beet is used to make a type of rum which is now known as tuzemak. On the Åland Islands, a similar drink is made under the brand name Kobba Libre. In some European countries, especially in the Czech Republic and Germany, sugar beet is also used to make rectified spirit and vodka.

Sugar Beet Syrup

An unrefined sugary syrup can be produced directly from sugar beet. This thick, dark syrup is produced by cooking shredded sugar beet for several hours, then pressing the resulting sugar beet mash and concentrating the juice produced until it has the consistency similar to that of honey. No other ingredients are used.

In Germany, particularly the Rhineland area, this sugar beet syrup (called Zuckerrüben-Sirup in German) is used as a spread for sandwiches, as well as for sweetening sauces, cakes and desserts.

Commercially, if the syrup has a Dextrose Equivalency above 30 DE, the product has to be hydrolyzed and converted to a high-fructose syrup, much like high-fructose corn syrup, or iso-glucose syrup in the EU.

In Saint John, New Brunswick, sugar beet molasses is used as a de-icing product on the Harbour Bridge. The molasses has a lower melting point (-34 Celsius) than road salt and reduces corrosiveness.

Betaine

Betaine can be isolated from the by-products of sugar beet processing. Production is chiefly through chromatagraphic separation, using techniques such as the "simulated moving bed".

Uridine

Uridine can be isolated from sugar beet. Uridine in combination with omega-3 fatty acids has been shown to alleviate depression in rats.

Alternative Fuel

There are plans by BP and Associated British Foods to use agricultural surpluses of sugar beet to produce biobutanol in East Anglia in the United Kingdom.

The feedstock-to-yield ratio for sugarbeet is 56 : 9. Therefore it takes 6.22 kg of Sugarbeet to produce 1 kg of ethanol (approximately 1.27L at room temperature).

A large root vegetable in 4000-year-old Egyptian temple artwork may be a beet. Although beets have been grown as vegetables and for fodder since antiquity, their use as a sugar crop is relatively recent. As early as in 1590, the French botanist Olivier de Serres extracted a sweet syrup from beetroot, but the practice was not widely used. The Prussian chemist Andreas Sigismund Marggraf used alcohol to extract sugar from beets (and carrots) in 1747, but the methods did not lend themselves to industrial scale production.

Marggraf's former pupil and successor Franz Karl Achard began selectively breeding sugar beet from the White Silesian fodder beet in 1784. By the beginning of the 19th century, his beet was approximately five to six per cent sucrose by (dry) weight, compared to around 20 per cent in modern varieties. Under the patronage of Frederick William III of Prussia, he opened the world's first beet sugar factory in 1801, at Cunern in Silesia.

The beet sugar industry in Europe rapidly developed after the Napoleonic Wars. In 1807, the British began a blockade of France, which prevented the import of sugarcane from the Caribbean. Partly in response, in 1812 Frenchman Benjamin Delessert devised a process of sugar extraction suitable for industrial application. In 1813, Napoleon instituted a retaliatory embargo. By the end of the wars, over 300 sugar beet mills operated in France and central Europe.

Sugar beet was not grown on a large scale in the United Kingdom until the mid-1920s when 17 processing factories were built, following war-time shortages of imported sugar cane. One factory had, however, been built by the Dutch at Cantley in Norfolk in 1912. Sugar beet seed from France was listed in the annual catalogues of Gartons Agricultural Plant Breeders from that firm's inception in 1898 until the first of their own varieties was introduced in 1909.

The first sugar beet mill in the U.S. opened in 1838, and the first commercially successful mill was established by E.H. Dyer in 1879.

An injunction in the base Center for Food Safety v. USDA in September 2010 prevented farmers from planting Roundup Ready sugar beets across the United States until a remedial environmental impact report could be filed, prompting some fear of a sugar shortage.

AGRICULTURE

Sugar beet is an important part of a rotating crop cycle. Sugar beet plants are susceptible to rhizomania ("root madness") which turns the bulbous tap root into many small roots making the crop economically unprocessable. Strict controls are enforced in European countries to prevent the spread, but it is already endemic in some areas. It is also susceptible to the beet leaf curl virus which causes crinkling and stunting of the leaves.

Continual research looks for varieties with resistance as well as increased sugar yield. Sugar beet breeding research in the United States is most prominently conducted at various USDA Agricultural Research Stations, including one in Fort Collins, Colorado, headed by Linda Hanson and Leonard Panella; one in Fargo, North Dakota, headed by John Wieland; and one at Michigan State University in East Lansing, Michigan, headed by J. Mitchell McGrath.

Other economically important members of the Cheno-podioideae subfamily:

- Beetroot
- Chard
- Mangelwurzel or Fodder Beet

GENETIC MODIFICATION

In the United States, genetically modified sugar beet, engineered for resistance to glyphosate, a herbicide marketed as Roundup, was developed by Monsanto. Glyphosate controls weeds by interfering with the 5-enolypyruvylshikimate-3-phosphate (EPSP) synthase enzyme, which is involved in the production of amino acids. These amino acids, tryptophan, tyrosine and phenylalanine, are synthesized in plants and bacteria, not humans or animals. Glyphosate-resistant sugar beet contains a biosynthetic gene that protects it from the effects of glyphosate when it is applied to the crop as a means to control weeds. In 2005, the United States Department of Agriculture-Animal and Plant Health Inspection Service (USDA-APHIS) deregulated glyphosate-resistant sugar beet after it conducted an Environmental Assessment and determined glyphosate-resistant sugar beet were highly unlikely to become a plant pest.

Nutritional Value

Sugar from glyphosate-resistant sugar beet has been approved for human and animal consumption in the European Union and the United States. Studies have concluded that sugar from glyphosate-resistant sugar beet has the same nutritional value as sugar from conventional sugar beet not genetically modified or non-GMO. Potential weed resistance and scientific evidence of super weeds has hindered public acceptance of glyphosate-resistant sugar beet.

Role of Glyphosate-Resistant Sugar Beet in the United States

Glyphosate-resistant sugar beet plays an important role in the United States' sugar industry. The United States imports 10 per cent of its sugar from other countries, while the remaining 90 per cent is extracted from domestically grown sugar beet and sugarcane.

Of the domestically grown sugar crops, half of the extracted sugar is derived from sugar beet, and the other half is from sugarcane. After deregulation in 2005, glyphosate-resistant sugar beet was extensively adopted in the United States. By the 2010, growing season, 95 per cent of sugar beet acres were planted with glyphosate-resistant sugar beet seed.

Weed Control

The ability to effectively and efficiently control weeds in glyphosate-resistant sugar beet is one of the many reasons why glyphosate-resistant sugar beet has been widely adopted in the United States. Elimination of weeds is important in sugar beet fields because they compete with the crop for water, nutrients and light. Weeds may be chemically controlled using glyphosate (Roundup) without harming the crop. After planting sugar beet seed, weeds emerge in fields and growers apply glyphosate to control them. Glyphosate is commonly used in field crops because it controls a broad spectrum of weed species and has a low toxicity.

Conventional

Prior to glyphosate, growers used other herbicides to control weeds in conventional sugar beet fields. While these chemicals are still available in small quantities, they are not as effective as glyphosate and require stricter application procedures. They also tend to injure the sugar beet crop.

Since herbicide options are limited in conventional sugar beet fields, growers rely on different methods to control their weeds. One method to reduce weed populations is mechanical control. Mechanical control uses tillage equipment to move soil and disturb weeds. Tillage equipment is necessary in both glyphosate-resistant and conventional sugar beet fields, but it is used more frequently in conventional systems. This may be problematic because greater use of tillage equipment directly correlates to higher input production costs as more fuel is required to run the equipment.

In addition to greater use of tillage equipment in conventional sugar beet fields, hand labor is another useful approach to control weeds. Each year, thousands of migrant workers travel around the United States to work in agricultural fields, including sugar beet fields. The widespread adoption of glyphosate-resistant sugar beet however has decreased the demand for migrant workers. Unlike conventional sugar beet, there is greater weed control in glyphosate-resistant sugar beet fields and migrant workers are no longer needed.

Higher's Yield

Glyphosate-resistant sugar beet allows growers to achieve higher yields and recoverable white sucrose than conventional sugar beet. Higher yields are achieved from greater weed control in glyphosate-resistant sugar beet field.

Weed Resistance

Many weeds in the United States and worldwide are resistant to glyphosate. Resistance develops when growers use the same herbicide, or mode of action, every year to control their weeds. Applying different herbicide modes of action reduces the risk of resistance.

The introduction of glyphosate-resistant sugar beet may contribute to the growing number of glyphosate-resistant weeds because sugar beet may be rotated with other glyphosate-resistant crops, such as soybean. If using all glyphosate-resistant crops, growers may control their weeds every year solely using glyphosate—a weed control strategy that is not recommended because it increases the likelihood of resistance.

Monsanto has developed a programme to encourage growers to use different herbicide modes of action to control their weeds in all cropping systems. Growers receive financial support when purchasing multiple herbicides.

Preventing Glyphosate-Resistant Sugar Beet

On January 23, 2008 the Center for Food Safety, the Sierra Club, and the Organic Seed Alliance and High Mowing Seeds filed a lawsuit against USDA-APHIS regarding their decision to deregulate glyphosate-resistant sugar beet in 2005. The organizations expressed concerns regarding glyphosate-resistant sugar beets' ability to potentially cross pollinate with conventional sugar beet.

On September 21, 2009 U.S. District Judge Jeffrey S. White, U.S. District Court for the Northern District of California, ruled that USDA-APHIS had violated Federal law in deregulating glyphosate-resistant sugar beet without adequately evaluating the environmental and socio-economic impacts of allowing commercial production.. The USDA estimated a sugar shortage would cost consumers $2.972 billion in 2011.

On August 13, 2010 Judge White revoked the deregulation of glyphosate-resistant sugar beet and declared it unlawful for growers to plant glyphosate-resistant sugar beet in the spring of 2011. As a result of this ruling, growers were permitted to harvest and process their crop at the end of the 2010 growing season, yet a ban on new plantings was enacted. After the ruling, glyphosate-resistant sugar beet could not be planted until USDA-APHIS filed an Environmental Impact Statement.

The purpose of an Environmental Impact Statement is to determine if environmental issues have negative effects on humans and the environment, and it may take two to three years to complete the study. After the Environmental Impact Statement is completed, USDA-APHIS may petition to deregulate glyphosate-resistant sugar beet.

After Judge White's ruling, USDA-APHIS prepared an Environmental Assessment seeking partial deregulation of glyphosate-resistant sugar beet. The Assessment was filed based on a request received from Monsanto and KWS SSAT AG, a German seed company. Both companies, as well as the sugar beet industry employees and growers, believed a sugar shortage would occur if glyphosate-resistant sugar beet could not be planted. As a response to this concern, USDA-APHIS developed three options in the Environmental Assessment to address the concerns of environmentalists, as well as those raised by the industry.

The first option was to not plant glyphosate-resistant sugar beet until the Environmental Impact Statement was completed. The second option was to allow growers to plant glyphosate-resistant sugar beet if they obtained a USDA-APHIS permit and followed specific mandates. Under the third and final option, glyphosate-resistant sugar beet would be partially deregulated but monitored by Monsanto and KWS SSAT AG. USDA-APHIS preferred the second option. They placed the Environmental Assessment in the Federal Register on November 4, 2010 and received public comment for thirty days.

On February 4, 2011, the USDA-APHIS announced glyphosate-resistant sugar beet had been partially deregulated and growers would be allowed to plant seed from spring 2011 until an Environmental Impact Statement is completed. USDA-APHIS developed requirements that growers must follow if handling glyphosate-resistant sugar beet and will monitor growers throughout the partial deregulation period.

The requirements are classified into categories which include planting glyphosate-resistant sugar beet for seed production, planting for sugar production, and transporting sugar beet across state lines. Failure to follow the requirements set by USDA-APHIS may result in civil or criminal charges and destruction of the crop. The lawsuit is an ongoing case and changes are expected to continue until the environmental impact statement is complete.

Coffee Plant Disease

It has been commonly said that coffee (*Coffea arabica*) is a tree practically free from disease. Actually, the coffee plant is subject to more than 40 diseases ailments due to lack of minor elements, virus troubles, mild bacterial infections of roots and fruits, and attacks by fungi and parasitic flowering plants. A century of effort has been expended on agronomic and horticultural problems in coffee, but only in the past fifty years has intensive work been done on its diseases.

In 1952, the Office of Foreign Agricultural Relations (now the Foreign Agricultural Service) of the Department of Agriculture sent a mission to study coffee diseases in all parts of the world. The mission was sponsored by the Point IV programme and financed by the Institute of Inter-American Affairs. Information gathered on the trip has been incorporated into this chapter, which is based primarily on study and experience in Latin America.

Coffee Rust, also called the oriental leaf disease, is by all odds the most serious disease of coffee. It does not occur in the Western Hemisphere, maybe just by pure luck. There are two species of rust: The classic Hemileia vastatrix, which is so destructive and is found in most of the coffee regions of Africa, the Near East, India, Asia, and the Pacific Islands, and *H. coffeicola*, an equally dangerous rust but still confined to the Cameroons of West Africa and the nearby island of Sao Tome. This discussion deals with the first species.

Ceylon, once one of the world's greatest coffee-producing countries, has had to become an exporter of tea when its coffee crops failed because of rust. The disease was first discovered in Ceylon in 1867. Between 1879 and 1893, after it had become well established, exports of coffee dropped to less than seven per cent of former shipments. In the Philippines in 1881 rust cut the harvest 35 per cent. In Java, too, rust practically wiped out the coffee plantations, and the planters turned to hevea rubber as a substitute crop.

The first symptoms are small, yellowish, translucent, oily spots on the leaves. They expand into rather large, round spots and early show a powdery coating of spores on the under surface. As the spores mature, the spots gradually turn bright orange to red. With age the lesions become brown and surrounded with a yellow rusted band. Defoliation occurs to such an extent that many trees retain only two or three pairs of leaves on their branches where they might ordinarily have 15 or 20. Such affected trees are stunted, cannot produce, and usually die after a few years.

The disease was not present in 1953 in the western Hemisphere. It was brought to Puerto Rico in 1903 but prompt and drastic action by O. W. Barrett, the horticulturist there who also dealt with pathology, destroyed all diseased material. He saved untold wealth for the coffee industry in the American Tropics and for centers of world trade.

In some eastern countries, notably the French Cameroon, Kenya, and Tanganyika in Africa, and in the states of Mysore and Coorg and in the Nilgiri Hills of southern India, growers control the rust by two or three annual spray applications of bordeaux mixture. The sprays are put on just before the heavy monsoon rains begin and again in the short dry spell that intervenes before the light monsoon rains fall. Sometimes a third spray is used after the light rains end. In countries that have extremely dry seasons, few rust spores are produced in these periods. Likewise little new leaf surface is developed by the coffee trees. When rains begin, both the parasite and the coffee take on new life, but by well-timed sprays the planters plan to keep about seventy per cent of their coffee foliage free from rust infections.

Where the seasons are not so well defined, such as in Ceylon, Java, Malaya, and the Philippines, weekly or monthly sprayings are needed to control rust. They increase tremendously the cost of growing coffee. Some plantations in some of those countries have been moved to high altitudes, where cool temperatures reduce the inherent producing capacity of the coffee tree but do permit it to grow with less trouble from the rust.

Spores of the rust are long-lived, withstand drying and other vicissitudes, and may be easily transported on live plants or as invisible dust from one country to another. Quarantines have been instituted, and many research workers in the western Tropics have repeated warnings of the danger. All varieties of coffee grown commercially in the Americas are highly susceptible to Hemileia. Increasing transportation between East and West by air as well as by sea multiply the hazards of reintroducing the disease and establishing it this time on western shores.

For more than a half century it has been known that highly tolerant and rust-resistant types of coffee exist. Those better strains, one after another, have been brought to afflicted areas in the Orient. There, at first, they were grown with success, only to succumb later to the rust. Beginning some thirty years ago intensive study was devoted to the phenomenon in India. It was learned that the rust, like others, had biologic races, which attacked new coffee varieties that had been selected for their resistance to the old populations of rust. Moreover, the races were probably the result of mutations, as no one has ever been able to discover an alternate host relationship, which ordinarily is fruitful in producing new races of rust.

Coffee breeders have been able to secure trees with enough resistance in them to be in time the basis for developing improved and acceptable coffee types that will grow well in the presence of rust. Through the work of the mission that studied the rust in the astern Hemisphere, seeds from all the rust-resistant coffees, and many more, have been obtained for growing in the Americas. After careful disinfection and other prophylactic measures to assure freedom from all diseases and insects, these new coffees are now growing in the Western Hemisphere. They are insurance against the time that the rust comes to this part of the world if it does.

The American Leaf Spot is recognized as the most serious disease of coffee in the Occident. It was discovered and studied by N. Saenz in Colombia in 1876. He sent herbarium species from Colombia and Costa Rica to Europe for identification. The causal fungus, Mycena citricolor (Omphalia flavida), is an inhabitant of wet mountains and woodlands and has a phenomenally wide range of wild hosts, from which it has spread to coffee. Its attack has been particularly severe because coffee culture has been concentrated in cool, moist mountain regions. It may cause losses of 75 per cent or more of the crop in some districts. In Costa Rica it takes an annual toll of about 20 per cent of the crop: It occurs in all leading coffee countries of the Americas.

The first symptom is a small, dark area on a leaf. In the center of the spot is a yellow infection body. The tiny lesion grows into a round, grayish spot. On the spot are produced a number of fine, yellowish, hairlike stalks, which at one time are tipped with a large, pear-shaped fruiting body. The infection body is not always present in field material but is large enough to be seen with the unaided eye. It is readily detached by water and carried by splashing droplets of rain practically the only means of distribution.

The disease progresses slowly in coffee plantations. Wide roadways, rows of closely set banana plants, thick hedges of old shade trees, and narrow fields of annual crops are barriers against its movement. Rarely in nature does the fungus produce the characteristic brilliant-yellow, miniature mushrooms. They bear few spores. Some bear none at, all.

The large infection bodies carry the disease from plant to plant. They cause excessive defoliation and fruit drop. They also attack flowers and green stems and produce lesions on fruits. The trees finally die if serious infection continues. Because the fungus has a comparatively narrow temperature range, the disease is more severe in cool highland areas and does not occur in warm places at low altitudes. It grows fairly well under conditions as cool as 54°F.; well at 61 to 75, reaching an optimum at 75 and poorly at 83. At 86 to 90, it stops growing.

The disease thus far is confined to the Americas. With care it can probably be kept from spreading to the oriental Tropics. The disease can be restrained somewhat in countries of its origin if the coffee is grown at warm, low altitudes, and if the dense protecting shade trees are thinned by severe pruning.

Spraying with bordeaux mixture has been recommended. Tests of other fungicides have been started. It is ordinarily considered that costs of materials, employment of untrained labor, and difficulties of terrain make adequate and regular spray applications practically impossible.

Several years of research under Point IV in cooperative stations by the Office of Foreign Agricultural Relations have resulted in developing a control that does not employ spray methods but is accomplished by removing leaves.

During the first two weeks of the rainy season, diseased trees are stripped of all leaves, flowers, and fruits, which fall to the ground, carrying the inoculum with them.

There the fungus is destroyed by natural means by insects, slugs, and bacterial action before the six weeks elapse that are required for new leaves to appear on the denuded trees. The current crop is sacrificed, of course, but the larger harvests in the following years compensate for the destruction of the one poor crop. If careful watch is maintained and reinfected trees are defoliated as soon as they are found in the old treated area, the disease apparently may be kept in check indefinitely.

Dieback, or anthracnose, caused by the fungus Colletotrichum coffeanum, is common in all countries where coffee is grown. It apparently causes injuries at irregular times to seedlings in the seedbed and nursery, to old bearing trees, and to new supplies transplanted in the field. In the places where it has been studied, the fungus has been found to be present on all trees. Losses are hard to measure, because the disease is still not well understood, but the trouble doubtless cuts substantially into profits year after year.

First symptoms of anthracnose are the dark lesions, usually large, which appear on seedling leaves. On weakened or older plants leaf lesions of anthracnose often spread into the stem tissues to which the leaves are attached. Those parts are killed, and the blackened dieback spreads down into branches and stems. When conditions of moisture and temperature favor the disease, it produces profuse masses of sticky spores. The spores are spread by rains, insects, and other means. A variable interval elapses between the period of inoculation with fungus spores and the visible appearance of disease symptoms.

Latent infections, which involve the presence of the organism in apparently healthy plants, may therefore occur. Intensive dieback of stems often is found that is unrelated to Colletotrichum infection under conditions adverse to tree growth. In Africa and India dieback is often due to plant exhaustion, following heavy crops. That is true also to some extent in tropical America. Instances are encountered in which the condition known as dieback results as a complex of both widespread infection by the causal fungus and from unfavorable growth conditions or physiological disturbances of infected plants.

There are hundreds of bacterial, fungal and pest-caused diseases that can affect a coffee crop. However, the four major coffee plant destroyers are coffee leaf rust, coffee berry disease, bacterial blight and leaf miner insects.

COFFEE LEAF RUST

Coffee leaf rust, also known as Hemileia vastatrix, is a devastating coffee disease that is highly contagious. The disease is carried by wind and rain through spores that come from legions found on the underside of an affected plant.

The disease destroyed Brazil's coffee crop during the 1970s and has since been found in almost every coffee-growing country in the world. It is prevented by spraying a fungicide that is copper based. Other countries, including Ethiopia and Sri Lanka, have begun planting a disease-resistant strain of robusta coffee to prevent the spread of leaf rust.

COFFEE BERRY DISEASE

Coffee Berry Disease, also known as Green berry anthracnose and caused by Colletotirchum coffeeanum, is a fungal-based disease. The fungi grow on affected plants and then spread through wind or splashing rain.

This disease can also be spread by animals. For example, if a coffee picker touches an affected plant, he or she can then spread the disease to every other coffee plant they touch.

The danger of Coffee Berry Disease is that it's virtually undetectable until the coffee plant blooms. At that point, the fungus becomes aggressive, covering the whole berry and even turning it black.

Typically, this powerful disease is found in Africa, but can be prevented through fungicides and limiting the instance of standing water.

Bacterial Blight

Bacterial Blight, also known as Pseudomanas syringae garcae, is a bacterial disease that flourishes under cold and wet conditions.

Most recently, Bacterial Blight had an incredibly detrimental effect on Kenya's coffee crop. However, the disease can be nominally prevented with copper-based fungicides.

LEAF MINERS

While leaf miners aren't technically a disease, they are still pests that can devastate a coffee crop. Because these insects are protected by a hard shell and feed right inside the plant itself, they can be very difficult to eradicate with pesticides.

Typically, leaf miner infestations are prevented or treated by planting tastier distraction crops or plants next to and amongst the coffee crop. For example, in Brazil, smart plantation owners are planting Columbine and velvet leaf among their coffee plants to remove the leaf miner threat.

Though these diseases do not inherently harm people, they can contribute to lower coffee supplies and higher prices.

MAJOR DISEASES

Hemileia vastatrix : Leaf Rust A Fungus

Spores are very light and spread by winds or passing animals. Simply touching the diseased tree will attach spores the toucher and will flick spores into the atmosphere. Spores move from the ground up to the leaves during rain periods. Spores will also move up the plant from rain. Spores last a long time on the ground. An area affected by Hemileia Vastatrix may never recover.

This disease is temperature related. The spore gets on the leaf, germinates, and sucks nutrition out of the leaf. This turns the leaf brown, thus, the term leaf rust. At colder temperatures, the germination process is slow. At higher altitudes, the temperature and humidity is such that the spores germinate so slow that the leaf dies of natural causes before its life is sucked out of it. The plant then replenishes the leafs before the leaf dies of the disease.

Generally speaking, leaf rust affects arabica coffea and not robusta coffea. Leaf rust is prevalent in many areas around this world. This disease is similar to that which affects wheat, and has many different races.

A particular survivor plant, of arabica type was found on a plantation owners crop which was wiped out by this disease, but this particular plant wasn't affected. The owner was named Mr. Kent, and hence the name, Kent's coffea. This plant has been sent to India, East Africa and many other areas where Hemileia Vastatrix is a problem. It was found that Kent's coffea is resistant all but two of the varieties of Hemilea Vastatrix.

Mycena flavida : American Leaf Spot

This is a fungus. The process which kills the plant is faster than leaf rust. Defoliation can be swift and sever. The particular disease is prevalent in the Americas. There are regions in Mexico, Guatemala, Costa rica, Colombia, and Brazil which whole plantations have been wiped out because of this disease. The spores will live indefinitely in the ground and make the area permanently troubled.

This disease will kill other crops as cacao and citrus. In general, it affects only the arabica variety and not the robusta variety.

The only effective method of control is choosing the correct environment. Perenox, Captan, and the concoction of two pounds of copper sulphate, two pounds of lime, in 40 gallons of water sprayed in a mist works to retard the disease.

Colletotrichum coffeanum : Coffee Berry Disease

This is a fungi belonging to the genus Colletotrichum and generally considered an active race to the above fungi. The difference is it tend only to attack the berries. And, it attacks at various times, such that it is believed to be caused something lacking in the environment.

Coffee berry disease attacks the green tissues at the beginning stage of berry development and often penetrating into the interior of the berry destroying the bean. It appears at the base berries then moves up the stalk. The berry will have brown patches which seem to have small punctures. Lesions form on the darker areas of the berry and in time the berry turns ash gray.

Coffee berry disease has caused sever losses in Kenya and the Congo. Varieties of coffee such as Jamaican Blue Mountain show inherited resistance to this disease.

Control of this disease is again by choosing the right environment. This disease is a cold temperature disease and may be avoided is the temperature never drops below 65 degrees fahrenheit. Perenox spray and other copper fungicides in four applications during the year tends to reduce the affects.

Fusarium xylorioides : Tracheomycosis Wilt

This is a microbe disease which is in the soil and enters a low surface wound or a shallow root. The disease spreads up through the stem into the vascular strands. Symptoms are yellowing and collapse of the leaf.

This disease affects plants in dry warm soils of Africa's equatorial areas. It attacks robusta coffea and has wiped out 100,000 acres at a time.

Once this disease has been diagnosed, it is contained by fire. Pull the affected plant, the plants around the affected plant, water the ground to keep down dust, dig up about three feet deep of ground from all the area, take the whole pile somewhere else and burn it to fine ash, throw some gas on the dirty ash and burn it some more.

Rosellinia bunodes : Collar-rot

This disease affects forest planted coffees. It is accompanied by fungus growth and internal discoloration of the roots. Its symptoms are wilting of the leaves.

The disease has attacked coffee all over the world. It will attack rubber tree too. It will also kill the shade trees Leucaena glavca. Apparently, Leucaena glavca seem to act as centers of infection.

To prevent this disease, one must properly prepare the soil. Remove any dead stumps and their roots. In area where trees are to be removed, it means ring-barking a year in advance in order that the dead tree's roots are exhausted of all nutrients. This disease is easier to prevent than to eradicate.

Armillaria Mellea : Root Rot

It is a widespread occurrence in the world. It attacks many orchard crops. It starts with dead or dying stumps and roots. It is a common saprophyte in forest soils and spread by the wind easily. Generally does not affect strong healthy plants but weak plants are susceptible and get it started. It then becomes aggressive.

It becomes a toadstool, rhizomorphs, which drives a strand of mycelium into the soil for a considerable distance.

Symptoms on the coffee plant are yellowing and wilting of the foliage followed by death. Symptoms on the ground are toadstool clusters of pale yellow.

To prevent this disease, one must properly prepare the soil. Remove any dead stumps and their roots. In area where trees are to be removed, it means ring-barking a year in advance in order that the dead tree's roots are exhausted of all nutrients. This disease is easier to prevent than to eradicate.

MINOR DISEASES

Rhizoctonia bataticola or *Rhizoctonia solani* : Damping-off Disease

A faily common disease caused by over watering, over crowding, over shaded or sitting on continually damp ground. Generally occurs to seedlings soon after germination. Symptoms are the seedling collapses. A compound of 2 ounces of copper sulphate, 11 ounces of ammonium carbonate, in 26 gallons of water poured at the seedlings base.

Rhizoctonia lamellifera : Root Disease

This is an ant and termite transported disease. It starts at the thinner roots and spreads to the base of old trees. Trees should be burnt and the soil deeply cultivated, in a year or so, the space may be replanted with some success. This is somewhat a mysterious disease. That is to say, plants mysteriously die and the generally have these insects around them.

Although, not a formal solution, kill the insects before they destroy the plant.

Rhizoctonia : Tip Die-back

A sudden die-back progressing from the tip of the upright branches downwards. Dense shade and humid conditions are predisposing factors. Prune away affected tissues well beyond the diseased area and burn immediately.

Ceratostomella Fimbriata : Trunk and Shoot Canker

Affects arabica coffea much more than robusta. Generally believed to be a physical wound, possibly by insects, animals, or humans gnawing, cleaving, or scraping the trunk. The bark grows gnarly, develops cracks like being hacked with a machete.

All diseased parts should be cut and burnt. The remaining plant be treated with a 10 per cent solution of formalin. Afterward, a paste made with copper sulphate and calcium carbide be applied to that affected areas. Prevention by proper training of labor and proper animal and insect control.

Helicobasidium compactum : Root-collar disease

This disease occurs when coffee plants are growing near tea plants. It is believed to be a disease of Java, and the coffee plant is the host. Young trees wilt and die at the start of the dry season. In India it is known as violet root rot because of the mycelium which grows on the stem. Wet or alkaline soil predisposes the attack. The cure is to improve growing conditions, add acidity to the soil, and eliminate diseased material.

Fomes lamaoensis : Brown Root Rot

It is a fungus said to be caused by FOMES NOXIUS. It is common in Mysore India, and is often attacks rubber trees too. It occurs in Java, Malaya, and the Philippines.

Fomes lignosus : White Root Rot

It is a fungus generally associated with rubber plants. However, it has been found in the Congo where there are no rubber plants. It is spotted when the root area has mycelium threads of yellowish-white.

Xylaria thwaitesii : Black Root Rot

It also is a fungus spread from rubber trees.

Nutrient Disorders

Like all plants, too much or too little of the right nutrient causes poisoning or starvation. Typical nutrients are nitrogen, phosphorous, potash, iron, and boron, etc. Numerous symptoms from yellowing of the leaves, whitening of the leaves, browning of the leaf, either the whole leaf or just at the tips. Some trace elements if totally devoid in the soil will also cause problems. The cure or prevention is proper fertilization.

Berry and Leaf Fall

Excessive shedding of berries and leaves if not caused by insects is caused by too alkali soil. Proper pH must be maintained by fertilization.

Die-back

The five general causes of a plant just dying off is either too hot or too cold, or not giving time for the plant to build up its strength before it bears fruit, or bad lighting or bad watering. These plants can be fried from the sun and get sun burn in a single day if for some reason the atmosphere does not filter the light right. For example, a bunch of years the humidity is high and there is light clouding, then one day the humidity drops to zip and there isn't a cloud in sight, wake up in the morning and a lot, if not all, the plants are gone. Let it drop below freezing and it is just that fast. Let the subsoil dry out real good and the plant starts to die right now too.

Virus Blister and ring spots have been known to be caused by various viruses. Generally, viruses are carried by insects, such that eradicating the insect, eradicates the virus. The coffee plant has a good immune system toward viruses and when the fresh source of viruses is removed, the plant recovers.

PEST DISEASES

The word pest covers mites, aphids, caterpillars, slugs, snails, beetles, flies, moths, butterflies, nematodes, bugs, rats, monkeys, grazers and humans.

There are many more pests which will not be mentioned here. These are the worst. Some of these pests have been responsible for wiping out whole plantations.

Diarthrothrips coffeae : *Taeniothrips xanthoceros*; Coffee Thrips

These are small active insects usually found underneath the leaves. They suck the life out of the leaf so a symptom is dying leaves. The are sucker type insects that like dry draughty periods. Proper mulching which keeps the humidity up generally thwarts their appearance. A small amount of these pests can do a large amount of damage. An eighteen per cent strength solution sprayed on leaves from underneath tends to inhibit the thrips.

Antestiopsis lineaticollis; Antestiopsis faceta; The Variegated Coffee Bug

They feed voraciously by piercing the fruit and sucking the inner juices. They tend to feed on young green berries but will eat ripe berries. Symptoms are a good deal of berry shedding, or when the fruit is pulped, there is no bean or badly shaped beans. The bugs are so ferocious that two or three on a tree can wipe out the berries. When there are no berries, the adult insect will attack the buds, shoots and the leaves.

No amount of pruning will bring the trees back to normal until this bug is eradicated. Five per cent aldrin powder and a six per cent solution of pyrethrum in 40 gallons of water sprayed on the tree then powdered will kill this bug. However, more troublesome bugs as leaf miners are usually present in areas antestopsis is, so killing leaf miners takes out these things too.

Leucoptera; Leaf Miner

This moth is the problem with insects affecting coffee plants. The larvae of the moths do the damage by tunnelling into the leaf and resides between two leaf surfaces. Hence the name 'miner.' Because it resides inside the plant, it is hard to kill.

Natural insect control by parasites has been accomplished in some areas. However, organo-phosphorus spays give sufficient penetration for control. Parathion, Methyl-Parathion, or Diazinon are some chemicals sprayed in low volume which do the job.

Planococcus; Ferrisiana; Mealybugs

Mealybugs are generally kept under control of other parasites and larger animals. Birds, reptiles, and mammals all eat these things. But, from time to time, an ant colony starts to protect and propagate these bugs, in which case, they get out of control. They simply eat the plant.

Many countries promote the concept of banding the tree such that ants can't get into it. This seems to work. But killing the ants works to. Dieldrin or Chlordane into the soil does the job.

Coccus; Green Scale

This insect encourage a black sooty fungus to grow which kills the plant. This insect is spread and protected by ants. Banding the plant tends to control this insect, thus controlling the fungus. Dieldrin, Diazinion, Malathion, or Parathion sprayed on the plant kills the insect. Dieldrin or Chlordane into the soil kills the ants.

Asterolecanium coffeae; Star Scale

This is a pest in Kenya. It is controlled by trunk banding with a brown tar oil solution. Diazion also kills this bug.

Stephanoders hampei; Coffee Berry Borer

A minute beetle which is capable of immense damage as an adult and as larvae. A small dark brown, almost black beetle which bores into the fruit. Symptoms are small holes in the fruit and the fruit has discoloration. When the fruit is pulped, it has varying quantity of beans. It is a ground beetle which likes weedy areas. Generally, an infestation is caused by poor ground keeping. The beetle itself eats the berry and the larvae eats the berry.

Natural parasites may hold the pest in control. The best prevention is proper grounds care. Dieldrin sprayed twice during harvest tends to control the pest.

Xylotrechus quadripes; White Stem Borer

An insidious pest of older coffee trees. It is a beetle with long antennae curving over their back. They lay their eggs under the bark of the thicker main stems. The grubs, white colored, tunnel into the wood and progressively burrow their way around in the tree. Symptoms are small amounts of woody waste around small holes in the trees. Unfortunately, once deep inside the tree, the larvae are hard to kill. If not stopped early, this pest can kill whole areas of trees.

Dieldrin spray mixed with Methylene and blue dye is applied to the trunk and main stems of the tree with a brush to kill these best when outside the tree. This concoction should be applied once or twice a year, just before it rains. For plants that the larvae has already penetrated deep into it, there isn't much that can be done. Uproot and destroy the tree.

APATE; Black Stem Borers

These beetles like a single tree or small group of trees. The tend not to do extensive damage but can affect the small group of trees. This is a boring type beetle and to kill it, one pushes a think steel wire into the hole and stabs it. Generally found in Africa but have been seen in other areas.

Bixadus sierricola; Stem Borer

Another African beetle which generally is a sign of poor husbandry and unsuitable environment. This beetle generally resides in shade trees and attacks the coffee tree from them. Constant spraying with Dieldrin or several other type chemicals will control this pest.

Xyleborus; Twig Borers

These type of insects and other like it are generally small suckers. They can be controlled by proper pruning and spraying with Dieldrin or several other type chemicals.

Habrochilla; Lace Wing Coffee Bug

Several species generally found in Africa. These bugs live off the leaf and suck the life out of the leaf. Found in Uganda and Kenya although have been know to frequent other areas. This pest is usually depressed by other insects, but when the other insects which do damage are killed off, these flourish. Malathion or Parathion controls these pests but applications must be made more often because these pests generate fast.

Euxoa; Cutworms

These are sluggish caterpillar like larvae which curl up just under the soil. Fat greenish or brownish crawlers which feed on young tender shoots near the ground. Easily controlled by a deep manure cover crop just before planting. Dusting the soil with Aldrin at regular intervals until young plant have gotten large and tougher.

Thlipteceras; Virachola

Moths and Butterflies: There are many types of moths and butterflies who's larvae attack the coffee plant. Generally speaking, these larvae are caterpillars. These buggers both eat the leaf and the berry. An infestation can be controlled with Diazinon.

Flute-holing and Shot-holing Beetles

There are many of these pests which tend to flourish when their predatory feeders are killed off. These bugs larvae bore into the branches and lay eggs inside the plant on the bark. Constant spraying with Dieldrin, Malathion, Parathion, and Diazion is advise. So, this is the age old story, when the bigger pests are killed off, those of lesser known nature take over.

Nematodes

Generally worms or worm-like pests which eat the roots of the plants. These are usually the result of killing off the higher order predators as birds and grubbing type animals by eradicating an insect with a poison.

Everything Else

Many other minor pests from red spiders to weeds choking the plants can be a problem. It is the same with every crop; if there isn't one thing it's another.

COFFEE PRODUCTION IN INDIA

Indian coffee is said to be the finest coffee grown in the shade rather than direct sunlight anywhere in the world. It is dominated in the hill tracts of South Indian states, with the state of Karnataka accounting 53 per cent followed by Kerala 28 per cent and Tamil Nadu 11 per cent of production of 8,200 tonnes. There are approximately 250,000 coffee growers in India; 98 per cent of them are small growers.

As of 2009, the production of coffee in India was only 4.5 per cent of the total production in the world. Almost 80 per cent of the country's coffee production is exported. Of that which is exported, 70 per cent is bound for Germany, Russian federation, Spain, Belgium, Slovenia, United States, Japan, Greece, Netherlands and France, and Italy accounts for 29 per cent of the exports. Most of the export is shipped through the Suez Canal.

Coffee is grown in three regions of India with Karnataka, Kerala and Tamil Nadu forming the traditional coffee growing region of South India, followed by the new areas developed in the non-traditional areas of Andhra Pradesh and Orissa in the eastern coast of the country and with a third region comprising the states of Assam, Manipur, Meghalaya, Mizoram,

Tripura, Nagaland and Arunachal Pradesh of Northeastern India, popularly known as "Seven Sister States of India".

Indian coffee, grown mostly in southern India under monsoon rainfall conditions, is also termed as "Indian monsooned coffee". Its flavour is defined as: "The best Indian coffee reaches the flavour characteristics of Pacific coffees, but at its worst it is simply bland and uninspiring". The four well known varieties of coffee grown are the Arabica, robusta, the first variety that was introduced in the Baba Budan Giri hill ranges of Karnataka in the 17th century marketed over the years under the brand names of Kent and S.795.

The shoots may be prepared in several ways to make black or green tea. To make the former, the leaf is usually withered and rolled or distorted by rolling in the conventional tea rollers, or is passed through tea machines, the 'rotorvane' and CTC rollers which exert drastic action on the withered leaves. The juice of the leaf cells is exposed in the air to oxidize (fermentation) when important changes take place. When the optimum fermentation is reached, the action of enzyme is arrested by drying the fermented leaf in a current of hot air in suitable tea-dryers. In the production of green tea, the shoots are steamed as soon as possible after plucking and the leaf oxidized is soon destroyed so that fermentation does not take place on rolling.

The processed tea is passed through a series of meshes, sorting out leaf grades and dust. The tea leaves are sorted into different grades , for example, pekoe, Orange pekoe, Flowery pekoe, Broken Orange pekoe and Fannings.

Tea intended for export is packed in plywood chests and shipped directly to various centres or sold through auctions at centres like Calcutta and Cochin.

Instant tea, soluble in water, tea bag and ready mix tea are new developments.

Tea Research

Tea research is carried out in the country at two centres: Tocklai Experimental Station of the tea research association , Jorhat (Assam) and the Tea Research Station of the United Planters Association of Southern India (UPASI) Cinchona P.o., Coimbatore district, Tamil Nadu.

Certain adhoc schemes on tea research are carried out at centres such as the Central Food Technological Research Institute at Mysore and the Department of Applied Chemistry, Calcutta University.

The Tocklai Experimental Station publishes its findings in its annual reports, bulletin the Tea Encyclopedia and in the journal Two and a Bud. The UPASI tea Research Station publishes the results of research in its annual reports, bulletins Handbook of tea Culture and in the Planter's Chronicle.

Coffee

Coffee is cultivated commercially in the four southern States of Karnataka, Tamil Nadu, Kerala and Andhra Pradesh. It is also grown on a limited scale in some non-traditional areas of Orissa, West Bengal, Assam and Madhya Pradesh.

Arabica (*Coffee arabica*) and robusta (*Coffee canephora*) are the two principal economic species extensively cultivated in India. While 90,211 hectare area (57.98%) is under arabica, 65,365 hectares (42.02%) are under robusta. India produces 85,000 to 100,000 tonnes of coffee and earns considerable foreign exchange. The details in respect of the area are given in Table 11.1.

Table 11.1: Area under Coffee (1973-74)

State	Arabica (in ha)	Robusta (in ha)	Total (in ha)
Karnataka	62,844	28,470	91,314
Tamil Nadu	21,619	2747	24,366
Kerala	4550	33,808	38,358
Andhra Pradesh	808	8	816
Assam	116	22	138
Orissa	201	–	201
Madhya Pradesh	45	–	45
Maharashtra	23	–	23
Andaman Islands	5	1	6
Total	**90211**	**65056**	**1,55,267**

Coffee Soils

Coffee cultivation is confined to the hilly areas of the Western and Eastern Ghats. The annual rainfall ranges from 1250 to 3000 mm. A major portion of the area is under the south-westerly monsoon and only a small area is under north-easterly monsoon. This plant grows well at temperatures between 12 and 36 degrees celcius. Elevation above the sea level influences the quality of the coffee. Coffee arabica grows well at elevations between 900 and 1200 metres; Coffee canephora or robusta grows luxuriantly at the lower elevations (about 150 metres). Arabicas are more shade-loving than robustas under conditions in south India.

Coffee soils in India belong to the red and lateritic soils. The soils differ in texture from sandy loam to clayey loam. Red ferruginous clays occur in tracts e.g. Bababudangiris in Karnataka and the Nilgiris in Tamil Nadu. They have good aggregating ability and are generally well-drained. They are rich in organic matter and are acidic to neutral. The total soluble salts are well below the sensitivity limits. They are well stocked with potassium but low in available phosphorus. They are also poor in calcium, and magnesium. They respond well to liming, manuring and other soil management practices.

Climate and Environment

Climatic and environmental factors, like rainfall, temperature, elevation and aspect can influence the economic production of coffee much more than soil factors. Under conditions in southern India, summer temperatures combined with poor subsoil moisture can be a severe limiting factor, whereas at northern latitudes cold winter temperatures can be equally limiting.

Coffee growing has a long history that is attributed first to Ethiopia and then to Arabia, mostly to Yemen. However, the earliest history is traced to AD 875 according to the Bibliotheque Nationale in Paris. The original source is also traced to Abyssinia from where it was brought to Arabia in the 15th century. The Indian context started with an Indian Muslim saint, Baba Budan, while on a pilgrimage to Mecca, smuggled seven coffee beans (by tying it around his waist) from Yemen to Mysore in India and planted them on the Chandragiri Hills [(1,829 metres (6,001 ft)], now named after the saint as Baba Budan Giri ('Giri' means "hill") in Chikkamagaluru district.

It was considered an illegal act to take out green coffee seed out of Arabia. As number seven is a sacrosanct number in Islamic religion, the saint's act of carrying seven coffee beans was considered a religious act. This was the beginning of coffee industry in India, and in particular, in the then state of Mysore, now part of the Karnataka State. This was an achievement of considerable bravery of Baba Budan considering the fact that Arabs had exercised strict control over its export to other countries by not permitting coffee beans to be exported in any form other than as in a roasted or boiled form to prevent germination.

Systematic cultivation soon followed Baba Budan's first planting of the seeds, in 1670, mostly by private owners and the first plantation was established in 1840 around Bab Budan Giri and its surrounding hills in Karnataka. It spread to other areas of Wynad (now part of Kerala), the Shevaroys and Nilgiris in Tamil Nadu. With British colonial presence taking strong roots in India in the mid 19th century, coffee plantations flourished for export. The culture of coffee thus spread to South India rapidly.

Initially, Arabica was popular. However, as result of serious infestation caused to this variety by coffee rust, an alternative robust variety of coffee, appropriately named as robusta and another hybrid between liberica and Arabica, a rust-tolerant hybrid variety of Arabica tree became popular. This is the most common variety of coffee that is grown in the country with Karnataka alone accounting for 70 per cent of production of this variety.

In 1942, the government decided to regulate the export of coffee and protect the small and marginal farmers by passing the Coffee VII Act of 1942, under which Indian Coffee Board got established, operated by the Ministry of Commerce. The government dramatically increased their control of coffee exports in India and pooled the coffees of its growers. In doing so, they reduced the incentives for farmers to produce high-quality coffee, so quality became stagnant.

Over the past 50 years, coffee production in India has grown by over 15 per cent. From 1991, economic liberalization took place in India, and the industry took full advantage of this and cheaper labour costs of production. In 1993, a monumental Internal Sales Quota (ISQ) made the first step in liberalizing the coffee industry by entitling coffee farmers to sell 30 per cent of their production within India. This was further amended in 1994 when the Free Sale Quota (FSQ) permitted large and small scale growers to sell between 70 per cent and 100 per cent of their coffee either domestically or internationally. A final amendment in September 1996 saw the liberalization of coffee for all growers in the country and a freedom to sell their produce wherever they wished.

COMMERCIAL SUCCESS OF COFFEE

Like in Sri Lanka, coffee production in India declined rapidly from the 1870s and was massively outgrown by the emerging tea industry. The devastating coffee rust affected the output of coffee to the point that the costs of production saw coffee plantations in many parts replaced with tea plantations. However, the coffee industry was not as affected by this disease as in Ceylon, and although overshadowed in scale by the tea industry, India was still one of the strongholds of coffee production in the British Empire along with British Guiana. In the period 1910-12, the area under coffee plantation was reported to be 203,134 acres in the southern states, and was mostly exported to England.

In the 1940s, Indian filter coffee, a sweet milky coffee made from dark roasted coffee beans (70%-80%) and chicory (20%-30%) became a commercial success. It was especially popular in the southern states of Andhra Pradesh, Karnataka, Kerala and Tamil Nadu. The most commonly used coffee beans are Arabica and Robusta grown in the hills of Karnataka (Kodagu, Chikkamagaluru and Hassan), Kerala (Malabar region) and Tamil Nadu (Nilgiris District, Yercaud and Kodaikanal).

Coffee production in India grew rapidly in the 1970s, increasing from 68,948 tonnes in 1971-72 to 120,000 tonnes in 1979-80 and grew by 4.6 per cent in the 1980s. It grew by more than 30 per cent in the 1990s, rivalled only by Uganda in the growth of production. By 2007, organic coffee was grown in about 2,600 hectares (6,400 acres) with an estimated production of about 1700 tonnes. According to the 2008 statistics published by the Food and Agricultural Organization (FAO), the area of coffee green harvested in India was 342,000 hectares (850,000 acres), with yield estimates of 7,660 hectogram/ha, forming a total production estimate of 262,000 tonnes.

There are approximately 250,000 coffee growers in India; 98 per cent of them are small growers. Over 90 per cent of them are small farms consisting of 10 acres or fewer. According to published statistics for 2001-2002, the total area under coffee in India was 346,995 hectares with small holdings of 175,475 accounting for 71.2 per cent. The area under large holding of more than 100 hectares was 31,571 hectares (only 9.1% of all holdings) only under 167 holdings. The area under less than 2 hectares holdings was 114,546 hectares (33% of the total area) among 138,209 holders.

The most important areas of production are in the southern Indian States of Karnataka, Kerala, and Tamil Nadu which accounted for over 92 per cent of India's coffee production in the 2005-2006 growing season. In this same season, India exported over 440,000 pounds (200,000 kg) of coffee, with over 25 per cent destined for Italy. Traditionally, India has been a noted producer of Arabica coffee but in the last decade robusta beans are growing substantially due to high yields, which now account for over 60 per cent of coffee produced in India. The domestic consumption of coffee increased from 50,000 tonnes in 1995 to 94,400 tonnes in 2008.

According to the statistics provided by the Coffee Board of India, the estimated production of Robusta and Arabica coffee for the "Post-monsoon Estimation 2009-10" and "Post Blossom Estimation 2010-11" in different states accounted for a total of 308,000 tonnes and 289,600 tonnes, respectively. As of 2010, between 70 per cent and 80 per cent of Indian grown coffee is exported overseas.

Growing Conditions

All coffees grown in India are grown in shade and commonly with two tiers of shade. Often inter-cropped with spices such as cardamom, cinnamon, clove, and nutmeg, the coffees gain aromatics from the inter-cropping, storage, and handling functions. Growing altitudes range between 1,000 m (3,300 ft) to 1,500 m (4,900 ft) above sea level for Arabica (premier coffee), and 500 m (1,600 ft) to 1,000 m (3,300 ft) for *Robusta* (though of lower quality, it is robust to environment conditions).

Ideally, both *Arabica* and *Robusta* are planted in well drained soil conditions that favour rich organic matter that is slightly acidic (pH 6.0-6.5). However, India's coffees tend to be moderately acidic which can lead to either a balanced and sweet taste, or a listless and inert one. Slopes of Arabica tend to be gentle to moderate, while Robusta slopes are gentle to fairly level.

Blooming is the time when coffee plants bloom with white flowers which last for about three to four days (termed "evanescent" period) before they mature into seeds. When coffee plantations are in full bloom it is a delightful sight to watch. The time period between blooming and maturing of the fruit varies appreciably with the variety and the climate; for the Arabica, it is about seven months, and for the Robusta, about nine months. The fruit is gathered by hand when it is fully ripe and red-purple in colour.

Climatic Conditions

Ideal climatic conditions to grow coffee are related to temperature and rainfall; temperatures in the range of 73 °F (23 °C) and 82 °F (28 °C) with rainfall incidence in the range of 60-80 inches (1.5-2.0 m) followed by a dry spell of 2-3 months suit the Arabica variety. Cold temperatures closer to freezing conditions are not suitable to grow coffee. Where the rainfall is less than 40 inches (1.0 m), providing irrigation facilities is essential. In the tropical region of the south Indian hills, these conditions prevail leading to coffee plantations flourishing in large numbers. Relative humidity for Arabica ranges 70-80 per cent while for Robusta it ranges 80-90 per cent.

Coffee Diseases

The common disease to which the coffee plants are subjected to in India is on account of fungus growth. This fungus is called the *Hemileia vastatrix*, an endophytous that grows within the matter of the leaf; effective cure has not been discovered to eliminate this. The second type of disease is known as the coffee rot, which has caused severe damages during the rainy season, particularly to plantations in Karnataka. *Pellicularia kole-rota* is the name given to this rot or rust, which turns the leaves into black colour due to the coverage by a slimy gelatinous film. This causes the coffee leaves and the cluster of coffee berries to drop off to the ground. Snakes such as cobras can also cause a nuisance to coffee plantations in India.

Processing

Processing of coffee in India is accomplished using two methods, dry processing and wet processing. Dry processing is the traditional method of drying in the sun which is favoured for its flavour producing characteristics. In the wet processing method, coffee beans are fomented and washed, which is the preferred method for improved yields. As to the wet processing, the beans are subject to cleaning to segregate defective seeds. The beans of different varieties and sizes are then blended to derive the best flavour. The next procedure is to roast either through roasters or individual roasters. Then the roasted coffee is ground to appropriate sizes.

Varieties

The four main botanical cultivars of India's coffee include Kent, S.795, Cauvery, and Selection 9. In the 1920s, the earliest variety of Arabica grown in India was named Kent(s) after the Englishman L.R. Kent, a planter of the Doddengudda Estate in Mysore. Probably the most commonly planted Arabica in India and Southeast Asia is S.795, known for its balanced cup and subtle flavour notes of mocca. Released during the 1940s, it is a cross between the Kents and S.288 varieties.

Cauvery, commonly known as Catimor, is a derivative of a cross between Caturra with Hybrido-de-Timor, while the award-winning Selection 9 is a derivative from the crossing between Tafarikela and Hybrido-de-Timor. The dwarf and semi-dwarf hybrids of San Ramon and Caturra were developed to meet the demands for high density plantings. The Devamachy hybrid (*C. arabica* and *C. canephora*) was first discovered around 1930 in India.

The Indian Coffee Association's weekly auction includes such varieties as Arabica Cherry, Robusta Cherry, Arabica Plantation, and Robusta Parchment.

Regional logos and brands include: Anamalais, Araku valley, Bababudangiris, Biligiris, Brahmaputra, Chikmagalur, Coorg, Manjarabad, Nilgiris, Pulneys, Sheveroys, Travancore, and Wayanad. There are also several specialty brands such as Monsooned Malabar AA, Mysore Nuggets Extra Bold, and Robusta Kaapi Royale.

Organic coffee is produced with synthetic agro-chemicals and plant protection methods. A certification is essential by the accrediting agency for such coffee to market it (popular forms are of regular, decaffeinated, flavoured and instant coffee variety) as such since they are popular in Europe, United States and Japan. The Indian terrain and climatic conditions provide the advantages required for the growth of such coffee in deep and fertile forest soils under the two tier mixed shade using cattle manure, composting and manual weeding coupled with the horticultural operations practiced in its various coffee plantations; small holdings is another advantage for such a variety of coffee.

In spite of all these advantages, the certified organic coffee holdings in India, as of 2008, (there are 20 accredited certification agencies in India) was only in an area of 2,600 hectares (6,400 acres) with production estimated at 1700 tonnes. In order to promote growth of such coffee, the Coffee Board, based on field experiments, surveys and case studies has evolved many packages for adoption, supplemented with information guidelines and technical documents.

RESEARCH AND DEVELOPMENT

Coffee research and development efforts are well organized in India through its Coffee Research Institute, which is considered the premier research station in South East Asia. It is under the control of the Coffee Board of India, an autonomous body, under the Ministry of Commerce and Industry, Government of India, which was set up under an Act of the Parliament with the objective of promoting "research, development, extension, quality up gradation, market information, and the domestic and external promotion of Indian coffee".

It was established near Balehonnur in Chikmagalur district of Karnataka, in the heartland of coffee plantations. Prior to establishing this institute, a temporary research unit was established in 1915 at Koppa primarily to evolve solutions to crop infestation by leaf diseases. This was followed by the field research station established by the then Government of Mysore, titled "Mysore Coffee Experimental Station," in 1925. This was handed over to the Coffee Board which was formed in 1942, and regular research started at this station from 1944. Dr L. C. Coleman is credited as the founder of coffee research in India.

The Coffee Board of India is an autonomous body, functioning under the Ministry of Commerce and Industry, Government of India. The Board serves as a friend, philosopher and guide of the coffee industry in India. Set up under an Act of the Parliament of India in the year 1942, the Board focuses on research, development, extension, quality up gradation, market information, and the domestic and external promotion of Indian coffee.

The research activities covered by the Institute constitute research in seven disciplines such as Agronomy, Soil Science and Agricultural Chemistry, Botany, Entomology/Nematology, Plant Physiology, Biotechnology and Post Harvest Technology with the basic aim of increasing productivity and quality of coffee grown in India. The institute has sixty scientific and technical personnel involved in research activities.

The institute has a well established farm land of 130.94 ha for carrying out crop research, out of which 80.26 ha are dedicated to coffee research of arabica and 28.94 ha of robusta), 10 ha are used for growing CXR, 12.38 ha are apportioned for nurseries, roads and buildings, and the balance area of 12.38 hectares (30.6 acres) is a reserve area for future expansion.

The research farm has a well established network of check dams that provides a regulated water source to the plantations which offer a wide range of shade tree species under which coffee is grown, and germplasm and exotic material from all the coffee growing countries including Ethiopia which is known as the home land of Arabica. In addition, crop diversification with crops such as pepper and areca are also part of income generating programmes of the institute.

Part of the institute includes a research laboratory to carry out research in identified disciplines, as well as a stocked library with books and periodicals, not only on coffee but also on other crops. Training of personnel is an important activity of the institute. The training unit of the institute conducts regular training programmes for estate managers and supervisory personnel of the coffee plantations and also for the extension officers of the Coffee Board.

Recognised by UNDP and USDA, the training unit of the institute is providing training to foreign nationals on coffee cultivation in which personnel from Ethiopia, Vietnam, Sri Lanka, Nepal, and Nestle Singapore have been trained.

In addition, a plant tissue culture & biotechnology division, established in Mysore, is carrying out exclusive research in bio-technology and molecular biology to supplement/complement the conventional breeding programmes in developing high yielding, pest and disease resistant varieties. The Coffee Board of India maintains a Quality Control Division in its head office in Bangalore which plays an active role in collaborating with other research disciplines in upgrading the "quality of coffee in the cup."

Regional Research Stations

To cover research specific to each coffee growing region covering different agro-climatic conditions, the following five research stations are fully functional under the overall control of the Central Coffee Research Institute. Coffee Research Sub-station (CRSS), Chettalli in Coorg district of Karnataka, was established in 1946. The sub-station has a well equipped laboratory and covers an area of 131 ha out of which 80 hectares is exclusive to coffee research activities. Regional Coffee Research Station (RCRS), R.V. Nagar in Visakhapatnam district of Andhra Pradesh also covers the Orissa on the eastern coast.

The research station, established in 1976 to cater to the development of coffee in non-traditional areas has an area of 30 hectares under coffee plantation. The objective of introducing coffee in this area was to wean away the tribal population from growing crops under the 'Podu' cultivation (shifting cultivation) in the forest areas, not only to preserve the forest ecology but also to improve the economic condition of the tribal people of the region. Regional Coffee Research Station (RCRS), Chundale village in Wayanad district of Kerala was established primarily to develop appropriate technologies to suit the region where robusta is the dominant crop. Kerala is reckoned as the second largest coffee producing state in the country with robusta variety of coffee.

The station covers an area of 116 ha with 30 ha of farm with an adequate laboratory support for research. Regional Coffee Research Station (RCRS), Thandigudi in Dindigul district of Tamil Nadu. The research station was established with the sole aim of evolving suitable practices for the cultivation of coffee area in Tamil Nadu which receives major rainfall (but scanty) during the Northeast monsoon, unlike the other regions of the country. This station is spread over an area of 12.5 ha including a research farm of 6.5 ha with laboratory facilities.

Regional Coffee Research Station (RCRS), Diphu in Karbi Anglon district of Assam was established to support coffee plantations which were established in the Northeast region in 1980 to provide an alternate, economically viable agricultural practice to the shifting or jhum cultivation, widely practiced by the tribals in the forested hills, which was a cause of concern to preserve the ecology of the region. This regional station is spread over an area of 25 ha.

Diseases of Sorghaum

The diversity of environments in which sorghum is cultivated expose the crop to a number of disease causing pathogens. In the areas where sorghum is traditionally grown, plants may be attacked by five or six foliar diseases, an array of soil-borne organisms, several diseases infesting earheads and grain, and one or more viruses.

Overlap of disease symptoms is very common. Variations in maturity, plant height, vigour, pigmentation of both seed and plant, and other plant characteristics affect disease expression and complicate accurate identification of the disease.

Fortunately many sorghum diseases do not affect the yields significantly except the ones which infest the earheads and developing grain.

A sorghum plant growing under optimal conditions can withstand the effects of a disease. Good root development and regeneration greatly reduce the severity of attack by root-rotting diseases. An abundance of leaves diminishes the impact of foliar diseases on yields. Healthy plants often grow to compensate for neighboring plants killed by diseases.

For example, downy mildew disease may infect as many as 50 per cent of the plants early in the season but may not affect yield when the disease is uniformly distributed in the fields.

Consequently many potentially serious diseases are avoided because of the natural ability of sorghum to yield well.

Diseases are estimated to reduce sorghum productivity by 15 per cent.

However, the extent of any single disease varies yearly so that losses from a given disease may be low in one year and may be serious in another year.

Absolute or accurate values for losses caused by sorghum diseases are not available. The three major sorghum disease control strategies available for farmers to practice are:

- Disease Resistance;
- Cultural Practices; and
- Use of chemicals.

Advance planning is required to follow these practices.

Cultural control measures are many times under recognized for their effectiveness in disease control. With proper crop management, the sorghum crop can escape most diseases or withstand them with negligible impact on yield.

Chemicals used for disease control are limited to seed treatments by fungicides.

Sorghum is the fifth most important cereal crop in the world after wheat, maize, rice, and barley.

Crop	Area (Million ha)	Production (Million MT)
Wheat	218	624
Rice	153	608
Maize	145	705
Barley	57	155
Sorghum	44	60

World Area and Production of Major Grain Crops during 2004.

Sorghum is cultivated for grain and as a major food crop in much of South Asia, Africa, and Central America.

In the USA, Australia and South America, sorghum is grown mainly for animal feed. In addition to these uses of the grain, sorghum crop residues and green plants also provide sources of animal feed, building material, and fuel for cooking, particularly dry land areas.

Sorghum is adapted to warm and dry climate but the greatest area of the crop is cultivated in drought-prone areas of the world.

In these areas, sorghum is usually grown with limited inputs in conditions of sparse rainfall, low soil fertility, and face a range of disease and pest problems, with correspondingly poor yields.

Table 12.1: Average Yields of Sorghum are Lower than Important Grain Crops

Crop (World)	Average Yield (kg/ha)
Maize	4859
Rice	3970
Wheat	2869
Barley	2720
Sorghum	1357

The lower average yields are primarily a result of the hot, dry conditions where sorghum is mostly grown, rather than sorghum plant's capability.

In fact, sorghum has high yield potential, comparable to rice, wheat and maize. On a field basis, sorghum yields have exceeded 11,000 kg/ha, with above average yields ranging from 7000 to 9000 kg/ha where moisture is not a limiting factor.

In areas where sorghum is commonly grown yields of 3000 to 4000 kg/ha are obtained under better conditions, dropping down to 300 to 1000 kg/ha as moisture and soil fertility become limiting.

A majority of the subsistence farmers who typically cultivate this crop are unable to take advantage of high yield potential because they have limited options for improving their management practices.

Sorghum production can be achieved through growing verities/hybrids with improved tolerance to drought and low soil fertility, and resistance to pests and diseases.

It is observed that of late food habits of sorghum eating people are changing towards rice and wheat products.

Perhaps this, and reduced market price for sorghum have resulted in the decline of area under sorghum cultivation.

Naturally, the poor farmers of rain fed areas who cannot grow crops other than sorghum are economically affected as they are not getting reasonable price for sorghum in the market.

However, there is hope. In addition to sorghum as a food crop, there are possibilities of other alternative uses of sorghum such as novel foods, processed foods, feed for dairy animals, and industrial uses - starch, beverages (beer) and ethanol.

Thus, commercialization of alternative food, feed, and industrial products is one of the ways to increase demand for sorghum.

Grain sorghum is planted under dryland and irrigated conditions. In 2007, total acreage harvested under dryland and irrigated conditions was 1.89 million and 565,000, respectively. Dryland areas produced 112.21 million bushels while irrigated areas accounted for 49.49 million bushels.

PRODUCTION REGIONS

The Coastal Bend, around Corpus Christi, produces 14 per cent of Texas sorghum. This region experiences temperate conditions with very high humidity. In the Coastal Bend approximately 25-32 inches of rainfall is received per year. Top-producing counties include Nueces, San Patricio, and Jim Wells counties.

The Lower Rio Grande Valley (LRGV) is located between McAllen and Brownsville, adjacent to the Mexico border. This region plants early due to the subtropical climate and insect problems. Average rainfall is between 25 and 30 inches per year and this area produces 16 per cent of the state's crop. Top-producing counties include Hidalgo, Willacy, and Cameron counties.

The High Plains region of Texas is located north and south of Lubbock, Texas between the Caprock and the New Mexico border. This area consists of 27 counties that produce 34 per cent of the state's sorghum crop. The hot days and cool nights plus loam and sandy soil types make it vital to implement water and soil conservation methods. Average rainfall is 16-22 inches, but there are wide year to year variations in both total and seasonal rainfall.

Top-producing counties include Deaf Smith, Hale, Lamb, and Floyd counties. The Upper Gulf Coast region is located south and southwest of Houston. This region produces 8 per cent of Texas' sorghum crop. Medium to heavy soils and relatively high rainfall allows this area to consistently produce significant sorghum yields.

The Blacklands of Texas is located south of Dallas. This region produces 9 per cent of the state's total sorghum crop. Deep prairie soils predominate this region. Temperate, warm nights and rainfall of 30-36 inches a year lead to the fact that only five per cent of this region is irrigated.

Cultural Practices

Sorghum is well-adapted to Texas, and its ability to yield consistently in harsh environments makes it popular with growers. Grain sorghum is generally grown as an annual crop, although there has been some ratoon production in Texas.

Cultural practices frequently employed in Texas sorghum production cover a wide range of production systems. Tillage systems include conventional tillage, reduced tillage, conservation tillage, strip-till, and no-till. While the majority of grain sorghum is grown in rows with spacings ranging from 27" to 40", some sorghum is planted broadcast.

Sorghum may be planted as early as February in the Lower Rio Grande Valley or as late as June in the Plains regions.

Crop rotation is a very important aspect of sorghum production in Texas. The most commonly rotated crop with sorghum is cotton. Other crops rotated with sorghum include corn, soybean, wheat, and peanut. Sorghum-cotton rotation allows growers to decrease grassy weed competition in sorghum. Similarly, sorghum rotated with herbicide-tolerant corn or soybean also provides sorghum growers opportunities to decrease grassy weed populations in sorghum fields.

The vast majority of worker activities associated with sorghum production in Texas will involve mechanized operations, therefore, there is very little potential for worker exposure to pesticides. Planting, cultivation, spray application, and harvest are all completed using either tractor or combine. Hand-hoeing is virtually non-existent in sorghum. The only potential for exposure would be during scouting activities or equipment maintenance in the field during a tractor-assisted operation.

INSECT PESTS

Insect pest problems in sorghum can vary widely across the state, as well as from one season to the next. The insect pests with the greatest potential to decrease yield are the greenbug and the sorghum midge, the latter is particularly important in the southern half of the state. In 2003, twenty per cent of sorghum acres in Texas were treated with an insecticide. Terbufos was the most commonly applied insecticide on about four per cent of planted acres. Chlorpyrifos was applied to one per cent of sorghum acres in 2003.

Seed and Root Insect Pests

Wireworms

True and false wireworms feed on planted sorghum seed, preventing germination. To a lesser degree, they feed on seedling plant roots, reducing plants stands and vigour.

- *Cultural control:* promote rapid germination, rotate with tap-rooted crop such as cotton
- *Chemical control:* (Name IRAC group)

Seed treatment -imidacloprid (Gaucho) 4A -thiamethoxam (Cruiser) 4A

At planting-terbufos (Counter) 1B

Red Imported Fire Ant

Under certain conditions in the eastern and southern parts of the state, red imported fire ants feed on planted seed. They prefer water-soaked or germinating seeds, but also damage dry seeds.

- *Cultural control:* promote rapid germination, rotate with tap-rooted crop such as cotton
- *Chemical control:* Seed treatment -imidacloprid (Gaucho) 4A-thiamethoxam (Cruiser) 4A

At planting-terbufos (Counter) 1B

White Grubs

Normally white grubs are not a serious pest of sorghum, however, if present, grubs can damage sorghum by feeding on roots.

- *Cultural control:* planting sorghum in rotation with non-grass crop
- *Chemical control:* Seed treatment -clothiandin (Poncho) 4A

At planting-terbufos (Counter) 1B

Southern Corn Rootworm

Southern corn rootworms burrow into germinating seeds, roots, and crowns of sorghum plants. They can cause reduced stands, lower plant vigour, and the occurrence of 'dead heart' in young plants. Damage is most likely in the Coastal Bend production region.

- *Cultural control:* none
- *Chemical control:* Seed treatment-clothiandin (Poncho) 4A

  At plantin

  - terbufos (Counter) 1B
  - chlorpyifos (Lorsban) 1B
  - carbofuran (Furadan) 1A

STEM AND LEAF INSECTS

Cutworms

Several species of sorghum can damage sorghum. Cutworms cut sorghum plants off at, slightly above or below the surface of the soil.

- *Cultural control:* plowing or herbicides to control weeds in late summer of early fall, and thoroughly prepare seedbed at least 4-6 weeks before planting.
- *Chemical control:*
  - chlorpyifos (Lorsban, NuFos) 1B
  - cyfluthrin (Baythroid) 3
  - cyhalothrin (Karate, Warrior) 3
  - zeta-cypermethrin (Mustang Max) 3

Yellow Sugarcane Aphid

Yellow sugarcane aphids feed on sorghum and inject toxin into leaves of seedlings and older plants. Damage often leads to delayed maturity and plant lodging that may be worsened by associated stalk rots.

- *Cultural control:* none
- *Chemical control:* Seed treatment
  - clothiandin (Poncho) 4A
  - imidacloprid (Gaucho) 4A
  - thiamethoxam (Cruiser) 4A

    Postemergence

    - dimethoate 1B
- carbofuran (Furadan) 1A

Corn Leaf Aphid

Corn leaf aphids often infest the whorls and undersides of sorghum leaves in great numbers. They suck plant juices but do not inject toxin; the most apparent damage is yellow mottling of leaves that unfold from the whorl.

- Cultural control: none.
- Chemical control: Seed treatment
  - imidacloprid (Gaucho) 4A
  - thiamethoxam (Cruiser) 4A
- At planting
  - terbufos (Counter) 1B
  - phorate (Thimet) 1B
  - carbofuran (Furadan) 1A

GREENBUG

The greenbug is an aphid that sucks plant juices and injects a toxin. Many greenbugs on booting and older plants can reduce yields and weaken plants that may later lodge. Using resistant varieties is suggested but new greenbug biotypes consistently occur.

- Cultural control: Resistant varieties
  - only provide tolerance
- Chemical control: Seed treatment
  - imidacloprid (Gaucho) 4A
  - thiamethoxam (Cruiser) 4A
  - clothiandin (Poncho) 4A
- At planting
  - terbufos (Counter) 1B
  - phorate (Thimet) 1B
  - carbofuran (Furadan) 1A
  - aldicarb (Temik) 1A
  - chlorpyrifos (Lorsban) 1B
- Postemergence
  - dimethoate 1B
  - carbofuran (Furadan) 1A
  - chlorpyrifos (Lorsban, NuFos) 1B
  - malathion 1B
  - phorate (Thimet) 1B

Chinch Bug

Chinch bugs are sporadic pests of sorghum in Texas. They suck juices from stems, leaves, or underground plant parts.

- Cultural control: promote dense, vigorous plant stands
- Chemical control: Seed treatment
  - imidacloprid (Gaucho) 4A
  - thiamethoxam (Cruiser) 4A
  - clothiandin (Poncho) 4A

- At planting
  - terbufos (Counter) 1B
  - aldicarb (Temik) 1A
  - chlorpyrifos (Lorsban) 1B
- Postemergence
  - carbofuran (Furadan) 1A
  - chlorpyrifos (Lorsban, NuFos) 1B
  - carbaryl (Sevin) 1A
  - cyfluthrin (Baythroid) 3
  - cyhalothrin (Karate, Warrior) 3

Banks Grass Mite

Large numbers of Banks grass mite sometimes occur on sorghum, especially in more arid areas such as the Plains production regions.

- Cultural control : resistant varieties
  - only provide tolerance
- Chemical control:
- Postemergence
  - dimethoate 1B
  - phorate (Thimet) 1B
  - propargite (Comite) 12C

GRAIN HEAD INSECT PESTS

Sorghum Midge

The sorghum midge is probably the most damaging insect pest of sorghum in Texas. The adult is a small, fragile-looking orange-red fly with a yellow head and gray, membranous wings. During the single day of adult life, each female lays about fifty eggs in flowering spikelet of sorghum.

- Cultural control: promote uniform heading and flowering in sorghum fields as well as control johnsongrass in and around fields.
- Chemical control:
  - methomyl (Lannate) 1A
  - chlorpyrifos (Lorsban, NuFos) 1B

- malathion (Fyanon) 1B
- cyfluthrin (Baythroid) 3
- cyhalothrin (Karate, Warrior) 3
- zeta-cypermethrin (Mustang Max) 3
- esfenvalerate (Asana) 3

Corn Earworm and Fall Armyworm (Headworms)

Corn earworms and fall armyworm infest the whorls and grain heads of sorghum plants.

Insecticide application may be justified if larval feeding reduces leaf area by more than 30 per cent or is damaging the developing grain head within the whorl.

- Cultural control: none.
- Chemical control:
  - methomyl (Lannate) 1A
  - cyfluthrin (Baythroid) 3
  - cyhalothrin (Karate, Warrior) 3
  - zeta-cypermethrin (Mustang Max) 3
  - esfenvalerate (Asana) 3
  - carbaryl (Sevin) 1A

Sorghum Webworm

Sorghum webworms occasionally infest grain heads of sorghum planted 2 to 3 weeks later than normal.

- Cultural control: none.
- Chemical control:
  - methomyl (Lannate) 1A
  - cyfluthrin (Baythroid) 3
  - cyhalothrin (Karate, Warrior) 3
  - carbaryl (Sevin) 1A

GRAIN HEAD FEEDING BUGS

Rice stink bug, southern green stink bug, conchuela stink bug, leaffooted bug, and false chinch bug These species of bugs may move in relatively large numbers from alternate host plants into sorghum during kernel development.

- Cultural control: none.
- Chemical control:
  - cyfluthrin (Baythroid) 3
  - cyhalothrin (Karate, Warrior) 3
  - carbaryl (Sevin) 1A

Stalk-boring insect Pests

Sugarcane borer, southwestern corn borer, European corn borer, Mexican rice borer, lesser cornstalk borer, and neotropical borer. These closely related insects tunnel into the stalks of sorghum.

- Cultural control: none.
- Chemical control:
  - cyfluthrin (Baythroid) 3
  - cyhalothrin (Karate, Warrior) 3

Diseases

Sorghum hybrids are bred for genetic resistance to most diseases. However, several sorghum diseases still cause yield loss to growers. Management of sorghum diseases is generally accomplished through resistant varieties and seed protectant fungicides. Foliarapplied fungicides are not used on sorghum in Texas. The most common seed treatment fungicides are below: (name FRAC group)

- Captan M4
- Metalaxyl (Apron) 4
- Fludioxonil 12

Common Diseases of Sorghum in Texas

Seed rots and seedling diseases (*Rhizoctonia solani*, *Fusarium* sp., *Pythium* sp. and others). Seed rots and seedling diseases are more prevalent when seed is planted in cool, wet soils, and especially when packing rains seal the soil surface.

Use of high quality treated seed is the best control method.

Sorghum downy mildew (Peronosclerospora sorghi). Young, systemically infected plants have light green to yellowish stripes lengthwise in the leaves often with a grayishwhite downy fungal growth consisting of numerous tiny spores on the lower surface of the leaf opposite the pale striped areas.

Use seed treated with a systemic fungicide containing metalaxyl and resistant hybrids to control this disease.

Maize Dwarf Mosaic Virus (MDMV)

Maize dwarf mosaic is a virus disease that occurs over all the sorghum producing areas of Texas. Its ability to cause damage is dependent on the presence of an overwintering virus host (mainly Johnsongrass), aphid populations to facilitate virus transmission and the susceptibility of the hybrid being grown.

Use tolerant hybrids and control Johnsongrass in and around the field to manage this disease.

Head Smut (Sporisorium reilianum)

This disease is characterized by the large, darkbrown smut galls that emerge in place of the panicle. Different races of the fungus exist which may result in a sorghum hybrid being resistant in one area but not another.

Use resistant varieties to minimize losses.

Bacterial Stripe (*Pseudomonas andropogoni*)

This is the most common bacterial disease of sorghum. The disease is characterized by long narrow stripes that vary from red to black depending on the type of sorghum.

This disease has not been a serious enough problem to warrant specific control in Texas.

Anthracnose (*Colletotrichum graminicola*)

The anthracnose fungus damages foliage and stems of grain sorghum. On susceptible hybrids, the stem holding the head (peduncle) becomes infected and a brown sunken area with distinct margins develops. In Texas, anthracnose is restricted mostly to the gulf coast areas.

The use of resistant hybrids and good management of crop residue are effective control measures.

Rust (*Puccinia purpurea*)

Rust appears on leaves as small raised pustules or blisters that rupture and release many reddish-brown spores. Grain yield losses are usually not serious and occurrence of the disease is sporadic. Forage sorghum yields may be affected most.

Charcoal Rot (*Macrophomina phaseolina*)

Grain sorghum plants affected by the charcoal rot fungus fail to fill grain properly and may lodge in the latter part of the season. Infected stalks show an internal shredding at and above the ground line. Host plants are usually in the early-milk to late-dough stage when infection occurs. The fungus is common and widely distributed in nature.

Avoiding moisture stress, proper management of crop residue, crop rotation, avoiding excessive plant populations, balancing nitrogen and potassium fertility levels, and growing drought-tolerant, lodging-resistant hybrids represent the best means of control.

Fusarium Stalk Rot (*Fusarium moniliforme*). Like charcoal rot, Fusarium stalk rot usually develops on mature to nearly mature plants that have been subjected to some form of stress.

Avoiding stress problems by proper use of cultural practices is the best approach to control.

Ergot Sorghum

Ergot is a disease caused by a fungus (Claviceps africana) that infects the ovaries of sorghum flowers and often converts them into a white, fungal mass (sphacelia). The most obvious external symptom of infection is the abundant exudation from infected flowers of an amber-colored, sticky fluid, or "honeydew," which often drips onto the leaves and soil.

- Time planting to avoid low evening temperatures (below 55 degrees F) during the period 3 to 4 weeks prior to flowering and from flowering to 5 days thereafter.
- When planting in ergot-free areas, use seed treatment fungicides.
- After harvest, disk the fields to prevent sorghum ratoon and sorghum volunteer development.
- Manage johnsongrass within and around the borders of the field.

Controlling Weeds

Controlling weeds in sorghum in Texas is one of the most critical aspects of successful production. Unchecked weed populations can rob valuable moisture and nutrients from the crop as well as cause significant quality reductions at harvest. Recent technological advancements have changed many aspects of weed control in cotton, corn and soybeans but these advantages are absent for grain sorghum. Crop rotation is an extremely important tool for weed management in sorghum. Crop rotation with broadleaved and/or glyphosate-tolerant crops is critical to manage perennial grassy weeds such as johnsongrass and others. There are no biological control methods for weed control in sorghum.

The lack of herbicide-tolerant sorghum varieties requires producers to be vigilant in their weed control programmes or risk losing production. Herbicides are by far the most widely used pesticide in sorghum production in Texas. According to NASS data, in 2003 78 per cent or sorghum acres in Texas received at least one herbicide application. This translated into 2.88 million pounds of herbicides applied to sorghum in 2003. The most commonly used herbicides were atrazine, glyphosate, s-metolachlor, 2,4-D, and prosulfuron.

COMMON WEEDS IN TEXAS SORGHUM FIELDS

Common Annual Grasses

- Texas panicum (*Panicum texanum*) or Colorado grass is a native weed found in every region of the state. Seeds are the only source of reproduction. It flourishes in warm conditions and competes very well with sorghum.
- Crabgrass (*Digitaria* spp.) species are mostly native warm season weeds.

Crabgrass produces large numbers of seed and can have both erect and decumbent growth habits.

- Browntop panicum (*Panicum fasciculatum*) is also a native warm season grassy weed. It is found in nearly every region of the state and can cause yield loss to sorghum.
- Sprangletops (*Leptochloa* spp.) such as red sprangletop, green sprangletop, bearded sprangletop, and Mexican sprangletop are native grassy weeds.

Commonly found across the state, these weeds compete with sorghum for water and light.

- Broadleaf signalgrass (*Brachiaria platyphylla*) is a large-seeded annual weed that is native to Texas. Fine hairs on the wide leaves increase the competitive ability of this weed with sorghum.

Common Perennial Grasses

- Johnsongrass (*Sorghum halapense*) is an introduced grassy weed that is probably the worst weed plaguing sorghum production in Texas. Reproducing either by seed or underground rhizomes, johnsongrass is a fierce competitor in sorghum fields. Belonging to the same genus as sorghum, johnsongrass control is difficult but left unchecked can severely decrease yield.

- Bermudagrass (*Cynodon dactylon*) is also an introduced perennial grassy weed that can be found in every area of the state. Commonly found in roadsides, ditches, lawns, and pastures bermudagrass is drought-tolerant and difficult to control.

Common Annual Broadleaf Weeds

- Pigweed (*Amaranthus* spp.) including Palmer amaranth, prostrate pigweed, spiny amaranth, tumble pigweed, smooth pigweed, redroot pigweed and common waterhemp are troublesome small-seeded broadleaf weeds. Pigweeds are prolific seed producers and can cause serious yield reduction if left uncontrolled.
- Common sunflower (*Helianthus annuus*) is an extremely troublesome broadleaf weed across Texas. Sunflowers are native to North America and have been cultivated for centuries for their edible seeds. They are commonly found in fields, roadsides, ditches, and waste areas.
- Cocklebur (*Xanthium strumarium*) is another native annual belonging to the sunflower family. Cocklebur fruit are one inch long, woody, with hooked prickles covering the outside of the fruit. The burs are irritating to humans and animals and seeds and seedlings contain a glycoside that is toxic to all classes of livestock.
- Devil's claw (*Proboscidea louisianica*) is a foul-smelling native annual sometimes referred to as unicorn plant. Plants are covered with glandular hair causing them to be very sticky. The fruit splits at maturity forming two claws, therego the common name.
- Smellmelon (*Cucumis melo var. Dudaim*) is a vining weed that reduces crop yields by competing for sunlight and moisture. Smellmelon also interferes with crop harvest by clogging and fouling combines with vines. Each plant may produce as many as 40 melons, each containing approximately 400 seed. Mature melons will float, as will the dried sacks of seed following rotting of the melons. This weed has become a serious pest in cotton, sorghum and corn and appears to be increasing.
- Kochia (*Kochia scoparia*) is an annual weed growing from 2-5 feet tall and begins growth in late spring. Kochia is an annual plant originating in Eurasia, and introduced into America in the early 1900's. Primarily a weed pest in West Texas, its appearance was first recorded in Texas during the late 1940s.

Common Perennial Broadleaf Weeds

- Silverleaf nightshade (*Solanum elaeagnifolium*) is a creeping perennial spreading by roots or seeds. Silverleaf nightshade is native to the central United States and can be found in pastures, rangeland, waste areas, and cropland. The berries and foliage are poisonous to livestock.
- Perennial morningglory (*Ipomoea* spp.) species such as sharppod morningglory are weedy vines that can cause significant yield reductions and harvest difficulties for sorghum growers. Sharppod morningglory develops extensive underground perennial roots that can regenerate repeatedly after removal or disturbance of top growth.
- Field bindweed (*Convolvuvis arvensis*) is a perennial from an extensive root system often climbing or forming dense mats. Field bindweed was introduced from Europe and has become a widespread and serious weed pest in many parts of the United States. It is difficult to control because of a root system that can penetrate the soil to a depth of 20 feet and which gives rise to numerous long lateral roots.

Common perennial monocot weeds:

- Yellow nutsedge (*Cyperus esculentus*) is an aggressive perennial superficially resembling a grass. Yellow nutsedge can spread by seed, creeping rootstocks, or by small underground tubers or nutlets. The many hard brown tubers may lie dormant in the soil for many years before producing new plants.
- Purple nutsedge (*Cyperus rotundus*) is another spreading perennial similar to yellow nutsedge. The underground tubers are oblong and covered by persistent reddish scales and are often formed in chains that remain connected underground. Purple nutsedge is commonly found in turf, ornamental areas, cultivated fields, and ditches.

Pre-emergence (PRE) Herbicides

Atrazine

- Trade name: Aatrex, many others.
- WSSA MOA: 5
- Application timing and target weed: preplant, preemerge, early preemergence.

- Very good broadleaf herbicide. Controls many broadleaf and some small-seeded annual grasses.
- Component of other products: Bicep II Magnum, Cinch ATZ, Bicep Lite II Magnum, Cinch ATZ Lite, Bullet 4EC, Lariat 4EC, Guardsman Max, Marksman.

In 2003, atrazine was applied to 59 per cent of sorghum acres in Texas. At an average rate of 0.87 lb this translated into 1.83 million pounds of atrazine applied.

s-Metolachlor

- Trade name: Dual Magnum, many others.
- WSSA MOA: 15
- Application timing and target weed: preplant, preemerge. Very good grass herbicide. Controls many annual grasses and some small-seeded broadleaf weeds.
- Component of other products: Bicep II Magnum, Cinch ATZ, Bicep Lite II Magnum, Cinch ATZ Lite.

In 2003, s-metolachlor was applied to 8 per cent of sorghum acres in Texas. At an average rate of 0.77 lb this translated into 208,000 pounds of s-metolachlor applied.

Alachlor

- Trade name: Micro-Tech, Intrro.
- WSSA MOA: 15
- Application timing and target weed: preplant, preemerge. Very good grass herbicide. Controls many annual grasses and some small-seeded broadleaf weeds.
- Component of other products: Bullet 4EC, Lariat 4EC.

In 2003, alachlor was applied to 6 per cent of sorghum acres in Texas. At an average rate of 1.25 lb this translated into 229,000 pounds of alachlor applied.

Dimethenamid

- Trade name: Outlook.
- WSSA MOA: 15
- Application timing and target weed: preplant, preemerge. Very good grass herbicide. Controls many annual grasses and some small-seeded broadleaf weeds.

- Component of other products: Guardsman Max, Guardsman Max Lite.

In 2003, dimethenamid was applied to 3 per cent of sorghum acres in Texas. At an average rate of 1.0 lb this translated into 60,000 pounds of dimethenamid applied.

Propazine

- Trade name: Milo-Pro.
- WSSA MOA: 5
- Application timing and target weed: preplant, preemerge. Good broadleaf herbicide. Controls many broadleaf and some small-seeded grass weeds.
- Component of other products: none.

Postemergence (POST) herbicides

Pendimethalin

- Trade name: Prowl, Prowl H20.
- WSSA MOA: 3
- Application timing and target weed: POST to 4 inch sorghum, must cultispray.
- Control many small-seeded grassy weeds.
- Component of other products: none.

Metsulfuron-methyl

- Trade name: Ally + 2,4-D.
- WSSA MOA: 2, 4
- Application timing and target weed: POST to weeds less than 6 inches.
- Controls many broadleaf weeds.
- Component of other products: none.

In 2003, metsulfuron-methyl was applied to 7 per cent of sorghum acres in Texas. At an average rate of .002 lb this translated into 1,000 pounds of metsulfuron-methyl applied.

Carfentrazone

- Trade name: Aim.
- WSSA MOA: 14

- Application timing and target weed: POST to small broadleaf weeds. Control some broadleaf weeds.
- Component of other products: none.

Fluroxypyr

- Trade name: Starane.
- WSSA MOA: 4
- Application timing and target weed: POST to small broadleaf weeds. Control some broadleaf weeds.
- Component of other products: none.

Bromoxynil

- Trade name: Buctril.
- WSSA MOA: 6
- Application timing and target weed: POST to small broadleaf weeds. Control some broadleaf and grassy weeds.
- Component of other products: none.

Prosulfuron

- Trade name: Peak.
- WSSA MOA: 2
- Application timing and target weed: POST. Controls many broadleaf weeds.
- Commonly tank-mixed with atrazine.
- Component of other products: none.

In 2003, prosulfuron was applied to 10 per cent of sorghum acres in Texas. At an average rate of .02 lb this translated into 6,000 pounds of prosulfuron applied.

Dicamba

- Trade name: Banvel, Clarity.
- WSSA MOA: 4
- Application timing and target weed: POST. Controls many broadleaf weeds.
- Component of other products: Marksman, Yukon.

In 2003, dicamba was applied to 6 per cent of sorghum acres in Texas. At an average rate of 0.12 lb this translated into 22,000 pounds of dicamba applied.

Quinclorac

- Trade name: Paramount.
- WSSA MOA: 27, 4
- Application timing and target weed: POST to sorghum up to 12 inches.
- Controls many broadleaf weeds and suppresses some grasses.
- Component of other products: none.

2,4-D

- Trade name: various.
- WSSA MOA: 4
- Application timing and target weed: POST to sorghum 6 - 15 inches.
- Controls many broadleaf weeds. Do not treat during boot stage.
- Component of other products: none.

In 2003, 2,4-D was applied to 9 per cent of sorghum acres in Texas. At an average rate of 0.35 lb this translated into 113,000 pounds of 2,4-D applied.

Halosulfuron

- Trade name: Permit.
- WSSA MOA: 2
- Application timing and target weed: POST to sorghum from 2 leaf stage through boot. Controls many broadleaf weeds and yellow and purple nutsedge.
- Component of other products: Yukon.

Glyphosate

- Trade name: various.
- WSSA MOA: 9
- Application timing and target weed: POST to sorghum after it has reached physiological maturity. Glyphosate is commonly used as a harvest aid primarily in southern portions of the state. The primary objective is to accelerate the drying process (decrease seed moisture

content). However, late-season glyphosate application also improves harvest efficiency as well as controlling late-season grass and broadleaf weeds.

- Component of other products: none.

In 2003, glyphosate was applied to 12 per cent of sorghum acres in Texas. At an average rate of 0.57 lb this translated into 302,000 pounds of glyphosate applied.

Tobacco Plant Diseases

The plant disease caused by tobacco mosaic virus is found worldwide. The virus is known to infect more than 150 types of herbaceous, dicotyledonous plants including many vegetables, flowers and weeds. Infection by tobacco mosaic virus causes serious losses on several crops including tomatoes, peppers, and many ornamentals. Tobacco mosaic virus is one of the most common causes of virus diseases of plants in Minnesota.

Many viruses produce mosaic-like symptoms on plants. Mosaic-like symptoms are characterized by intermingled patches of normal and light green or yellowish colors on the leaves of infected plants. Tobacco mosaic damages the leaves, flowers, and fruit and causes stunting of the plant. The virus almost never kills plants but lowers the quality and quantity of the crop, particularly when the plants are infected while young.

Virus-infected plants often are confused with plants affected by herbicide or air pollution damage, mineral deficiencies, and other plant diseases. Positive identification of tobacco mosaic virus in infected plants often requires the services of a plant pathologist and the use of an electron microscope. Although, it may take a plant pathologist to diagnose tobacco mosaic virus in many ornamental plants, the majority of tomato plants showing mosaic symptoms usually are infected by tobacco mosaic virus.

Tobacco mosaic virus (TMV) is a positive-sense single stranded RNA virus that infects plants, especially tobacco and other members of the family Solanaceae. The infection causes characteristic patterns (mottling and discoloration) on the leaves (hence the name). The TMV was the first virus to be discovered. Although it was known from the late 19th century that an infectious disease was damaging tobacco crops, it was not until 1930 that the infectious agent was determined to be a virus.

In 1883, Adolf Mayer first described the disease that could be transferred between plants, similar to bacterial infections. Dimitri Ivanovski gave the first concrete evidence for the existence of a non-bacterial infectious agent, showing that infected sap remained infectious even after filtering through Chamberland filter candles, in 1892. However, he remained convinced despite repeated failures to produce evidence, that bacteria were the infectious agents. In 1898, Martinus Beijerinck showed that a filtered, bacteria-free culture medium still contained the infectious agent.

Wendell Meredith Stanley crystallized the virus in 1935 and showed that it remains active even after crystallization. For his work, he was awarded one-fourth of the Nobel Prize in Chemistry in 1946, even though it was later shown some of his conclusions (in particular, that the crystals were pure protein, and assembled by autocatalysis) were incorrect. The first electron microscopical images of TMV were made in 1939 by Gustav Kausche, Edgar Pfankuch and Helmut Ruska - the brother of Nobel Prize winner Ernst Ruska.

In 1955, Heinz Fraenkel-Conrat and Robley Williams showed that purified TMV RNA and its capsid (coat) protein assemble by themselves to functional viruses, indicating that this is the most stable structure (the one with the lowest free energy). The crystallographer Rosalind Franklin worked for Stanley for about a month at Berkeley, and later designed and built a model of TMV for the 1958 World's Fair at Brussels. In 1958, she speculated that the virus was hollow, not solid, and hypothesized that the RNA of TMV is single-stranded. This conjecture was proven to be correct after her death and is now known to be the + strand.

Tobacco mosaic virus has a rod-like appearance. Its capsid is made from 2130 molecules of coat protein and one molecule of genomic single strand RNA 6400 bases long. The coat protein self-assembles into the rod like helical structure (16.3 proteins per helix turn) around the RNA which forms a hairpin loop structure. The protein monomer consists of 158 amino acids which are assembled into four main alpha-helices, which are joined by a prominent loop proximal to the axis of the virion. Virions are nearly 300 nm in length and ~18 nm in diameter.

Negatively stained electron microphotographs show a distinct inner channel of ~4 nm. The RNA is located at a radius of ~6 nm and is protected from the action of cellular enzymes by the coat protein. There are three RNA nucleotides per protein monomer. X-ray fiber diffraction structure of the intact virus was studied based on an electron density map at 3.6 Å resolution. TMV is a thermostable virus. On a dried leaf, it can withstand up to 120 (50 °C) for thirty minutes. TMV has an index of refraction of about 1.57.

DISEASE CYCLE

TMV does not have a distinct over-wintering structure. Rather, it will over-winter in infected tobacco stalks and leaves in the soil, on the surface of contaminated seed (TMV can even survive in contaminated tobacco products for many years). With the direct contact with host plants through its vectors (normally insects such as aphids and leaf hoppers), TMV will go through the infection process and then the replication process.

Infection

After its multiplication, it enters the neighboring cells through plasmodesmata. For its smooth entry, TMV produces a 30 kDa movement protein called P30 which enlarge the plasmodesmata. TMV most likely moves from cell-to-cell as a complex of the RNA, P30, and replicase proteins.

It can also spread through phloem for longer distance movement within the plant. Moreover, TMV can be transmitted from one plant to another by direct contact. Although TMV does not have defined transmission vectors, the virus can be easily transmitted from the infected hosts to the healthy plants, by human handling.

Replication

Following entry into its host via mechanical inoculation, TMV uncoats itself to release its viral RNA strand. Then the viral genome will further replicate to produce multiple mRNAs. The resulting mRNAs encode several proteins, including the coat protein and an RNA-dependent RNA polymerase (RdRp), as well as the movement protein. Thus TMV can replicate its own genome.

After the coat protein and RNA genome of TMV have been synthesized, they spontaneously assemble into complete TMV virions in a highly organized process.

The protomers come together to form disks composed of two layers of protomers arranged in a helical spiral. The helical capsid grows by the addition of protomers to the end of the rod. As the rod lengthens, the RNA passes through a channel in its center and forms a loop at the growing end. In this way, the RNA can easily fit as a spiral into the interior of the helical capsid.

HOST AND SYMPTOMS

Like other plant pathogenic viruses, TMV has a very wide host range and has different effects depending on the host being infected. The tobacco mosaic virus has been known to cause a production loss for flue cured tobacco of up to two per cent in North Carolina. It is known to infect members of nine plant families, and at least 125 individual species, including tobacco, tomato, pepper (all members of the useful Solanaceae), cucumbers, and a number of ornamental flowers.

There are many different strains. The first symptom of this virus disease is a light green coloration between the veins of young leaves. This is followed quickly by the development of a "mosaic" or mottled pattern of light and dark green areas in the leaves. Rugosity may also be seen where the infected plant leaves display small localized random wrinkles.

These symptoms develop quickly and are more pronounced on younger leaves. Mosaic does not result in plant death, but if infection occurs early in the season, plants are stunted. Lower leaves are subjected to "mosaic burn" especially during periods of hot and dry weather. In these cases, large dead areas develop in the leaves. This constitutes one of the most destructive phases of tobacco mosaic virus infection. Infected leaves may be crinkled, puckered, or elongated. However, if TMV infects crops like grape and apple, it is almost symptomless.

Consumption of tobacco products infected with the tobacco mosaic virus has not been found to have any effect on humans. TMV is known as the one of the most stable viruses. It has a very wide survival range. As long as the surrounding temperature remains below approximately 40° C, TMV can sustain its stable form. All it needs is a host to infect. If necessary, greenhouses and botanical gardens would provide the most favorable condition for TMV to spread out, due to the high population density of possible hosts and the constant temperature throughout the year.

One of the common control methods for TMV is sanitation, which includes removing infected plants, and washing hands in between each planting. Crop rotation should also be employed to avoid infected soil/seed beds for at least two years. As for any plant disease, looking for resistant strains against TMV may also be advised. Furthermore, the cross protection method can be administered, where the stronger strain of TMV infection is inhibited by infecting the host plant with mild strain of TMV, similar to the effect of a vaccine.

In the past one decade, the application of genetic engineering on a host plant genome has been developed to allow the host plant to produce the TMV coat protein within their cells. It was hypothesized that the TMV genome will be re-coated rapidly upon entering the host cell, thus it prevents the initiation of TMV replication. Later it was found that the mechanism that protects the host from viral genome insertion is through gene silencing.

In some cases, spraying milk on the host plant is known to inhibit the TMV infection. The large amount of literature about TMV and its choice for many pioneering investigations in structural biology (including X-ray diffraction), virus assembly and disassembly, and so on, are fundamentally due to the large quantities that can be obtained, plus the fact that it does not infect animals. After growing a few infected tobacco plants in a greenhouse and a few simple laboratory procedures, a scientist can easily produce several grams of virus. As a result of this, TMV can be treated almost as an organic chemical, rather than an infective agent.

Due to its cylindrical high aspect ratio, self-assembling nature, and ability to incorporate metal coatings (nickel and cobalt) into its shell, TMV is an ideal candidate to be incorporated into battery electrodes. Addition of TMV to a battery electrode increases the reactive surface area by an order of magnitude, resulting in an increase in the battery's capacity by up to six times compared to a planar electrode geometry.

Common Plant Hosts

In Minnesota, common plant hosts for the mosaic virus are tomato, pepper, petunia, snapdragon, delphinium, and marigold. Tobacco mosaic virus also has been reported to a lesser extent in muskmelon, cucumber, squash, spinach, celosia, impatiens, ground cherry, phlox, zinnia, certain types of ivy, plantain, night shade, and jimson weed. Although tobacco mosaic virus may infect many other types of plants, it generally is restricted to plants that are grown in seedbeds and transplanted or plants that are handled frequently.

Symptoms

In tomatoes, the foliage shows mosaic areas with alternating yellowish and dark green areas. Leaves are sometimes fern-like in appearance and sharply pointed. Infections of young plants reduce fruit set and occasionally cause blemishes and distortions of the fruit. The dark green areas of the mottle often appear thicker and somewhat elevated giving the leaves a blister-like appearance. Symptoms on other plant hosts include various degrees of chlorosis, curling, mottling mosaic, dwarfing, distortion, and blistering of the leaves. Many times the entire plant is dwarfed and flowers are discolored. Symptoms can be influenced by temperature, light conditions, nutritional factors, and water stress.

Disease Cycle

Viruses differ from fungi and bacteria in that they do not produce spores or other structures capable of penetrating plant parts. Since viruses have no active methods of entering plant cells, they must rely upon mechanically caused wounds, vegetative propagation of plants, grafting, seed, pollen, and being carried on the mouth parts of chewing insects. Tobacco mosaic virus is most commonly introduced into plants through small wounds caused by handling and by insects chewing on plant parts.

The most common sources of virus inoculum for tobacco mosaic virus are the debris of infected plants that remains in the soil and certain infected tobacco products that contaminate workers hands. Cigars, cigarettes, and pipe tobaccos can be infected with tobacco mosaic virus. Handling these smoking materials contaminates the hands, and subsequent handling of plants results in a transmission of the virus. Therefore, do not smoke while handling or transplanting plants.

Once the virus enters the host, it begins to multiply by inducing host cells to form more virus. Viruses do not cause disease by consuming or killing cells but rather by taking over the metabolic cell processes, resulting in abnormal cell functioning. Abnormal metabolic functions of infected cells are expressed as mosaic and other symptoms as previously described. Infected plants serve as reservoirs for the virus and the virus can be transmitted easily either mechanically or by insects to healthy plants.

Control

Unlike fungicidal chemicals used to control fungal diseases, to date there are no efficient chemical treatments that protect plant parts from virus infection. Additionally, there are no known chemical treatments used under field conditions that eliminate viral infections from plant tissues once they do occur. Practically speaking, plants infected by viruses remain so.

Thus, control of tobacco mosaic virus is primarily focused on reducing and eliminating sources of the virus and limiting the spread by insects. Tobacco mosaic virus is the most persistent plant virus known. It has been known to survive up to fifty years in dried plant parts. Therefore, sanitation is the single most important practice in controlling tobacco mosaic virus.

Control for Seedling Growers and Gardeners

The most common method of transferring the virus from plant to plant is on contaminated hands and tools. Workers who transplant seedlings should refrain from smoking during transplanting and wash their hands frequently and thoroughly with soap and water. Tools used in transplanting can be placed in boiling water for five minutes and then washed with a strong soap or detergent solution. Dipping tools in household bleach is not effective for virus decontamination. Any seedlings that appear to have mosaic symptoms or are stunted and distorted should be removed and destroyed. After removing diseased plants, never handle healthy plants without washing hands and decontaminating tools used to remove diseased plants.

Persons purchasing small tomato plants for transplanting should beware of any plants showing mottling, dwarfing, or stunting. Avoid the purchase of any affected plant. Gardeners are advised to follow the same procedures recommended for greenhouse workers when handling tomato transplants.

Other control methods for home gardeners include roguing (removal of diseased plants), destruction of diseased and infected plants, and control of weeds and chewing insects. When roguing and destroying mature diseased plants from the home garden, be sure to wash hands and decontaminate any tools used in the process before contacting healthy plants.

Bacterial Diseases

Angular Leaf Spot

Pseudomonas syringae pv. tabaci (Wolf & Foster) Young et al.

Granville Wilt

Pseudomonas solanacearum (Smith) Smith

Hollow Stalk

Erwinia carotovora subsp. carotovora (Jones) Bergey et al.

E. carotovora subsp. atroseptica (van Hall) Dye

Leaf Gall

Rhodococcus fascians (Tilford) Goodfellow

Wildfire

Pseudomonas syringae pv. tabaci (Wolf & Foster) Young et al.

Fungal Diseases

Anthracnose

Colletotrichum destructivum O'Gara

(teleomorph: *Glomerella glycines* F. Lehm. and F.A. Wolf)

Barn Spot

Cercospora nicotianae Ellis & Everh.

Barn Rot

Several fungi and bacteria

Black Root Rot

Thielaviopsis basicola (Berk. & Broome) Ferraris

Black Shank

Phytophthora parasitica Dastur var. nicotianae (Breda de Haan) Tucker

P. nicotianae Breda de Haan var. nicotianae G.M. Waterhouse

Blue Mold (downy mildew)

Peronospora tabacina D.B. Adam

= *P. hyoscyami de* Bary f. sp. tabacina

Brown Spot

Alternaria alternata (Fr.:Fr.) Keissl.

Charcoal Rot

Macrophomina phaseolina (Tassi) Goidanich

Collar Rot

Sclerotinia sclerotiorum (Lib.) de Bary

Damping-off, Pythium

Pythium spp.

P. aphanidermatum (Edson) Fitzp.

P. ultimum Trow

Frogeye leaf spot

Cercospora nicotianae Ellis & Everh.

Fusarium Wilt

Fusarium oxysporum Schlechtend.:Fr. (several f. sp.)

Gray Mold

Botrytis cinerea Pers.:Fr.

(teleomorph: Botryotinia fuckeliana (de Bary) Whetzel)

Olpidium Seedling Blight

Olpidium brassicae (Woronin) P.A. Dang.

Phyllosticta Leaf Spot

Phyllosticta nicotiana Ellis & Everh.

Powdery Mildew

Erysiphe cichoracearum DC.

Ragged Leaf Spot

Phoma exigua Desmaz. var. exigua

= Ascochyta phaseolorum Sacc.

Scab

Hymenula affinis (Fautrey & Lambotte) Wollenweb.

= Fusarium affine Fautrey & Lambotte

Sore Shin and Damping-off

Rhizoctonia solani Kühn

(teleomorph: Thanatephorus cucumeris (A.B. Frank) Donk)

Southern Stem Rot (southern blight)

Sclerotium rolfsii Sacc.

(teleomorph: Athelia rolfsii (Cursi) Tu & Kimbrough)

Stem Rot of Tranplants

Pythium spp.

Target Spot

Rhizoctonia solani Kühn

Verticillium Wilt

Verticllium albo-atrum Reinke & Berthier

V. dahliae Kleb.

Miscellaneous Diseases Or Disorders

Brown Root Rot

Pratylenchus spp. (nematodes)

Drought Spot

Drought

False Broomrape

Unknown

Frenching

Metabolite of *Bacillus cereus* Frankland & Frankland

Stem Break (in Europe)

Ditylenchus dipsaci (Kühn) Filipjev (nematodes)

Sunscald

High light intensity and high temperatures

Weather Fleck

Ozone

Nematodes, Parasitic

Bulb and Stem (Stem Break)

Ditylenchus dipsaci (Kühn) Filipjev (in Europe)

Cyst

Globodera solanacearum (Miller & Gray) Behrens

= *G. virginiae* (Miller & Gray) Behrens

G. tabacum (Lownsbery & Lownsbery) Behrens

Dagger, American

Xiphinema americanum Cobb

Foliar

Aphelenchoides ritzemabosi (Schwartz) Steiner

Lesion

Pratylenchus brachyurus (Godfrey) Filipjev & Schuurmans-Stekhoven

P. penetrans (Cobb) Filipjev & Schuurmans-Stekhoven

Pratylenchus spp.

Reniform

Rotylenchulus reniformis Linford & Oliveira

Root-knot

Meloidogyne arenaria (Neal) Chitwood

M. hapla Chitwood

M. incognita (Kofoid & White) Chitwood

M. javanica (Treub) Chitwood

Spiral

Helicotylenchus spp.

Stubby-root

Paratrichodorus spp.

Trichodorus spp.

Stunt

Merlinius spp.

Tylenchorhynchus spp.

PARASITIC HIGHER PLANTS

Broomrape

Orobanche ramosa L.

O. ludoviciana Nutt.

Dodder

Cuscuta spp.

Witchweed

Striga gesnerioides (Willd.) Vatke

Virus Diseases

(Also mycoplasmalike organisms [MLO])

Alfalfa Mosaic

Alfalfa mosaic virus

Aster Yellows

MLO

Beet Curly Top

Beet curly top virus

Bushy Top

Tobacco vein distorting virus and tobacco bushy top virus in combination

Cucumber Mosaic

Cucumber mosaic virus

Peanut Stunt

Peanut stunt virus

Rosette Disease

Tobacco vein distorting virus and tobacco mottlevirus in combination

Stolbur (Europe only)

MLO

Tobacco etch

Tobacco etch virus

Tobacco Leaf Curl

Tobacco leaf curl virus

Tobacco Mosaic

Tobacco mosaic virus

Tobacco Necrosis

Tobacco necrosis virus

Tobacco Rattle

Tobacco rattle virus

Tobacco Ring Spot

Tobacco ring spot virus

Tobacco Streak

Tobacco streak virus

Tobacco Stunt (Japan only)

Tobacco stunt virus

Tobacco Vein Mottling

Tobacco vein mottling virus

Tomato Spotted Wilt

Tomato spotted wilt virus

Vein Banding

Potato virus Y

Wound Tumor

Wound tumor virus

CONTROL FOR COMMERCIAL PRODUCERS

Commercial greenhouse producers of tomatoes should follow control practices for seedling production as stated above. It is essential for commercial growers to constantly inspect and rogue diseased production plants while the plants are in the seedling stage. An experienced individual, who is familiar with the tobacco mosaic virus symptoms, should do the initial inspection.

Roguing of young production plants is recommended and should take place before workers are allowed to prune or tie up production plants. When removing diseased plants, also remove one plant on either side of the diseased one. The reason for this is that it is almost impossible to remove a diseased plant and not contaminate the healthy adjacent plants. Never attempt to transplant a healthy tomato into the soil from which a diseased plant was removed. Roots from diseased plants will remain in the soil and provide the virus inoculum for the new transplant.

As a matter of routine, soils from which production plants have been removed, following harvest, should be steam sterilized before the introduction of new seedlings. Steam sterilization can be accomplished by steam or air-steam mixtures. In the preparation of soil for steam sterilization, sift it to remove clumps and large pieces of organic matter. The total soil mixture will have to be heated to a temperature of 200□ F for fourty minutes. Since high temperatures are required, steam sterilization must be done in an enclosed system.

Temperatures within the steam sterilization system should be monitored by high temperature thermometers to make sure the desired temperature has been reached. Steam sterilization of soil also will eliminate fungi, insects, nematodes, and weeds from the soil. Steam sterilization also is recommended for gravel mixtures used in hydroponic operations following the same procedure described above.

Grow individual production plants in separate containers so that the soil or growing media can be removed when roguing infected production plants. Remember that the soil harbors old root tissues that may serve as inoculum when new roots are introduced. Growing production plants in separate containers is also useful for the control of root diseases caused by fungi and bacteria.

Bibliography

Alcamo IE, Pommerville J. (2004). *Alcamo's Fundamentals of Microbiology*. Boston, Massachusetts: Jones and Bartlett. p. 590. ISBN 0-7637-0067-3.

Blackwell M, Vilgalys R, James TY, Taylor JW. (2009). "Fungi. Eumycota: Mushrooms, Sac Fungi, Yeast, Molds, Rusts, Smuts, etc." *Tree of Life Web Project*. Retrieved 2009-04-25.

Brundrett MC. (2002). "Coevolution of Roots and Mycorrhizas of Land Plants". *New Phytologist* 154 (2): 275-304.

Butterfield NJ. (2005). "Probable Proterozoic Fungi". Paleobiology 31 (1): 165-182.

Chang S-T, Miles PG. (2004). *Mushrooms: Cultivation, Nutritional Value, Medicinal Effect and Environmental Impact*. Boca Raton, Florida: CRC Press. ISBN 0-8493-1043-1.

Christensen MJ, Bennett RJ, Ansari HA, Koga H, Johnson RD, Bryan GT, Simpson WR, Koolaard JP, Nickless EM, Voisey CR. (2008). "Epichloë Endophytes Grow by Intercalary Hyphal Extension in Elongating Grass Leaves". *Fungal Genetics and Biology* 45 (2): 84-93.

Dadachova E, Casadevall A. (2008). "Ionizing Radiation: How Fungi Cope, Adapt, and Exploit with the help of Melanin". *Current Opinion in Microbiology* 11 (6): 525-531.

Daniels KJ, Srikantha T, Lockhart SR, Pujol C, Soll DR. (2006). "Opaque Cells Signal White Cells to form Biofilms in Candida Albicans". *EMBO Journal* 25 (10): 2240-2252.

Dennis RL. (1970). "A Middle Pennsylvanian Basidiomycete Mycelium with Clamp Connections". Mycologia 62 (3): 578-584.

Desjardin DE, Oliveira AG, Stevani CV. (2008). "Fungi Bioluminescence Revisited". Photochemical & Photobiological Sciences 7 (2): 170-182.

Donoghue MJ, Cracraft J. (2004). Assembling the Tree of Life. Oxford (Oxfordshire), UK: Oxford University Press. p. 187.

Dotzler N, Walker C, Krings M, Hass H, Kerp H, Taylor TN, Agerer R. (2009). "Acaulosporoid Glomeromycotan Spores with a Germination Shield from the 400-million-year-old Rhynie Chert". *Mycological Progress* 8 (1): 9-18.

Eshet Y, Rampino MR, Visscher H. (1995). "Fungal Event and Palynological Record of Ecological Crisis and Recovery Across the Permian-Triassic boundary". *Geology* 23 (1): 967-970.

Farrar JF. (1985). "Carbohydrate Metabolism in Biotrophic Plant Pathogens". *Microbiological Sciences* 2 (10): 314-317.

Fischer R, Zekert N, Takeshita N. (2008). "Polarized Growth in Fungi-interplay Between the Cytoskeleton, Positional Markers and Membrane Domains". *Molecular Microbiology* 68 (4): 813-826.

Foster CB, Stephenson MH, Marshall C, Logan GA, Greenwood PF. (2002). "A Revision of Reduviasporonites Wilson 1962: Description, Illustration, Comparison and Biological Affinities". *Palynology* 26 (1): 35-58.

Furlaneto MC, Pizzirani-Kleiner AA. (1992). "Intraspecific Hybridisation of Trichoderma Pseudokoningii by Anastomosis and by Protoplast Fusion". FEMS Microbiology Letters 69 (2): 191-196.

Gill EE, Fast NM. (2006). "Assessing the Microsporidia-fungi Relationship: Combined Phylogenetic Analysis of Eight Genes". *Gene* 375: 103-109.

Guarro J, Gené J, Stchigel AM. (1999). "Developments in Fungal Taxonomy". Clinical Microbiology Reviews 12 (3): 454-500.

Hawksworth DL. (2006). "The Fungal Dimension of Biodiversity: Magnitude, Significance, and Conservation". *Mycological Research* 95 (6): 641-655.

Heitman J. (2005). "Sexual Reproduction and the Evolution of Microbial Pathogens". *Current Biology* 16 (17): R711-R725.

Heynes MJ. (1994). "Regulatory Circuits of the amdS Gene of Aspergillus Nidulans". Antonie Van Leeuwenhoek 65 (3): 179-182.

Hibbett DS, Grimaldi D, Donoghue MJ. (1995). "Cretaceous Mushrooms in Amber". *Nature* 377 (6549): 487.

James TY, Kauff F, Schoch CL, Matheny PB, Hofstetter V, Cox CJ, et al. (2006). "Reconstructing the Early Evolution of Fungi Using a Six-gene Phylogeny". *Nature* 443 (7113): 818-822.

Le Calvez T, Burgaud G, Mahé S, Barbier G, Vandenkoornhuyse P. (2009). "Fungal Diversity in Deep Sea Hydrothermal Ecosystems". *Applied and Environmental Microbiology* 75 (20): 6415-6421.

Linder MB, Szilvay GR, Nakari-Setälä T, Penttilä ME. (2005). "Hydrophobins: The Protein-amphiphiles of Filamentous Fungi". *FEMS Microbiology Reviews* 29 (5): 877-896.

Looy CV, Twitchett RJ, Dilcher DL, Van Konijnenburg-van Cittert JHA, Visscher H. (2005). "Life in the End-Permian Dead Zone". *Proceedings of the National Academy of Sciences USA 162* (4): 7879-7883.

López-Gómez J, Taylor EL. (2005). "Permian-Triassic Transition in Spain: A Multidisciplinary Approach". *Palaeogeography, Palaeoclimatology, Palaeoecology* 229 (1-2): 1-2.

Lucking R, Huhndorf S, Pfister D, Plata ER, Lumbsch H. (2009). "Fungi Evolved Right on Track". *Mycologia* 101 (6): 810-822.

Marzluf GA. (1981). "Regulation of Nitrogen Metabolism and Gene Expression in Fungi". *Microbiological Reviews* 45 (3): 437-461.

Metzenberg RL, Glass NL. (1990). "Mating Type and Mating Strategies in Neurospora". *Bioessays* 12 (2): 53-59.

Mihail JD, Bruhn JN. (2005). "Foraging Behaviour of Armillaria Rhizomorph Systems". *Mycological Research* 109 (11): 1195-1207.

Money NP. (2002). "Mushroom Stem Cells". Bioessays 24 (10): 949-952.

Moore RT. (1980). "Taxonomic Proposals for the Classification of Marine Yeasts and Other Yeast-like Fungi including the Smuts". *Botanica Marine* 23: 361-373.

Moss ST. (1986). *The Biology of Marine Fungi*. Cambridge, UK: Cambridge University Press. p. 76. ISBN 0-521-30899-2.

Mueller GM, Schmit JP. (2006). "Fungal Biodiversity: What do we know? What can we Predict?". *Biodiversity and Conservation* 16: 1-5.

Parniske M. (2008). "Arbuscular Mycorrhiza: The Mother of Plant Root Endosymbioses". Nature Reviews. *Microbiology* 6 (10): 763-775.

Peñalva MA, Arst HN. (2002). "Regulation of Gene Expression by Ambient pH in Filamentous Fungi and Yeasts". *Microbiology and Molecular Biology Reviews* 66 (3): 426-446.

Pringle A, Patek SN, Fischer M, Stolze J, Money NP. (2005). "The Captured Launch of a Ballistospore". *Mycologia* 97 (4): 866-871.

Raghukumar C, Raghukumar S. (1998). "Barotolerance of Fungi Isolated from Deep-sea Sediments of the Indian Ocean". *Aquatic Microbial Ecology* 15 (2): 153-163.

Redecker D, Kodner R, Graham LE. (2000). "Glomalean Fungi from the Ordovician". *Science* 289 (5486): 1920-1921.

Redecker D, Raab P. (2006). "Phylogeny of the Glomeromycota (arbuscular mycorrhizal fungi): Recent Developments and New Gene Markers". *Mycologia* 98 (6): 885-895.

Remy W, Taylor TN, Hass H, Kerp H. (1994). "4-hundred million year old vesicular-arbuscular mycorrhizae". *Proceedings of the National Academy of Sciences USA* 91 (25): 11841-11843.

Sancho LG, de la Torre R, Horneck G, Ascaso C, de Los Rios A, Pintado A, Wierzchos J, Schuster M. (2007). "Lichens Survive in Space: Results from the 2005 LICHENS Experiment". *Astrobiology* 7 (3): 443-454.

Schaller M, Borelli C, Korting HC, Hube B. (2007). "Hydrolytic Enzymes as Virulence Factors of Candida Albicans". *Mycoses* 48 (6): 365-377.

Taylor JW, Berbee ML. (2006). "Dating Divergences in the Fungal Tree of Life: Review and New Analyses". *Mycologia* 98 (6): 838-849.

Vaupotic T, Veranic P, Jenoe P, Plemenitas A. (2008). "Mitochondrial Mediation of Environmental Osmolytes Discrimination during Osmoadaptation in the Extremely Halotolerant Black Yeast Hortaea werneckii". *Fungal Genetics and Biology* 45 (6): 994-1007.

Ward PD, Botha J, Buick R, De Kock MO, Erwin DH, Garrison GH, Kirschvink JL, Smith R. (2005). "Abrupt and Gradual Extinction Among Late Permian Land Vertebrates in the Karoo Basin, South Africa". *Science* 307 (5710): 709-714.

Xu H, Andi B, Qian J, West AH, Cook PF. (2006). "The a-aminoadipate Pathway for Lysine Biosynthesis in Fungi". *Cellular Biochemistry and Biophysics* 46 (1): 43-64.

Yuan X, Xiao S, Taylor TN. (2005). "Lichen-like Symbiosis 600 Million Years Ago". Science 308 (5724): 1017-1020.

Zabriskie TM, Jackson MD. (2000). "Lysine Biosynthesis and Metabolism in Fungi". *Natural Product Reports* 17 (1): 85-97.

Index